D1243704

Workers' management
in Yugoslavia
Recent developments
and trends

WORKERS' MANAGEMENT IN YUGOSLAVIA

RECENT DEVELOPMENTS AND TRENDS

EDITED BY
NAJDAN PAŠIĆ
STANISLAV GROZDANIĆ
MILORAD RADEVIĆ

INTERNATIONAL LABOUR OFFICE   GENEVA

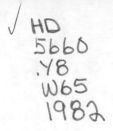
ISBN 92-2-103035-0 (limp cover)
ISBN 92-2-103034-2 (hard cover)

First published 1982

Photocomposed in India
Printed in Switzerland

The ILO has a long-standing interest in workers' participation. After adopting various international instruments dealing with industrial relations,[1] the International Labour Conference went on in 1966 to adopt a resolution calling upon the Governing Body of the International Labour Office to request the Director-General to undertake studies of the various methods currently used throughout the world to enable workers to participate in decisions within undertakings and to consider the convening of international seminars to discuss problems involved and hold an exchange of views and experience.

In keeping with that resolution, the ILO has published a number of studies on workers' participation[2] and organised four international meetings, held in Geneva (1967), Belgrade (1969), Oslo (1974) and The Hague (1981).

Sequel to a previous ILO study

Four years before the adoption of the 1966 resolution, the ILO had already published a study on the system of workers' management introduced in Yugoslavia in 1950.[3] The study reflected the evolution of the system during the early years of its development and described its basic principles and goals. It stressed repeatedly that workers' management was a dynamic process rather than a set of institutions and that it was bound to change and develop gradually as it moved towards the achievement of its long-term aims. As stated in the last paragraph of the study—

From the point of view of industrial relations, the Yugoslav system of workers' management of autonomous undertakings seems in the last analysis to be a vast melting-pot for concepts which originated in widely differing economic and social systems and which are often considered to be incompatible. Nationalisation of the means of production, over-all planning, industrial democracy, autonomy of undertakings, market

1

competition, remuneration of workers according to production and profits are the main ingredients of a new alloy whose durability only the future can show but whose originality and interest can hardly be denied even today.

Need for a new work

Since the publication of that ILO study, workers' management in Yugoslavia has, indeed, continued to evolve towards a more complex and comprehensive system of self-management extending beyond the enterprise to many other aspects of relationships within society as a whole. The 1960s and 1970s saw an impressive succession of developments in legislation and practice in this field, culminating in the new Constitution of 1974 and the adoption in 1976 of the Associated Labour Law, which consolidated the important changes already introduced and pointed the way towards future developments. In the 30 years that have elapsed since its inception, workers' management has already evolved from a form of workers' participation in decisions into a social system which permeates all aspects of Yugoslav life.

Authorship

In the light of these changes and in view of the continuing interest which the Yugoslav system arouses in many countries throughout the world, it was felt that a new study should be prepared, describing workers' management as it is today, after three decades of experience. Given the unique character and complexities of the Yugoslav system it was considered necessary to entrust this study to Yugoslav authors who could fully describe the system from within. In co-operation with the Confederation of Trade Unions of Yugoslavia, this task was entrusted to a group of Yugoslav experts,[4] of whom the following three acted as editors: Professor Najdan Pašić, Professor Stanislav Grozdanić and Milorad Radević. The group prepared the original draft study, in Serbo-Croatian. The English text was largely recast and in some respects shortened by Mrs. E. Epstein, formerly of the Labour Law and Labour Relations Branch of the International Labour Office.

Purpose

The present volume is in no sense intended to be a complete critical or comparative analysis of the Yugoslav workers' management system. A large number of critical works already exist on the subject, including many from Yugoslav sources. The purpose of this book is therefore to give to readers in other countries as clear a picture as possible of the main features of the Yugoslav system, its aims and structure and its historical development, together with as much factual information as is available concerning its functioning and some of the current difficulties of workers' management in practice as noted by the Yugoslavs themselves.

Terminology

To make it easier for the reader to cope with the complexity of the subject and the special vocabulary used, a very full table of contents is provided, as well as a terminological index which contains some brief definitions, brief descriptions including statistics in two cases, and references to the parts of the book in which the fullest descriptions of particular concepts and institutions are to be found.

It may be added that ordinary English terms have been used whenever they will best convey the meaning to readers who are new to the subject. Thus, whereas most published works on the Yugoslav system refer to "workers' self-management", the International Labour Office has preferred to follow the precedent set in its earlier study on the subject, and to use the simpler expression "workers' management"; also in the interests of clarity, the "organ of self-management workers' control" is referred to as the "workers' supervisory commission".

Notes

[1] See, for instance, the Right to Organise and Collective Bargaining Convention, 1949 (No. 98), the Collective Agreements Recommendation, 1951 (No. 91), the Co-operation at the Level of the Undertaking Recommendation, 1952 (No. 94), the Communications within the Undertaking Recommendation, 1967 (No. 129), the Examination of Grievances Recommendation, 1967 (No. 130), the Workers' Representatives Convention, 1971 (No. 135), and the Workers' Representatives Recommendation, 1971 (No. 143).

[2] See, for instance, ILO: *Participation of workers in decisions within undertakings*, Documents of a technical meeting, Geneva, 20–29 November 1967, Labour-Management Relations Series, No. 33 (Geneva, 1969); ILO and United Nations Development Programme: *Report on the international seminar on workers' participation in decisions within undertakings, Belgrade*, 2–11 December 1969 (Geneva, ILO, 1970); ILO: *Workers' participation in decisions within undertakings, Oslo symposium*, Summary of discussions of a symposium on workers' participation in decisions within undertakings, Oslo, 20–30 August 1974, Labour-Management Relations Series, No. 48 (Geneva, 1976); J. Schregle: "Workers' participation in decisions within undertakings", in *International Labour Review* (Geneva, ILO), Jan.-Feb. 1976, pp. 1–15; "Co-determination in the Federal Republic of Germany: A comparative view", ibid., Jan.-Feb. 1978, pp. 81–98; ILO: *Workers' participation in decisions within undertakings* (Geneva, 1981).

[3] ILO: *Workers' management in Yugoslavia*, Studies and Reports, New Series, No. 64 (Geneva, 1962).

[4] The group included Prof. Najdan Pašić, Prof. Stanislav Grozdanić, Peter Toš, Dr. Aleksandar Vacić, Dr. Slobodan Ostojić, Drago Gorupić, Milorad Radević, Dr. Mijat Šuković, Albina Tušar, and Ruža Banjac. Andrej Grahor, at that time a member of the Presidium and a secretary of the Confederation of Trade Unions of Yugoslavia, was in charge of co-ordination.

CONTENTS

Tables

Diagrams

HISTORY AND BASIC PRINCIPLES OF WORKERS' MANAGEMENT IN YUGOSLAVIA

1

ORIGINS AND DEVELOPMENT

In its present form, workers' management in Yugoslavia is the outcome of an evolutionary process that has extended over a period of some 30 years. The process has included horizontal and vertical expansion, quantitative growth and qualitative changes. Since the main purpose of this volume is to describe the present system, it would be fastidious to enter into much detail concerning all the changes that have taken place. However, in order to understand the present system it is necessary to survey briefly its origins and the main lines along which it developed.

War, revolution and administrative socialism (1941–49)

While some of the philosophical ideas underlying the concept of workers' management date back to the nineteenth century, in Yugoslavia workers' management and some of its basic tenents grew out of an uprising against foreign occupying forces in the Second World War. From a very early stage that four-year struggle for the liberation of the country took on the character of a socialist revolution. "National liberation committees", chosen wherever possible by direct and secret ballot, were set up in the freed territories to mobilise resources for the liberation struggle as well as to organise economic affairs in the freed territories and manage publicly owned goods and property. It was in these circumstances, and in the extremely difficult wartime conditions, that the workers in some cases took over the management of factories. For example, the National Liberation Committee decided that a workers' council should be set up in the antimony factory in the town of Krupanj, in the liberated territory of Western Serbia. It was elected in September 1941, and successfully managed the factory until the territory was later re-occupied by the enemy. Other forms of workers' management were also introduced in some undertakings in the freed territories. But perhaps even more important for the development of workers' management was the widely felt need for self-reliance and independent initiative among the population actively supporting the "partisans" in their fight for independence and fundamental human rights.

After the war, a brief period of highly centralised management and planning followed, from 1945 to 1949. Yugoslavia, which was one of the least developed countries economically in Europe at the time, had suffered enormous human and material losses: according to official estimates, the country had lost about 1.7 million people—more than a tenth of its population—in the war, and about 3.5 million people were left homeless; mines and industrial plants were heavily damaged; on the railways only 23.4 per cent of the locomotives and 16.1 per cent of the stations were still in working order after the war. Centralised planning and management of the economy appeared at the time to provide the best solution for the reconstruction of the country. A large state-owned sector was rapidly created by confiscating the property of the occupiers and of the people who had collaborated with them, by appropriating war profits and by nationalising the means of production in industry, transport, banking and commerce. Family land holdings were limited to 10 hectares and the number of employees in small, artisan-type private enterprises was also strictly limited by law. Yet despite the creation of large state-owned farms over 80 per cent of arable land remained in the hands of small farmers, and a substantial number of small private undertakings also continued to function in industry and commerce.

The organisation of the economy was based on the principle of centralised socio-administrative management. The state-owned sector was intended to supply the motive force for the entire economy and to play the main role in carrying out state plans for the industrialisation of the country. State enterprises were subject to a complex hierarchical administrative apparatus which included planning commissions, ministries for the various sectors of the economy, and administrators in charge of every sector of the economy at the federal, republican and local levels. Within the undertaking, all authority was invested in the general manager, whose appointment was made and terminated by the competent organ of government. All workers were responsible to the manager, who was the highest disciplinary authority, and labour relations and wages were uniformly subject to government regulation.

The initiative and revolutionary zeal developed in the population by the war were channelled into productive efforts for reconstruction through the existing socio-political organisations: the trade unions, youth organisations and special cells and committees of the Communist party that existed within almost all undertakings had a powerful influence on working conditions and the status of workers. They were significant factors on which managers depended for steady production and government agencies for the implementation of economic policies. These socio-political organisations participated in the proceedings of the workers' consultation bodies which existed at the time. Such bodies assessed the achievement of production objectives and discussed the organisation of work, the application of new methods, work discipline, the economical use of raw materials, innovations in production and other relevant matters. Although considerable importance was attached to these consultation procedures, they remained entirely advisory in character. The managers of undertakings and the heads of major government agencies had the decisive say in the management of all economic activity.

This system of "administrative socialism", or state ownership and centralised administrative management of the major portion of the economy, proved capable of mobilising the creative forces needed for an economic recovery; by the end of 1949, total production had reached the pre-war level of 1939 and the first five-year industrialisation plan had been put into effect. However, certain anomalies and deficiencies soon emerged. The economy was overburdened by an increasingly weighty administrative apparatus for the regulation and control of production and distribution. Centralised planning, disproportionately oriented to-wards "state priorities", tended to favour some economic sectors, such as heavy industry, and to ignore the needs of popular consumption and the raising of living standards. Thus, despite a high rate of growth in total production, the people lived poorly in an atmosphere of want and severely restricted consumption. The uniformity and centralisation inherent in the system came into conflict with the aspirations and expectations of the people, and in the long run affected productivity.

These problems were intensified after 1949, when, as a result of the break with the Cominform, Yugoslavia found itself in a position of economic isolation. That was a decisive turning-point: once again the country had to mobilise its own internal creative forces and to appeal directly to the energy and initiative of its people in order to redesign its political and social institutions along independent lines.

Establishment of workers' councils and related political changes (1948–53)

The relatively short period from 1948 to 1953 constituted the first phase in the development of the workers' management system, and was marked by the legislative and other measures that laid the foundations for it. It began with the directive of the Federal Government and the trade unions concerning the experimental formation of workers' councils in state economic enterprises, and included the first changes in the

3

centralised administrative system of economic management, designed to open the way for the development of workers' management. This period came to an end with the adoption in 1953 of the constitutional law which confirmed the changes introduced in the intervening years in both economic and political institutions.

The early months of 1949 saw the formation, in some 215 large state enterprises throughout the country, of workers' councils with broad though still mainly advisory functions. This movement, promoted by recommendations of the Federal Government and the trade unions, met with strong support among the workers, so that by June 1949, when a law concerning the surrender of state economic enterprises and groups of enterprises to the management of the work collectives was passed, workers' councils had already been formed on an experimental basis in 520 enterprises. The passage of that law, handing over the management of factories to the workers, marked the first decisive step towards the building of a society in which the workers themselves are to become the direct masters of the conditions and fruits of their work. The law clearly stated in its first article that manufacturing, mining, communications, transport, trading, agriculture, forestry, municipal and other public undertakings should, as the property of the whole nation, be administered on behalf of the community by their work collectives under the economic plan and on the basis of rights and duties established by law. Each work collective (i.e. the workers of an enterprise, collectively) managed its affairs through a workers' council, elected by secret ballot by all the workers in the enterprise, or for each enterprise in a group of enterprises, for a period of one year,[1] and a board of management appointed by the workers' council.

The work collective had the right to recall the entire council or individual members of it at any time, and the board of management was likewise answerable to the workers' council. The main functions of the latter were to approve the outline plan and balance sheet of the enterprise or undertaking and to take decisions concerning the management of the undertaking and the attainment of production objectives, to adopt rules of operation (approved by the board of management and the supervisory public authority or by the group of undertakings) and to discuss the reports of the board of management and evaluate its work. Depending on the size of the undertaking, the workers' council could have from 15 to 150 members; in small undertakings with no more than 30 workers the entire workforce made up the workers' council. The board of management was composed of from three to 11 members, including the manager. It had extensive duties and powers concerning all phases of production planning and the operation of the undertaking as well as certain aspects of personnel management and work discipline.

4

Over-all responsibility for the management of the undertaking was vested in the general manager, who carried out the decisions of the board of management as well as the instructions and directives emanating from the management of the group of which the undertaking was a member and from the appropriate government agencies. Within the framework of the economic plan, and in harmony with the decisions of the board of management, the manager was authorised to conclude contracts and dispose of the resources of the undertaking. He was bound to act as the guardian of legality in business transactions and the observance of labour legislation, with power to refuse to carry out any decisions of the board of management that were in his judgement unlawful, the final decision in the event of a conflict of opinion of this nature lying within the competence of the group of undertakings or of the competent government agency. The position of the manager illustrates the hybrid nature of the relations established in this phase, when workers' management was being introduced into the economic organisations which, by virtue of their ownership and the directives received from government departments, were still state undertakings. The manager served as a link between the two systems, acting as the executive organ of the internal workers' management machinery while at the same time being .a government employee responsible for the execution of government economic policy in supervising the operation of the undertaking. As will be seen below, later changes in the position of the manager reflected continued attempts to eliminate this dualism and strengthen workers' management.

The first elections to workers' councils were held from August to October 1950. In undertakings where workers' councils of a consultative nature had already been set up earlier, the terms of reference and powers of those councils were brought into line with the provisions of the 1949 law. The organs of workers' management thus began to operate within the existing system of centralised government management of the economy; but it quickly became evident that in order to provide a basis for the favourable development of workers' management, it was necessary to change the status and character of state undertakings, as well as the economic system as a whole. In these early years, immediately after the introduction of workers' councils, some preliminary but important steps began to be taken in this direction. The complex hierarchical structure of government management in which the undertaking was the lowest unit was gradually dismantled. A series of ministries in charge of various sectors of the economy were abolished and superseded by other administrative agencies, later transformed into the management of groups of undertakings which were, themselves, eventually broken up in the interests of fortifying the operational independence of individual undertakings. At the end of 1951 a new system of planning was introduced which gave undertakings greater freedom to decide on product choice in relation to market demands, while maintaining a mandatory minimum utilisation of productive capacity. Investment in new undertakings remained under the jurisdiction of government agencies, which also established the amount of the remuneration fund for each enterprise. During 1952 and 1953 a series of economic laws and regulations were passed which, taken together, significantly increased the independence of the undertaking and the rights of its workers' management organs, particularly with regard to the foundation and winding up of an undertaking and the distribution of wages and salaries within the framework of an approved remuneration fund. Of greatest importance was the fact that the undertaking's own income and expenditure ceased to be a part of the state budget, while it was obliged to fulfil its social obligations with proceeds from the sale of its products on the market.

Nevertheless, despite the many changes introduced, the individual undertaking continued to operate in a framework that was still largely determined by the Federal Government. The degree of involvement of the work collective in management decision-making still did not substantially or directly influence its financial position, since the Federal Government took over almost all its income over and above the centrally regulated remuneration fund. Thus in this first phase the economic system retained the essential characteristics of a centrally managed economy. It is important to note, however, that already at this first phase in the development of workers' management the changes introduced in the status of the worker in the undertaking were linked with broader changes, not only in the system of management of the economy but also in the country's political institutions. A new law adopted in 1952 designated people's committees as the basic organs of government, and laid the foundation for the extension of local self-government and the decentralisation of decision-making power on both the political and the economic plane. Under the constitutional law adopted in 1953, the new status of workers in production was given political expression by the introduction of the chamber of producers, a body of representatives, chosen directly by the workers in self-managed undertakings, as the second chamber of the assembly (the highest representative body) in the administrative districts, in the republics, at the federal level, and later in the "communes." At the same time, it was decided to change the role of the Communist Party, now the League of Communists, from one of direct management of social affairs through the machinery of government to one of ideological guidance and leadership in development activity within the new system of workers' management.

Rapid growth of the system (1953–63)

The second phase in the development of workers' management covers the ten-year period from 1953 to 1963, a period of dynamic change culminating in the adoption of the Constitution of 1963 which gave normative expression to the developments up to that time and opened up new perspectives for the future. The numerous changes that took place during this period may be seen to have evolved in four different directions.

Extension to the service sector

In the first place, workers' management was extended to new spheres of activity beyond the production of goods, in particular to apply to public and social services. By 1954 the system already covered rail transport, postal and telecommunication services and public utilities such as urban transport, water supply and sanitation. The constitutional law of 1953 had laid the basis for this development by specifying that workers' management should be guaranteed to working people in the fields of education, culture and social services. The process of transforming every school, hospital and scientific or cultural institution into a self-managing organisation was therefore undertaken. However, since these services could not, by their very nature, be administered entirely in the interests of the workers engaged in them nor on the basis of the principle of a commercial sale of services analogous to the sale of goods, special arrangements were made to enable the workers' management organs in these organisations "of special social interest" to include representatives of other institutions concerned and of consumers of the services provided, as well as the workers of the service organisations themselves.

The extension of workers' management to public and social services was handicapped in the beginning by the method of financing their activities through state budgeting, a factor which severely limited their financial base for self-management. A remedy was found for this difficulty through the setting up of separate, autonomous funds for financing public and social services, resources for which were collected from various fees or contributions and the administration of which was entrusted to boards composed of representatives of workers from the services in question and of consumers and other citizens concerned.

Decentralisation of decision-making within the undertaking

The second direction of development during this phase was the progressive decentralisation and democratisation of the decision-making process within undertakings. Changes were introduced which substantially modified the internal centralised, hierarchical structure of the enterprise, by continually enlarging the range of matters on which workers were empowered to take decisions within their workers' management bodies. In 1956, at the time of the fifth regular election of workers' councils, a decentralised system was introduced in all the larger and more complex organisations whereby some of the powers formerly concentrated in the hands of one central council were transferred to workers' councils elected by the various departments and shops in the enterprise. In many cases, these shop or department councils were also empowered to elect their own boards of management.

A further movement towards the decentralisation of workers' management and bringing decision-making power closer to the worker was the expansion of self-managing activities in the "economic work units" of the undertaking. Formed at first as accounting units for the purpose of analysing economic results and productivity, these units gradually took over other workers' management functions in the organisation of production and the distribution of income. The status and functions of these work units had become a subject of lively controversy towards the end of this period.

Experience gained in everyday practice contributed to the strengthening of workers' management during this phase, as the workers became more accustomed to assuming the responsibilities it entailed. For example, the submission of reports by the workers' councils and boards of management to general meetings of all the workers was becoming established practice, and the councils took it upon themselves to set up committees and other bodies where deemed necessary to help them carry out their functions more effectively. Finally, an important change which fortified the authority of workers' management bodies was introduced in 1958, by the Labour Relations Law which transferred the power to hire and fire workers from the general manager to the work collectives themselves, acting through their elected organs.

Increased autonomy of individual undertakings and their workforce

A third direction of development was a gradual increase in the independence of undertakings and expansion of the rights of the work collectives in decisions concerning the disposal of the income they earned. The evolution in this direction was relatively slow, marked during this ten-year period by a few reforms concerning the economic system as a whole, particularly in the machinery for the concentration and use of capital accumulation.

Although the work collectives were legally empowered to dispose freely of the means of production entrusted to them, under legislation of 1954 the governments retained almost complete control over the disposal

8

of the surplus value created by the undertaking. The income remaining after payment of such expenses as interest on loans, sales taxes and payments into the remuneration fund was divided into two parts, one of which went to the federation and republics in the form of taxes while the remainder was distributed between local authorities and the undertaking, in accordance with decisions taken jointly by local authorities and responsible self-management bodies of the undertaking. As has already been noted, the Federal Government retained almost complete monopoly of investment funds, which were derived from accumulated interest on the sums set aside by undertakings for depreciation of fixed assets and from certain other sources. The influence of the Government was even stronger in respect of distribution of resources for personal income in the undertaking: while the workers' council could propose scales of remuneration, they could not be put into effect until approved by the local authority and the local council of the trade union. Only a few years later, however, in 1957–58, regulations substantially enlarged the rights of the work collectives, which were empowered to allocate freely the net income of the undertaking (after payment of operating expenses and taxes) for personal consumption and for reserve funds of capital accumulation, as they saw fit. Control by outside political organisations was limited to the right of the local authorities to make comments or recommendations on decisions of the collectives regarding distribution of income among funds and earnings. The collectives were also entitled to establish freely their own scales of personal income. Another major step forward towards greater independence for individual undertakings was taken by legislation passed in March 1961, under which the work collectives gained the right to decide freely on the distribution of their net income, after deducting a 15 per cent tax on total income, and the authorities finally abandoned their remaining rights regarding the determination of the distribution of the income of enterprises as between personal income and the various types of funds.

There still remained, however, some important administrative limitations on the decision-making power of the work collectives. The Federal Government continued to regulate prices for about 70 per cent of the goods produced, and retained firm control over the foreign trade and foreign exchange systems. In order to avoid too great inequalities in the financial situation of different enterprises, a tax on "exceptional income" was imposed on the more prosperous undertakings, ostensibly as a temporary measure.

Political decentralisation and representation of work organisations

The fourth direction of development during this period concerns the evolution of the political organs, designed to expand the area of workers' management so as to encompass the organs of local government and the political decision-making system as a whole. Important structural reforms were introduced in 1955–56 at the level of "local communities", on the assumption that it was at this level that a direct link could be established between the interests of the working people organised in work collectives and the interest of the community at large, and that real participation of the workers in political decisions concerning social affairs could best be ensured. The focus of the reforms was on the decentralisation of decisions by transferring responsibility for all government matters that could reasonably be handled at the local level to the communes, and by the formation of groups of communes with responsibility for carrying out certain types of functions jointly in place of the previous centralised hierarchical structure of government in which the commune had been the lowest administrative unit. In particular, decisions relating to the workers' management institutions and enterprises were largely delegated to communal bodies, namely the communal assembly and its council of producers. These changes were aimed at establishing close and democratic relations between undertakings and political bodies. However, some difficulties arose at first because of a tendency to create centres of bureaucratic power within the communes themselves, and it was not until the workers' management bodies in undertakings were given greater economic independence, by the developments described above, that the new system of decision-making at the communal level took on a more democratic character.

The transformation of political institutions was not confined to the local level. To give political expression to the extension of workers' management to a variety of work organisations other than "economic" organisations engaged in the production of goods, the Constitution of 1963 provided for the formation of five-chamber federal, republican and provincial assemblies, to include, in addition to one political chamber elected by all citizens, chambers of delegates from "economic", educational and cultural, health and welfare, and administrative work organisations, elected by the self-managed work collectives in those organisations. At the commune level, the assembly still had two chambers, but the chamber of work communities (formerly the council of producers) was enlarged to include delegates from work organisations other than those engaged in the production of goods.[2]

Extension to investment policy and election of managers, and stimulation of market competition (1963–74)

The third phase in the development of workers' management covered the period from 1963 to 1974. It included the economic and social reforms of 1965 and further constitutional amendments, up to the passage of the new Constitution of 1974 which ushered in the current period. The main feature of this phase was an effort to put the entire capital of undertakings under workers' management, in order to give their workers the right to decide not only on matters of current production but also on development and investment policies. In addition, the independence of individual undertakings was further strengthened by the abolition of state controls and the rescinding of regulations regarding their internal organs of management and by measures to stimulate productivity and market competition.

As has already been indicated, up to 1963 the Yugoslav system was marked by a peculiar kind of dualism, in that although workers' management in economic and other types of activity was being extended and strengthened, the management of resources for the expansion of production had remained in the hands of the Government, primarily at the federal level. Since they were unable to plan and manage their investment and development themselves, there was no incentive for undertakings to take an interest in the efficient management of social resources. The ill-effects of this situation had become apparent as early as 1961, in a falling-off of the very high rates of economic growth achieved earlier, a decline in the rate of increase of productivity and a low level of utilisation of productive capacity. As a result, political pressures built up for greater freedom for undertakings to manage their entire revenue, radical changes in the system of economic planning, freer marketing, and the elimination of inequalities in the conditions applying to organisations in different sectors of economic activity. The achievement of these aims took up a full decade, during which many important changes were introduced that radically altered the economic foundations and method of operation of the workers' management system. A decisive step towards the elimination of state control of the capital accumulation of undertakings was taken in 1964 with the abolition of the investment funds held by government agencies and the transfer of those resources to independent banks organised on a self-managing basis. This led to a considerable change in the handling of resources for new investment, modernisation, and expansion of the productive capacity of undertakings. Whereas in 1961 government agencies held 61.7 per cent of all resources for the financing of investments, by 1971, 50.9 per cent of those resources had been transferred to the banks and only 15.2 per cent remained in the hands of the socio-political communities.

In 1965 a whole series of economic and social reforms were introduced in a relatively short period, with the aim of achieving—

(a) more efficient operation of undertakings and utilisation of social resources through more intensive use of productive capacity and stricter evaluation of economic results, with regard both to individual workers and to the groups of workers in different units of the undertaking;

(b) equality in conditions of operation for the different sectors of economic activity and different undertakings by the gradual elimination of government price-fixing for certain products and other forms of government intervention such as subsidies and special compensatory payments;

(c) greater freedom for undertakings to compete as commodity producers subject to the economic laws of the market; and

(d) liberalisation of export and import trade, in order to increase the competitivity of the Yugoslav economy on international markets and achieve convertibility of the currency.

This phase of development also saw the introduction of changes within the self-managing organisations which greatly increased the independence of the work collectives. Thus, a law on the election of self-management organs in work organisations, adopted in 1964,[3] made provision for the election of the manager of the undertaking every four or five years. A joint committee of representatives of the work collective and of government agencies was responsible for making recommendations regarding the appointment or dismissal of the manager, and the decision was then taken by the workers' council on the basis of that recommendation. Thus relations between the manager and the workers were reversed: whereas in the early phases of workers' management the manager had full authority to hire and fire workers, the workers had now gained the right to choose and dismiss the manager. Other administrative personnel having executive and supervisory functions were appointed by the board of management, but those decisions were also subject to the approval of the workers' council. In December 1968 a further important change in the internal organisation of work collectives was introduced by a constitutional amendment which gave the workers full rights to decide for themselves on the composition, structure, method of election, term of office and powers and functions of the workers' management organs within the work organisation. The election of a workers' council remained mandatory, but the constitution of other management organs and executive bodies, including the election of a manager, was left to the discretion of the work collective, to be decided independently by internally adopted by-laws or other self-management rules.

This period was also marked by the continued development of "self-managing communities of interest", linking the production of goods and other spheres of activity, in which working people were represented as both users and providers of services. These communities, which had grown up spontaneously to take the place of government agencies in the field of social services, were legally defined and made mandatory by a constitutional amendment of 1971.[4]

The economic and social reforms begun in 1965 greatly contributed to the emancipation of workers' management from the political and bureaucratic tutelage of government departments. Greater operational independence of enterprises and stricter application of market criteria in evaluating the results of labour gave a strong impulse to efficient management, initiative and increased productivity. The performance of the economy benefited from the modernisation of production and the elimination of outdated technology and unprofitable operations. However, the changes introduced also had some effects which were not always to the advantage of the work collectives. In particular, the transfer of investment funds from government agencies to the banks tended to create new centres of economic power on which undertakings depended for credit. Despite the introduction of self-management in the administration of the banks, with representatives of both organisations of associated labour and socio-political communities on their boards of management, the political authorities, represented by government officials, or managers of large undertakings, retained a dominant influence on investment policy. In addition, the increased reliance on the free functioning of a competitive market led to the accentuation of differences in the financial situation of individual undertakings and branches of the economy. These differences, combined with the serious inequalities that already existed in levels of economic development in the various parts of the country, the relative scarcity of resources for development and the arbitrary exercise of economic power on the part of the central banks, gave rise to widespread dissatisfaction, conflicts between regional or local and wider interests, and political dissension.

Workers' management was further undermined by the increasing tendency for a "technostructure" of professional managerial personnel to take over effective management of undertakings. The constitutional amendment which gave the work collectives the right to determine the composition and powers of the organs of management in the undertaking frequently resulted in the transfer of the right of decision on many important matters to boards of management or other organs which were more professional in character than representative of the workers in the undertaking. This took place with the formal agreement of the workers, who were persuaded that professional management with wide authority was essential to the efficient operation of the undertaking, on which their personal income depended, in a competitive market.

These shortcomings, anomalies and weaknesses, which gradually emerged in everyday practice over the period 1965 to 1971, and which were perceived as endangering the possibilities of a real transformation of society into a total system of workers' management, led to a new series of institutional changes, mainly in order to extend and protect the rights of workers in self-managed enterprises and to enable them to assume effective control of the entire income resulting from their labour. These changes were incorporated in various constitutional amendments adopted during the period and, finally, in the new Constitution of 1974[5] and the Associated Labour Law of 1976. Those provisions will be referred to where relevant in subsequent parts of the text, which describe the evolution of workers' management in the current phase.

SIGNIFICANCE OF WORKERS' MANAGEMENT IN YUGOSLAV SOCIETY

As described in the previous section, the history of the development of workers' management in Yugoslavia covers a period of about three decades. Once narrowly identified with workers' councils in government undertakings, workers' management has grown into a complex and highly involved system embracing the entire organisation of Yugoslav society. Despite the relatively short time that has elapsed since its inception in 1950, in Yugoslavia workers' management can no longer be regarded merely as an "experiment" with new forms of production relations. Indeed, from the very beginning, it was envisaged by its authors as a means of giving concrete expression to a historical process, "the social emancipation of labour", by creating a new status for working people both at the workplace and in the management of the affairs of the community at large.

The search for an alternative to technocratic, impersonalised labour relations and to the bureaucratisation of social relations in general is an important concern of modern society. Many countries in all parts of the world have been impelled to seek new methods of liberating workers from the constraints and alienation of modern industrial civilisation. Ideological, ethical and psycho-social concepts have converged in recent years to promote the democratisation of relations at the workplace and the humanisation of working conditions by various systems designed to enable workers to participate to an increasing degree in the determination of conditions of work and the management of the undertakings in which they work. In several countries of Europe and other parts of the world legislative measures or contractual arrangements on a national scale have introduced various institutional forms of workers' participation in decision-making in enterprises on a wide range of general matters, and there are countless examples of individual undertakings in which new internal systems of labour relations have been created whereby workers assume a greater share in management decisions relating to the operation of the undertaking.

While the principle that workers have a right to participate in the determination of working conditions and in other decisions that affect them directly is now widely accepted, and consultative or negotiating systems for this purpose are well entrenched, workers' participation in management none the less remains a highly controversial issue. Proposed measures relating to the representation of workers in management organs have given rise to wide popular debate and serious political dissensions in some cases, even where they were envisaged as being applicable only in certain sectors of the economy or to enterprises of a certain size. Thus, despite the widespread interest and concern aroused by these trends, practical measures to increase the workers' share in the management of undertakings are often partial, experimental, reactive or palliative in their effect. Moreover, although there have been an increasing number of cases in which workers in exceptional circumstances have themselves taken over the management of their undertaking, such instances are on the whole isolated and unusual. The originality of the Yugoslav system lies in its sustained effort to build up gradually an entire social system based on the workers' management principle.

The essence of the idea of workers' management in Yugoslavia is the creation of a system of relations in which individual workers, in association with their fellows, directly manage the means, conditions and results of their labour and thus achieve control over the totality of social relations in the community. Conceived in this fashion, workers' management seeks to do away with the wage labour relationship of subordination and dependency. Under the logic of the system, the means of production are no longer independent economic forces beyond the control of those who work with them; management is no longer separate from execution; and the disposal of the products of labour is no longer separated from direct participation in their production. The fundamental criterion for the achievement of workers' management is the degree to which participation of workers in "associated labour" ensures their direct participation, on a footing of equality, in the management both of work and of all the other affairs of the community. Workers' management is therefore not simply a series of measures designed to alleviate or partially compensate for the negative effects of the wage-labour status of the workforce, nor merely an institutional mechanism for popular decision-making in the economic or other spheres of social life. It represents a fundamental change in the basic relations in production, which in turn becomes the basis for all the other social rights and freedoms of the workers.

The workers' management system seeks to vest the social power that comes from the management and control of concentrated means of production in the hands of the workers themselves, under the system of associated labour. A consistent effort has been made to combat centralising tendencies and to find institutional means of returning decision-making power to the labour base. This is the focus of the reforms introduced by the Constitution of 1974 and the Associated Labour Law of 1976, which aim, on the one hand, to avoid the formation of a management élite and, on the other hand, to consolidate the links between the workers in "basic organisations of associated labour" and political organs, in order to build up a form of social organisation run entirely by the workers at the levels of the local communities, the communes, the provinces, the republics and the federation as a whole.

It goes without saying that the attainment of such an ideal presents enormous conceptual problems and practical difficulties. Such a workers' management system is not built up in a socio-political vacuum, and its progress does not depend wholly on the will of the parties concerned. The degree of development of productive forces in society, relations between different social groups, the level of social consciousness and mass culture, all influence the scope and pace of such progress.

When workers' management was introduced in Yugoslavia in 1950, the economy was in a poorly integrated state: large sectors of activity were divided up among small, autarchic groups, alongside of centrally administered sectors. In addition, the level of economic development varied widely among different parts of the country. There are few countries in Europe where economic development had been as uneven as in Yugoslavia and, as a result, the objective interests of different regions often conflicted, so that it was difficult to develop uniform economic policies for the country as a whole. Moreover, since Yugoslavia is a federation of republics and autonomous provinces which retain a large measure of sovereignty, it has been necessary to create new institutions and economic instruments in order to help promote economic relations between more and less developed regions and to establish workers' management on a basis of equality throughout the federation.

Partly as a consequence of this situation, one of the inherent contradictions remaining in the Yugoslav system is the continuing need for the State to set extensive and detailed norms concerning the status and activity of workers' management organisations. While in principle the laws regulating the relations of workers in associated labour are designed to protect the management rights of workers from bureaucratic or technocratic influences, in practice frequent and sudden changes in economic regulations to meet the day-to-day needs of economic policy tend to impede long-term planning of production and development in individual enterprises and thus have the effect of limiting the scope of workers' management, even though such decisions are taken by "socio-political bodies" constituted on the "delegation principle" and therefore directly linked to organisations of associated labour in all spheres of activity.

In Yugoslav theory the development of workers' management is inseparable from the elimination of the government monopoly over the expression "articulation", and interpretation of the general interests of society and the management of its economic and social affairs. These two trends are seen as the two complementary parts of the same socio-historical process.

However, the limitation and gradual elimination of government functions in the economic and other spheres of social life have not always been automatically accompanied by the development of workers' management machinery as a substitute for the machinery of government in carrying out these functions. Between the diminishing jurisdiction of the State and the sectors of the economy under workers' management there were at times gaps where unrestrained economic activity and improvised government intervention have occurred. Difficulties arose, for example, when the system of centralised administrative planning was abandoned before workers' management methods of development planning had become fully established, a situation which rendered the entire planning system insufficiently effective at certain periods. In the area of investment policy, the Government long continued to reserve for itself control over most of the resources available for investment. At first this was done directly, through state investment funds, and later by exercising direct or indirect influence on the investment policy of the banks in which these resources were deposited, while only a smaller portion of capital accumulation was left in the hands of economic enterprises under workers' management. This control had unfortunate economic results, in that enterprises showed less interest in the revenue they earned and a tendency towards a less responsible management of the social resources entrusted to them. Not only did these problems threaten the development of workers' management, but they also tended to restrain the hitherto dynamic expansion of the economy. As has been seen above, the economic reforms of 1965, the constitutional amendments of 1971, the new Constitution of 1974 and the Associated Labour Law of 1976 represent successive steps taken to overcome these problems and to pursue the development of self-management as a coherent system embracing society as a whole.

To sum up, three essential characteristics of the historical development of workers' management in Yugoslavia must be kept in mind.

In the first place the changes introduced at every phase in the evolution of the system were dictated both by the long-term socialist goal of the emancipation of labour in the management of production and by the need to solve practical problems at a given stage of social development in the interests of strengthening the control of workers over their working and living conditions and social affairs in general. The theoretical vision of a more just and humane society was thus linked directly with the struggle for social changes based on the aspirations, difficulties and everyday experience of millions of workers.

The second essential feature is the effect of workers' management in production relations on all other aspects of social relations. The establishment of a new status for working people in associated labour created the need to adapt the entire political system, its institutional structure and the way in which it functions in practice, to the new relations in production whereby the workers, organised in associated labour, took on the decision-making role in all economic and social matters. Every phase in the development of workers' management in production relations has been accompanied and supported by corresponding changes designed to democratise the organisation and functioning of the organs of government, the systems of planning and directing economic and social development, the composition of representative socio-political bodies, which have been linked ever more directly to their social base, and the nature and activities of the "socio-political organisations".

A third important characteristic is that every step in the development of workers' management has been aimed at extending the possibilities of free and direct expression of the numerous and different interests of people in associated labour, both as individuals and as members of particular social groups, and gradually eliminating the influence of external forces that run counter to these interests. Thus, the private or state monopoly of ownership of the means of production and the authoritarian structure of work organisations and other institutions, reflected in the separation and isolation of managerial functions, are gradually disappearing. The spread of workers' management to all sectors of the economy has made it possible to achieve a more democratic organisation of the process of political decision-making, since matters of everyday concern, whether at work or outside it, on which working people freely express their views and take decisions in the primary units of society, i.e. the basic self-managing organisations and communities, are to an increasing extent directly taken into account in decision-making on the problems and directions of the development of society as a whole.

BASIC PRINCIPLES AND KEY CONCEPTS

Workers' management in Yugoslavia has consistently evolved as an original economic and socio-political system, distinct from the market economy based on privately owned industry and from the centrally planned socialist systems, though containing elements of both. It is perhaps useful at this point to formulate briefly the basic concepts of the system which underlie the institutional structure and practice of self-management today.

Social ownership of the means of production

From the first, the concept of "social ownership" of the means of production has been a fundamental principle of the workers' management system. This means that all productive resources are collectively owned by the whole community; they are neither the property of the State, nor of private individuals, nor of the groups of associated workers who manage them.

In Yugoslavia, as in other socialist countries, private ownership of the means of production was abolished by the transition to state ownership through expropriation and nationalisation; but the system of state ownership guaranteed to the public authorities the right to dispose of the product of labour, while the workers using state-owned resources remained wage earners who could exert only indirect influence on the direction of social and economic policy. The aim of workers' management in Yugoslavia, however, is to place the responsibility for managing socially owned resources and the disposal of income derived from the use of those resources in the hands of the workers themselves, organised in associated labour. Associated labour is a system of relations, rights and responsibilities that people who jointly work with socially owned means of production establish among themselves, as well as with other groups of workers and socio-legal entities and with the community as a whole. Social ownership is expressed in the right of workers organised in associated labour to use, manage and dispose of the social resources entrusted to them and the product of their labour, including the right to appropriate resources for personal income and "joint consumption", in common with other workers, on a basis of equality. The concept of social ownership thus provides the economic basis for the entire self-management system.

Workers in associated labour also bear the responsibility for the social resources with which they work and are under an obligation to preserve their value and to expand and improve them. Any action that endangers social ownership undermines workers' management. Hence the need to protect and defend social ownership by legal and other means, since it is the economic foundation of workers' management. In addition to legal and judicial protection, special institutions have been created to safeguard social ownership.[6] All rights to use, manage and dispose of social assets and of the product of labour with social resources can only be founded on law or on general workers' management regulations adopted in conformity with the law.[7]

Associated labour

Associated labour is the general concept embracing all forms of relations and institutions established among working people who jointly manage the socially owned means of production and dispose of the income resulting from their labour, in conformity with the Constitution and the law. This term denotes a specific new form of production and social relations, linking equal, mutually dependent and responsible workers voluntarily and freely associated in the production process and in other forms of work, and in all decision-making connected with their management.

The status of individuals in associated labour is exclusively determined by their participation in the work and the management of social resources. All working people—all citizens—have an equal right to enter into associated labour and to take on the corresponding obligations in respect of work and workers' management. This constitutionally guaranteed right to work with socially owned resources or means of production is thus the foundation of all the other rights belonging to people working under the system of workers' management in associated labour, i.e. the right to manage jointly and on equal terms with other workers the work and business of the organisation of associated labour in which they work, to regulate mutual relations at work, and to earn a personal income. This right thus represents the legal expression of a permanent linkage between associated labour, social ownership and workers' management.

Organisations of associated labour

Workers exercise their management rights by associating in organisations of associated labour. There are three main levels and forms of organisations of associated labour, namely the basic organisation, the work organisation and the composite organisation of associated labour, and, in addition, the work community. The primary unit for associating labour is the basic organisation of associated labour within which working people exercise the rights and fulfil the obligations deriving from joint labour with socially owned means of production. They carry out their work, manage the operation and affairs of the organisation, decide on the pooling of their labour and resources with other basic organisations or in other forms of association, decide on the distribution of income (including allocation for personal incomes, joint consumption, and investments for expansion and reserves), distribute resources for personal incomes in conformity with the principle of distribution according to the work done, and regulate labour relations.

Organisations of associated labour are thus a radically different type of institution from the traditional privately owned or state-owned undertaking. In the first place, a system of voluntary association of workers, on the basis of "self-management agreements", and on terms of equality of status and rights, is substituted for wage-labour relationships and to a great extent for the hierarchical structure of authority. The same principle of voluntary association and equality of the associated parties applies to the association of basic organisations among themselves and with other types of socio-legal entities, for the pooling of labour and resources for joint production or other activities.

In the second place, through the decisions made by workers concerning the distribution of income in line with their own immediate and long-term interests, the basic organisations of associated labour themselves carry out the necessary concentration and allocation of investment resources. This they do by pooling their labour and resources with those of other such basic organisations either directly or through banks whose main management organs are composed of delegates from the basic organisations of associated labour that pool their assets in them.[8] Income created in all forms of associating labour and resources is distributed among the basic organisations of associated labour that participated in its formation in proportion to their contributions. They therefore retain the possibility of deciding on the pooling of their labour and resources, expanding thus the financial base for their own labour. According to the theory of workers' management, this would in turn enable workers to reach an ever higher level of satisfaction of personal and social needs on the basis of their own decisions.

The workers in organisations of associated labour who assume the tasks of management also assume the risks involved. Since decisions on the distribution of income between personal earnings, joint consumption and investment are taken by the workers themselves, and not by some higher authority or outside centre of economic power, they are motivated to strike a balance between their immediate interests and the long-term interests of the organisation. The principle that workers' earnings depend on their own good judgement in managing the affairs of the organisation is one of the basic driving forces behind the whole system of workers' management. This principle extends to the management of economic affairs on a broader scale, through the voluntary association of basic organisations that pool their resources in banks managed by their own representatives. The workers thus gain the right of decision in the allocation of social capital based on their own labour.

21

Income as the main economic incentive

The economic concept of profit has no place in the Yugoslav workers' management system. The new approach is expressed by the notion of income as the basic economic incentive for economic activity and for the measurement of its results. Income earned on the basis of labour performed is the property of working people and of society as a whole. It is managed by the workers themselves according to agreed social principles. Income is thus one of the key concepts of the system, embodying the workers' rights of management and decision-making with regard to the results of their labour. Also embodied in the concept of income is the interdependence of the personal interests of associated workers, the interests of the organisations in which they are associated, and the interests of the community both locally and on a wider scale.

The achievement of an increase in income is the basic incentive for associating labour and resources among basic organisations, by decision of the workers in the organisations concerned, taking account of their own interests and the wider interests of society. For this reason, every self-management agreement concerning the pooling of labour and resources concluded among self-managing organisations and communities must contain precise rules for the distribution of the jointly earned income.[9] The right and duty to decide on the allocation of income is one of the most important rights and obligations of the workers in basic organisations of associated labour. As it is exercised on a broader scale, they gain the opportunity of expressing their ideas and taking decisions concerning the key questions of the maintenance and development of society as a whole, and about all matters that directly or indirectly influence their conditions of life and work. Thus, the priorities of cultural and scientific development, health and welfare, the general needs of defence and security, and "social protection" in all its forms, are all matters for discussion and decision-making in the basic organisations of associated labour.

In practice, of course, there are very great differences with regard to the scope for direct decision-making by workers in the basic organisations on the allocation of income according to the particular questions at issue. Obligations to the community in the form of taxes and other contributions are not established directly by the workers, but are laid down by law in some cases and in others by binding self-management agreements or by-laws. However, the process of making these decisions does not by-pass the workers in associated labour whose income is directly in question. Through their delegates in the assemblies of the socio-political communities, from the communal to the federal level, and of the "self-managing communities of interest" which provide a meeting-ground for all interests concerned in the supply of public or social services, the workers in basic organisations participate indirectly in such decisions, although the scope of their influence and the extent of free decision-making they enjoy is much less in this case than it is in the allocation and distribution of net income within their own organisations.

Free exchange of labour through self-managing communities of interest

One of the original features of the Yugoslav workers' management system is the linkage of organisations engaged in production and those supplying social and public services. In the early years, workers' management was limited to the sphere of the production of goods, but one of the important facets of its development has been the gradual extension of workers' management to services such as education, health care, social security, the development and diffusion of science and culture, and essential public services, and the close integration of the production of goods with these other areas of work.

The provision of these services has ceased to be a domain of state control and budget financing, and has been included within the ambit of workers' management and decision-making concerning the disposal of social income. This is achieved by the so-called "free exchange of labour" between the providers and users of the services concerned. The institutional framework in which it is embodied is the self-managing community of interest, managed jointly by the workers in the organisation providing the service and those who consume the service and who contribute part of their personal income to its financing. In the assemblies of self-managing communities of interest, delegates of consumers and delegates of providers of services are equally represented and, proceeding from the guidelines laid down by the workers they represent, decide together about the financing, operation and development of services and conclude self-management agreements for the long-term regulation of these matters. The equal status of workers engaged in the production of goods and in other spheres of activity and their interdependence and mutual solidarity are thus given concrete expression. This manner of linking various fields of activity is designed to guarantee—

(a) that working people who contribute part of their income for social services may directly influence the satisfaction of their needs and control the use of the resources they contribute, thus strengthening their own management status;

(b) that, on the basis of their own labour, workers in the field of social services may earn incomes, derived partly from the contributions set aside from the income of basic organisations of associated labour and partly from contributions of individual workers, these contributions providing the financial basis for workers' management;

(c) the avoidance of arrangements that would imply a different status for workers engaged in production and those in other activities, or that would impose market pressures which should have no place in the satisfaction of social needs;

(d) that work in activities other than production may be linked as directly as possible with production, and may thus become an integral part of the socio-economic activity of the country as a whole and an important element in its productive and creative power.

It goes without saying, however, that this link between the production of goods and other work does not completely exclude government intervention in the field of social services. In matters deemed to be of particular social interest, the Government retains specific and very important regulatory and supervisory functions. Those functions do not necessarily disturb, but in fact serve to increase and further guarantee the essential reciprocal linkage and mutual dependence of all social labour within the workers' management system. This linkage finds its institutional expression in the constitutional device whereby the self-managing communities of interest are among the bodies that elect delegates to the chambers of associated labour of the commune and republican assemblies.[10]

As will be seen in more detail in Chapter 5, these communities of interest in the social services are only one, although the most important, of several forms of direct linkage of the interests of working people managing their own affairs without the intervention of the Government or through the market. These forms of self-managing organisations are being increasingly used in other fields, especially where the nature of activities is such that linkage of producers and users through the market does not sufficiently safeguard the general interest, as in public utilities, power production and supply, water management, housing, or highway maintenance.

Changing role of the State

The State, in the Yugoslav system of self-management relations, has a greatly reduced but still important role in the planning and management of the economy and social affairs. The theory of workers' management entails the withering away of state power, but the nature of social relations is such that there remain some conflicting interests that cannot be adjusted and general needs that cannot be guaranteed without leaning, however indirectly, on the coercive force of the State.

Two basic changes in the role of the State have marked the development of self-management. On the one hand, a series of important functions formerly carried out by government agencies have been transferred to organs of workers' management. As the quasi-universal owner of the means of production, the State used to manage and organise the production process. Now, however, the State is gradually losing all powers associated with monopoly ownership and all means of intervention in the social spheres. The Government can no longer dispose of the capital of organisations of associated labour, nor decide on financial investments or the establishment of banks or similar institutions. All these powers have been transferred to the self-managed organisations and communities.

On the other hand, the progressive decentralisation of the political decision-making process by the direct linkage of organs of government with organs of workers' management has substantially modified the character of the State itself. The characteristic features of this process have been the creation of a number of councils, commissions and co-ordinating bodies on which the Government is represented not as a fount of authority but as a partner in the democratic process of reaching consensus and joint decision-making, and changes introduced in the composition of the main representative bodies (the assemblies of the socio-political communities), which now include special chambers representing the self-managed organisations and communities.

The machinery of government is thus being gradually merged with the machinery for the workers' management of society, and the distinctions between the State, as a fount of authority, and society in general are being gradually erased. In order to emphasise this "socialisation" of the State, the Constitution of 1963 introduced the concept of the socio-political community, a uniform designation for all territorial-political units (local community, commune, province, republic and federation). In the organisational structure of each socio-political community, the central place is occupied by the elected body—the assembly—which the Constitution defines as "the organ of self-management and highest organ of authority" within the framework of the constitutionally established rights and obligations of the respective socio-political community. In constitutional language, "the organs of the socio-political community" are the organs of decision-making and management that, in addition to the characteristics and functions of workers' management, have the prerogatives of organs of state power. The institution of the delegate system has contributed to the establishment of permanent links between the process of political decision-making and the workers' management organisations and communities engaged in production and other spheres of activity.

As workers' management achieves the dimensions of a total system of social organisation, the State nevertheless retains some important functions that are indispensable to the functioning of that system:

(1) The legislative role of the State remains essential in supporting the development of workers' management and establishing its institutional forms. All important changes in social relations to the advantage of associated labour—for example, the expansion or formation of self-management relations and institutions—have their starting-point and support in laws and regulations, as well as in general self-management by-laws which, being legally binding, also rest on the political force of the State.

(2) The State also fulfils an important function in safeguarding the free development of workers' management and in protecting the foundations of workers' management institutions, i.e. the principle of social ownership and the rights of workers in associated labour. Although national defence and social protection are no longer exclusively state functions, the Government still provides organised, qualified professional bodies that play an important role in these activities.

(3) Government agencies are also involved directly as indispensable factors in certain self-management functions. For example in the planning process, which begins with the plans of basic self-managing organisations and agreements concluded between them, the organs of the socio-political communities adopt "social plans" and supervise their implementation. Socio-political communities are also represented by delegates on the boards of management or councils of self-managing organisations of special importance; and they are co-signers of "social compacts" under which they undertake certain specific obligations.

(4) In addition, the Government retains some latent or reserve powers, which it may use in order to intervene where workers' management does not give suitable results, whether because it is insufficiently developed or for some other reasons; for example, a self-managing community of interest may be established by law, where this is deemed to be essential and has not occurred spontaneously; or regulations may be adopted requiring organisations of associated labour to pool a part of their resources in order to finance the construction of roads, power-stations or other public works.

Consensus and interdependence among republics and provinces in the federation

The various peoples that live together in the federation of Yugoslavia have inherited differences not only in culture but in their level of economic development and in their resources. The development of workers' management as a social system has had a profound influence on the relations of those peoples with each other, primarily through the mode of distribution of the social product. The basic principle that working people in self-managing organisations of associated labour have the right and the duty to decide for themselves about the distribution of the total income they create by their labour is extended to the relations among the various peoples or nations within the federation. Since the workers take decisions not only about the allocation of income for personal and joint consumption but also on resources to be allocated for social needs, they are able to build up the economic foundations for the social development of the national communities to which they belong. This system thus seeks to guarantee the economic self-government of the national communities.

In order to further promote equality among the nations on the basis of their economic independence, changes have been introduced in the structure of decision-making at the level of the federation. According to the Constitution, all decisions regarding measures of government policy that influence the conditions applying to economic activity and the distribution of the social product must be taken on the basis of a consensus, with participation on equal terms and joint responsibility of all the republics and autonomous provinces, in the Chamber of Republics and Provinces of the Assembly of the Yugoslav federation. This Chamber is one of two chambers of the Assembly. Both are constituted on the parity principle, with an equal number of delegates from each republic or province, regardless of its size. No decision on important economic matters can be imposed by a majority vote; an expression of consensus is required.

Self-management agreements and social compacts

The instruments for regulating relations and adjusting the interest of workers and their organisations in associated labour are self-management agreements and social compacts. By means of self-management agreements, workers may—

(a) pool their labour in basic organisations of associated labour;

(b) pool their labour and resources in work organisations and other organisations of associated labour, in banks and other financial organisations, in self-managing communities of interest, insurance communities and other forms of association of labour and resources;

(c) establish a basic plan;

(d) adjust their interests to the social division of labour and the need to maintain and develop society as a whole;

(e) lay down the principles for the distribution of income;

(f) lay down principles of price formation;

(g) establish relations with other organisations on the basis of the free exchange of labour; and

27

(*h*) spell out the mutual rights, obligations and responsibilities of workers in associated labour and the measures for their exercise and discharge as well as the means of implementing them in the field of national defence and social self-protection.

Self-management agreements may be concluded by workers among themselves, in their basic organisation of associated labour, or they may be concluded by two or more organisations of associated labour. Every participant in a self-management agreement may institute proceedings for its revision, or may initiate the conclusion of other agreements. The trade union may also make proposals for the conclusion of self-management agreements, and it participates in concluding agreements to govern labour relations of workers in associated labour or to lay down the criteria and scales for the distribution of net income and the allocation of resources for personal income and joint consumption.

Social compacts are concluded on a broader scale, by organs of the socio-political communities and organisations of associated labour, chambers of industry and other economic associations, self-managing communities of interest, and trade unions and other socio-political organisations. They serve to regulate socio-economic relations of broader concern, in the areas of planning, price fixing, rules for the distribution of resources and the allocation of income, employment policy and other matters. All parties to self-management agreements and social compacts conclude them on an equal footing: agreements and compacts are concluded freely by consensus among the participants and in observance of the constitutionally established obligation that their contents be in conformity with the Constitution and not in conflict with the laws and moral principles of a socialist workers' management society. They are binding on the parties that have concluded or acceded to them, and all such parties must account for any failure to meet the requirements of the agreements or compacts to which they are pledged. The form of this liability and its implementation is specified in the agreements themselves.

Self-management agreements and social compacts play an important role in ensuring the limitation and gradual elimination of government regulation of relations in associated labour, both among workers and among their organisations and communities. At the same time, they guarantee the stable and lasting self-management regulation of relations on the basis of workers' management principles and means.

Planning and the market

The independence and powers of initiative which the workers in organisations of associated labour enjoy are exercised within a system which recognises freedom to produce and sell goods and services subject to the laws of the market. Competition is fundamental to the workers' management system. But at the same time, one of the principal components of socio-economic development is social planning, carried out on a workers' management basis.

One of the main goals of social planning is to bring about a balanced development of the various sectors of the economy and the various parts of the country, and in particular to promote the development of the more backward areas. Emphasis is therefore placed on the need to take all interests into consideration in the preparation of development plans. Thus, the provisions of the Constitution of 1974 and the Associated Labour Act of 1976 require organisations of associated labour to adopt and fulfil their own plans, while at the same time taking the necessary measures for the fulfilment of the plans of the socio-political communities of which they are a part. The latter, in turn, are responsible for adjusting as far as possible "the special interests and independent operation of organisations of associated labour and other self-managing organisations and communities to the common development interests and targets laid down by social plans".[11] Thus, the planning system does not have the character of central administrative direction resting on central government coercion; on the contrary, the responsibilities, rights and duties inherent in the preparation and implementation of plans lie with the organisations of associated labour and the organs of the socio-political communities. Moreover, the whole concept of planning is concerned not only with material development but also with the development of social relations.[12]

Delegation principle

Under the workers' management system, decisions on matters of common concern are taken on the basis of the delegation principle, a new form of decision-making based on workers' management and applied in every organisation of associated labour, whether engaged in the production of goods or not, and in every self-managing community of interest. Workers' councils in organisations of associated labour, assemblies of self-managing communities of interest, management organs of business communities, banks and other financial organisations, and managerial organs in all other forms of association of labour and resources, are constituted and act on the delegation principle of decision-making. All these organs—workers' councils and organs of management of matters of common concern—are composed of delegates of workers organised in self-managing bodies. Delegates are required to take decisions in accordance with the instructions drawn up by the workers who elected them.

The development of decision-making on the delegation principle ensures that both labour and management remain in the hands of the politically organised workers, and guarantees that in associated labour and in society as a whole they retain control over decisions concerning the distribution of gross income as well as over that part of income set aside for the satisfaction of common and general social needs. The delegate system is intended to ensure the personal participation of all workers on a footing of equality with each other, in decisions concerning the conditions, instruments and results of their labour, wherever such labour does not serve a purely personal purpose and in all forms of social organisation in which decisions are made by workers' councils, assemblies and other elected organs.

The delegate system also links self-managing work organisations with political decision-making; herein lies the profoundly original significance of this new form of decision-making on matters of common concern and on matters concerning society in general.

Socio-political organisations

In a complex multinational society like Yugoslavia, in which the level of economic development varies widely from one region to another and where market competition prevails, conflicts of interest are bound to occur among the national communities, among organisations of associated labour and among individual workers. In order to promote workers' management solutions to such problems, and to assist in removing anomalies in the long-term interests of the workers and of the community as a whole, considerable reliance is placed on the socio-political organisations. The League of Communists, the Confederation of Trade Unions, the Union of Socialist Youth and the Veterans' Federation each perform their functions independently in their own field, their activities being co-ordinated by the Socialist Alliance of Working People, which is the comprehensive organisation of all citizens, while the League of Communists is the militant political organisation of the working class.

The role of the socio-political organisations in society is conditioned by their historical development during the fight for independence and the struggle for social change, as well as by a conscious attempt to make them an integral part of the workers' management system. They have gradually shed their functions as forces of political direction and authority closely linked with government agencies, and have assumed the role of promoting workers' management and enlisting the direct participation of as much of the population as possible in all areas of political life. They are regarded not as mediators between the citizens and the Government, but as means of developing the social conscience of working people so as to improve their capacity for carrying out the functions required of them in their self-managing organisations independently and effectively.

The development of democratic decision-making processes in all areas of socio-economic and political activity that is characteristic of workers' management has opened up wide possibilities for the expression of different personal and group interests. If these interests dominate in decision-making, to the exclusion of the interests of the broader community, it becomes extremely difficult to adjust democratically the narrower and wider interests. This is why it is felt to be necessary that working people who are responsible for making management decisions should be organised not only within the framework of their self-managing organisations and communities but also politically, within the framework of the socio-political organisations.

These organisations are, however, required to act from within the system, in a manner consistent with the principles of workers' management, and not as an outside element exercising powers of direction or control. They must respect the right of the self-management bodies to take decisions independently, within the scope of their jurisdiction and responsibility; but they are obliged to influence these decisions so as to take into account not only the immediate sectoral interests of those directly concerned but also the broader interests of the community and the requirements of the development of workers' management. This influence is exercised by the direct involvement of their members in the proceedings of workers' management bodies, where they are expected to play a key role in the guidance of social development on workers' management foundations and along workers' management lines. They are also actively involved in the initiation and conclusion of self-management agreements, as well as in the selection of candidates for election to managerial bodies and delegations to the assemblies of the socio-political communities.

These and other functions and responsibilities of the socio-political organisations are laid down in the Constitution,[13] along with provisions concerning the composition and powers of workers' management institutions and organs. This highlights the fact that those organisations are regarded as an essential element in guaranteeing the democratic functioning of the workers' management system.

Notes

[1] As will be seen on p. 48, the length of the mandate of members of workers' councils has since been extended to two years.

[2] See tables 10 and 11 for the composition of delegations to the assemblies of the socio-political communities.

[3] *Službeni List Federativne Narodne Republike Jugoslavije* (cited hereafter as *Službeni List*), 8 Apr. 1964, pp. 277–287 (ILO translation published in its *Legislative Series* (cited hereafter as *LS*), 1964—Yug. 1).

[4] *Službeni List*, 8 July 1971, pp. 525–528.

[5] Ibid., 21 Feb. 1974 (*LS* 1974—Yug. 1). The adoption of the federal Constitution of 1974 was followed by the adoption of similar constitutions in the individual federated republics and autonomous provinces of Yugoslavia.

[6] See pp. 179–182.

[7] Associated Labour Law, art. 130.

[8] See pp. 145–149.

[9] See p. 105

[10] See pp. 152–153.

[11] Yugoslav Constitution of 1974, art. 74.

[12] See p. 126.

[13] Constitution of 1974, section VIII.

INSTITUTIONS AND FUNCTIONING OF THE WORKERS' MANAGEMENT SYSTEM

2

ORGANISATIONS OF ASSOCIATED LABOUR

As a result of the developments traced in the preceding chapter and the changes introduced by the Constitution of 1974 and the Associated Labour Law of 1976, the foundations have been laid for the transformation of all enterprises and institutions supplying goods or public or social services into self-managing organisations of associated labour. This transformation is a complex, ongoing process which cannot yet be said to have reached its final stage. The following paragraphs do no more than outline the institutions, the decision-making process, and the relations that exist under the workers' management system at present.

There are three main forms of self-managed organisations of associated labour, operating with socially owned resources, in which workers join together to pool their labour: they are the "work organisation" and the "basic organisation of associated labour", both of which are of an obligatory nature, and the optional form of association on a broader scale in "composite organisations of associated labour". Subject to the differences inherent in the Yugoslav system, these organisations correspond to the establishments, undertakings and conglomerates of other socio-economic systems.[1]

The workers who perform administrative and related functions (planning, analytical, book-keeping, legal, etc.) in work organisations or in composite organisations form special self-managing "work communities", which may in certain circumstances be converted into basic organisations.

A particular and rarer form of organisation of associated labour is the so-called "contractual organisation of associated labour", which concerns the pooling of labour and resources remaining in private ownership.

Organisations of associated labour may themselves join together in self-management association and co-operation, and form "business communities" and "communities of associated labour for joint planning and business co-operation"; "general associations" and "economic

33

chambers"; banks, "insurance communities" and other financial institutions; and "self-managing communities of interest" for the provision of public and social services. These wider forms of association will be described in Chapter 5.

All forms of associated labour, from the basic organisations to the large, composite organisations, come into being by decision of the workers concerned and with the signing of a self-management agreement.

Work organisations

The universal and obligatory[2] form of organisation of work is the work organisation, which may be a single unit or may be composed of two or more basic organisations of associated labour. For example, the Rakovica Engine Works, in Belgrade, is composed of five basic organisations and three work communities. The basic organisations include, for example, "Vozilo"—a basic organisation of associated labour for the production of tractors, transmissions, and agricultural vehicles (613 workers), and "Livnica"—a basic organisation of associated labour which is a specialised foundry (744 workers). For the provision of public and social services, workers are also organised in work organisations of associated labour, with or without basic organisations, that enter into relations with the users of the services either directly or through self-managing communities of interest. For example, the Faculty of Political Science of the University of Belgrade, as a work organisation, enters into relations with the users of its services both directly and through the Republican Community of Interest in Education (of the Socialist Republic of Serbia). Irrespective of whether they are engaged in the production of goods or of services, workers may associate their work organisations in composite organisations of associated labour and other broader forms of association and co-operation.

A work organisation is an independent, self-managing organisation of workers linked by common interests in their work and, as a rule, organised in basic organisations of associated labour. When the conditions do not exist for the formation of basic organisations within the framework of a work organisation, the latter may exist without them, its workers having the same rights, obligations and responsibilities as those in basic organisations. When two or more basic organisations are formed within a work organisation, linked by production, trade or other common interests, they regulate their mutual relations by a self-management agreement which constitutes the basic by-laws of the work organisation. Relations between the basic organisations that operate within a work organisation are also regulated by self-management agreements concerning the organisation's outline plan, which lays down the general lines of joint production and trade for a specific period, and by other internal self-management rules concerning, for example, the distribution of income. The main motive for associating or establishing basic organisations within a work organisation is the workers' interest in the efficient organisation of production and trade, the raising of productivity, and, hence, the increasing of the total income of the organisation and their own personal incomes, which are decided on by the workers themselves in their self-management bodies.

The internal cohesion of the work organisation is thus not based on a hierarchical structure or on ownership rights but on common interests of workers in the different parts of the work. The workers act as freely associated producers, taking decisions with regard to the conditions and results of their work and bearing full responsibility for such decisions. They also decide on the hiring of new workers and on the type of management organ to which they entrust the day-to-day running of the organisation; the personnel responsible for these functions is also appointed by and answerable to the workers.

A new work organisation may be established by existing organisations of associated labour or self-managing communities of interest. Socio-political communities and other legal entities of a social character that are responsible for the management of social resources may also set up work organisations. The law permits the establishment of a work organisation by independent workers and by legal entities that operate with resources in private ownership, but only on clearly specified conditions; for example, such organisations may not engage in export-import operations, whole-sale trade, brokerage in the sale of goods and services, or the production and distribution of arms or other military equipment.

The procedure for the establishment of a work organisation begins with the adoption of its constitution, i. e. the signing of a self-management agreement on association in a work organisation, and is concluded by the election of a workers' council and the appointment of the management organs. The name and activity of the work organisation are entered in a court register, together with particulars of the liability of each of the basic organisations within it, where such exist. All these requirements, including those for introducing changes in a work organisation and for its dissolution, are laid down in the Associated Labour Law.[3]

Basic organisations of associated labour

The primary institutional form in which workers pool their labour to work with socially owned resources and in which they exercise their self-management rights of decision on economic and social matters is the basic organisation of associated labour. According to the Constitution and the Associated Labour Law, a basic organisation of associated labour may not exist independently, outside a work organisation. On the other hand, workers have the right, and indeed are obliged, to form a basic organisation within a work organisation if the following three conditions are met:

(a) if the unit concerned is engaged in a part of the production process or of the activity of the work organisation that forms a coherent whole, in which workers are mutually interdependent in their work and directly linked as a group to the work process as a whole;

(b) if the gross income of the unit concerned can be calculated independently and separately and if it earns that income in a lawful manner; and

(c) if the workers can, freely and on an equal footing, exercise their management rights in the unit concerned, pool their labour and resources with other workers and manage the income earned by various forms of such association, regulate labour relations, and in general assume the responsibilities and obligations of a basic organisation.

A basic organisation may not associate several parts of the production process, but a basic organisation may be formed for each part separately. In addition to its principal activities, a basic organisation may also engage in ancillary activities (for example, transport of goods, machine maintenance and repair and similar services), in so far as they are related to and contribute to the performance of its main activities. Workers are also free to introduce changes in basic organisations. If at any time the three basic requirements are no longer fulfilled, they may dissolve their basic organisation or reorganise it into others, which may then be associated in the work organisation concerned. Workers in a basic organisation may also separate from the work organisation of which it is a part and pool their labour and resources with other basic organisations or work organisations. However, a basic organisation may not separate from a work organisation if the separation would cause substantial difficulties to the work organisation or to other basic organisations associated in it, that is, if its separation would disrupt the production or business activity of the work organisation within which it operates and thus diminish the efficiency of the use of social resources and the possibilities for the other basic organisations concerned of earning an adequate income. Only if the basic organisation has succeeded in raising labour productivity to an extent sufficient to compensate for such difficulties will it be allowed to separate from the work organisation concerned.

The initiative for the formation of basic organisations of associated labour lies mainly with the workers, who themselves judge whether the basic statutory prerequisites have been met. Such an initiative may, however, come from the trade union or the management organ of the work organisation; in certain circumstances it may be taken by outside authorities such as the "social attorney of self-management", a "court of associated labour", or the assembly of a socio-political community. A meeting of the workers in the unit for which it is proposed to form a basic organisation is then called; the workers consider the proposal, and if they agree that the statutory prerequisites have been met, they hold a referendum by which a decision is taken to form the organisation.

The next step is the adoption of the self-management agreement on the association of workers in a basic organisation, which establishes its basic by-laws. This agreement lays down the principles that will govern the socio-economic relations of workers in the basic organisation, with particular reference to the management of its resources, the allocation of gross and net income, the distribution of resources for personal income, and labour relations matters. The agreement also lays down the principles of workers' management and the means of keeping workers informed, as well as the rules for the association of labour and resources within the work organisation of which the basic organisation is a part.

After these matters have been agreed upon and the basic organisation constituted, its name and that of the work organisation to which it belongs are entered in the court register. A basic organisation of associated labour has legal personality and its own bank account.

Composite organisations of associated labour

A composite organisation of associated labour[4] is an independent, self-managed organisation formed voluntarily by the association of work organisations that are engaged in the same production process or have other common interests. For example, work organisations that are interdependent with regard to the production of raw materials and the supply of energy, the supply of raw materials and the production of intermediate goods, the production of semi-finished goods or parts and the manufacture of finished products, or the distribution and sale of goods produced and other services, may and often do associate in composite organisations. The UPI united agro-industrial combine of Sarajevo (with nearly 30,000 workers) is an example of this kind of organisation. It is composed of 49 work organisations, 213 basic organisations, and 49 work communities. UPI co-operates with more than 10,000 individual agricultural producers through 106 basic organisations of associated labour. In terms of number of workers the size of composite organisations of associated labour varies greatly. For example, the Iskra composite organisation of associated labour for the production of electronic and thermocaloric apparatus, in Ljubljana, has about 28,500 workers; the Trepča composite organisation of associated labour, a mining and metallic chemical combine in Kosovska Mitrovica, has about 16,000; the Minel composite organisation of associated labour for the production of industrial articles, in Belgrade, about 12,000; and the Brodogradilište 3 maj shipbuilding yard in Rijeka about 7,500. Organisations producing similar products or providing similar services may also associate in this way if the purpose of forming a composite organisation is to ensure the introduction of a more developed technology or a more effective division of labour based on specialisation and leading to higher productivity. Work organisations producing different kinds of products or services are also entitled to associate with the aim of earning joint income or for other common purposes.

Work organisations also have the right to associate with more than one composite organisation at the same time. However, this may be done only subject to conformity with the self-management agreement on association within the work organisation and with any agreements to which it has acceded in other composite organisations, as well as with the self-management agreement of the composite organisation with which it intends to associate.

As in the case of other forms of associated labour, the composite organisation comes into existence with the signing of the self-management agreement regulating mutual relations among the work organisations thus associated, the election of a workers' council and the appointment of a management organ.

Work communities

A work community for the administration of affairs of common interest[5] is a self-managing organisation formed by the association of workers performing certain specialised functions or common services for several basic organisations within a work organisation, or for several work organisations grouped in a composite organisation or in any other form of association of organisations of associated labour.

The functions in question, which are enumerated in the Associated Labour Law, are those related to the administration of the affairs of the organisation and the provision of certain professional and auxiliary services, for example functions connected with planning and analytical work, personnel matters, book-keeping, record-keeping and statistics, legal affairs, clerical and administrative duties, security and maintenance of premises. For example, the Rakovica Engine Works of Belgrade includes three work communities: for planning and development; for financial and commercial affairs; and for personnel, self-management, legal and other affairs. Work related to commercial affairs, design, scientific research and other matters may be performed within a work community where such work is of a limited nature and not extensive enough to justify the creation of a basic organisation. The law specifies, however, that in principle, workers providing technical services of common concern which are germane to the successful performance of the activities of the work organisation or basic organisation in which they operate should organise themselves in basic organisations rather than work communities. This provision concerns in particular such activities as commercial matters related to the sale of goods and services, market research, project design, engineering, scientific research and professional studies related to technological problems, electronic data processing and the organisation of vocational training.

The creation of work communities resulted from efforts to integrate administrative and professional personnel into the workers' management structure in such a manner as to avoid the transformation of their functions into ones of command, without denying this type of personnel workers' management rights and status. Work communities thus formed have, in principle, the same rights and obligations as basic organisations of associated labour. Its members regulate their mutual relations by a self-management agreement concluded within the work community, and their relations with the basic or work organisations for which they provide services are regulated by other such agreements which lay down the mutual rights and responsibilities of all the parties and govern, in particular, the allocation of income.

Work communities may also be organised for the provision of joint services in other types of organisations such as agricultural co-operatives, banks, insurance communities, self-managing communities of interest, socio-political organisations and organs of socio-political communities. There is, for example, a work community servicing the council of the Yugoslav Confederation of Trade Unions. This community, composed of experts, administrative employees and specialised staff, prepares analytical studies and drafts of documents concerning various fields of trade union activity, besides attending to certain administrative and financial matters.

Contractual organisations of associated labour

As has already been indicated above, the Yugoslav system leaves room for individuals or groups of individuals to set up an enterprise or a business, within certain limitations, using their own privately owned resources. The new Constitution and the Associated Labour Law provide for the integration of such enterprises into the self-management system in

39

the form of contractual organisations of associated labour. By the end of 1977 there were about 45 contractual organisations of associated labour in Yugoslavia. Most of them are in Slovenia, where there are at present 24 of these organisations.

Such an organisation may be formed by the pooling of the resources of the "manager", who sets up his business independently, using his own resources, and the labour of other workers who agree to work in the organisation. A contractual organisation may also be formed by several people who work independently with their own resources. Resources may also be invested in such contractual organisations by other organisations of associated labour, by socio-political communities, self-managing communities of interest, banks and other legal entities, subject to conditions laid down by law.

All persons concerned in the establishment of a contractual organisation, whether they contribute labour or resources, share in the joint risk. The manager is responsible for the legality of the operations of the organisation and has the same rights, obligations and responsibilities as the managing organ or manager of an organisation of associated labour.[6] The self-management rights of workers in such organisations are protected since they participate in the conclusion of the contract establishing the organisation, which is signed by the manager and by authorised representatives of the socio-political community, the trade union and the economic chamber. The contract lays down the basic conditions governing the work of the organisation and the rights based on the investment of resources as well as the obligations of workers and of the manager; the mutual relations, rights and responsibilities of the workers and the manager are further regulated by a self-management agreement concluded by them.

With regard to the disposal of income earned and the social resources invested in a contractual organisation, the manager and workers decide jointly on the portion of net income to be set aside for personal incomes and "joint consumption" in accordance with agreed principles and scales which must not be out of line with those applying in organisations of associated labour in general. The remainder is allocated partly to the resources invested by the manager and partly to those which remain in social ownership. Thus, while the manager is entitled to a return on his investment, the social character of the accrued incomes based on the labour of the workers concerned is preserved.

Developments and problems

Since the adoption of the constitutional amendments of 1971 and the new Constitution of 1974 organisations of associated labour have been set up on quite a wide scale: by the end of 1978 there were more than 40,000. Of that number, 18,528 were basic organisations (about 85 per cent of which were engaged in some stage of the production and distribution of goods—in mining, industry and transport); 13,707 work organisations without basic organisations; 3,660 work organisations with basic organisations; 280 composite organisations of associated labour; and 4,100 work communities. Since the process of transforming under-takings into organisations of associated labour represents a radical break with traditional forms of organisation of management, it is only natural that it has been accompanied by certain problems and difficulties. It has been observed, for example, that the basic principles governing the formation of basic organisations of associated labour are not always respected, with the result that in some instances an entire factory has been constituted as a single basic organisation although the conditions for the formation of several such organisations were present. On other occasions unwieldy work organisations have been formed, composed of more than 50 basic organisations, whereas the association of the latter in a number of work organisations themselves associated in a composite organisation would have been more appropriate; or, again, work organisations have failed to see the need for forming basic organisations within their framework. A report submitted to the Eighth Congress of the Confederation of Trade Unions indicated that there were "still quite a number of basic organisations" which did not constitute integrated technological and economic units. In some cases they consisted of so many workers that it was impossible to arrive at decisions in the workers' council. There were also unnecessarily small and fragmented organis-ations. A few basic organisations still did not generate and earn their own income, which was "allocated" to them by the work organisation, in which the former head office, though formally transformed, had in fact retained its authority over income.[7]

Efforts are constantly being made to improve the structure of work organisations and adapt them to changing needs. Thus, there is a trend towards the transformation of work communities into basic organis-ations; while in many cases large, unwieldy basic organisations have been broken up into smaller ones, or autonomous work units have been set up within them. The main principle motivating such changes appears to be the desire to bring decision-making closer to the worker. It has been found, for example, that where large basic organisations of associated labour were divided up many functional difficulties were overcome. For one thing, some people had been reluctant to speak up in large gatherings. For another, information on the functioning of a small work organisation proved easier to furnish and simpler to understand. And again, workers attending assemblies of a basic organisation or smaller units usually have first-hand knowledge of the matters to be discussed and are therefore better able to contribute to the discussion.

A problem which has been noted is the development of autarchical group-ownership attitudes, especially in basic organisations that are particularly successful and financially prosperous. Some of those organisations tend to treat socially owned resources as their own, neglecting the obligations that stem from the social character of ownership. Their workers often aspire to promote their own interests without taking sufficient account of those of workers in other basic organisations with which they are associated or of the work organisation as a whole, and thus fail to give due recognition to their common interests and the principle of interdependence in the generation of income.

Some weaknesses have also been seen to appear in the organisation of work communities. In some work organisations they are allowed to acquire dominant influence on decisions and a privileged position as regards distribution of income, since they are considered to be a vital factor in the successful operation of the entire organisation; whereas elsewhere, they are reduced to the status of technical services for the basic or work organisations and deprived of any scope for initiative or independent responsibility.

The socio-political organisations of Yugoslavia are well aware of these and other weaknesses in the functioning of the system and are constantly seeking to remedy them;[8] indeed, the Associated Labour Law of 1976 was adopted in this perspective, after widespread public discussion of the draft. However, the evolution of the self-management system is essentially a social process which demands not only a change in organisational forms but also fundamental changes in customary ways of behaving and thinking in everyday life; it may therefore be expected that more time will be needed before all the problems are solved.

SELF-MANAGEMENT AGREEMENTS

As indicated in the preceding section, the institutional forms of associated labour and the basic rights, obligations and relations of workers in organisations of associated labour are regulated by the Constitution and by legislation. This is designed to provide a uniform basis for the system and the necessary degree of unity in the regulation of the more important aspects of the relations concerned. However, statutory regulation of all such matters in detail is not possible, because of the differing conditions in which organisations of associated labour seek to implement these enactments, nor is it desirable since it would limit the workers' rights which the law seeks to extend. For this reason, it is laid down that all detailed, practical arrangements concerning the management and operation of the basic organisations of associated labour are to be worked out by the workers in those organisations, in conformity with the basic principles established in the Constitution and other statutes, and are to be laid down in self-management agreements and other internal rules.

Reference has already been made to the fact that basic organisations, work organisations and other forms of associated labour come into being with the adoption of a self-management agreement by the workers in the organisations concerned. Thus, for example, the self-management agreement on the pooling of workers' labour in a basic organisation of associated labour serves as the constitution of the organisation; at the same time it establishes the basis for all other self-management by-laws or rules which the basic organisation may later adopt. This general self-management agreement is adopted by the workers by referendum, after which all workers individually freely decide whether they accept it, and give their answers in special written statements.

In addition to this general agreement, the workers in a basic organisation adopt a series of other self-management agreements or by-laws concerning, for example, the organisation of work and systematisation of jobs and work tasks; the principles and scales for allocating the net income and measures for the distribution of resources for personal income; the utilisation of resources for joint consumption; principles for the allocation of housing or the grant of credit for home building; workers' supervision; workers' responsibility; labour relations; arrangements for keeping workers informed; workers' education and vocational training; standards applying to worker trainees; work safety; rationalisation and introduction of technical improvements; business and other secrets; book-keeping and similar tasks; and the election and recall of the organs of management.

Similarly in a work organisation the basic internal rules are the self-management agreement on association and the by-laws of the organisation. In addition, self-management agreements are adopted concerning the outlines of the plan of the organisation; the generation of joint income and the principles and scales for its allocation; the principles and scales for distribution of personal incomes; and such matters as "social self-protection" and national defence, as appropriate. Similar types of self-management agreements are adopted in the composite organisations and in the work communities, as already indicated. The principle underlying all such agreements for the joint regulation of matters of common concern is the participation of all the parties concerned, on a basis of equality, and the corresponding participation of the parties in the jointly earned income and joint sharing of the risks involved.

The preparation and adoption of self-management agreements on association and the by-laws of organisations of associated labour has become a complex process, in many cases necessitating the help of legal advisers to enable the workers' self-management organs to find their way in the maze of legislation and constitutional provisions to which they must conform. Most organisations, even small ones, employ full-time lawyers and other experts to assist in drafting these documents. For organisations that lack such assistance, there are a number of specialised institutions such as centres for legal and economic analysis, workers' universities, and others, that organise round tables, seminars and similar meetings for the exchange of opinions on questions relevant to the adoption of internal regulations on the subjects mentioned above. This kind of activity has proved to be of great help in practice.

However, despite the legalistic aspects, the preparation and adoption of self-management agreements is essentially a democratic process in which efforts are made to involve all the workers in the organisation. Drafts of self-management agreements and other internal rules are regularly brought up for public discussion in the general meetings of basic organisations and work communities at every stage before their final adoption. The trade union is closely involved in the preparation of these texts, organising public discussions and channelling workers' comments to the drafting committee of the workers' council. The final procedure for adoption of the agreements by referendum and written acceptance by each individual worker is designed to ensure that they are familiar with the rules governing their conditions of work and relations with other organisations, and that they accept the responsibilities these entail.

ORGANS AND PROCEDURES OF WORKERS' MANAGEMENT

Workers in organisations of associated labour of the types described above exercise their right to manage these organisations both directly, through the expression of their personal views at meetings or by referendums, and indirectly through elected delegates to workers' councils and delegations to the assemblies of self-managing communities of interest and socio-political communities. It is mainly in the basic organisations of associated labour and in work communities that management decision-making takes place in workers' meetings or by referendums, while delegates in the workers' councils exercise this right on behalf of the workers in basic and work organisations, work communities and composite organisations of associated labour. The delegates in these organs are bound to follow the general instructions given and abide by the decisions taken by the workers in the basic organisations who elected them. They may be recalled at any time if they fail to follow those instructions.

An important distinction is made between the type of decisions taken by these different organs and procedures: fundamental issues are dealt with by meetings and referendums; that is, they are submitted to the personal expression of views of the workers concerned, whereas operational questions concerning the functioning of the organisation are entrusted to the workers' councils and managerial organs. In keeping with the policy of bringing decision-making closer to the worker, the number of fundamental issues to be decided by the former procedures, which are enumerated in the Associated Labour Law, has been increased in recent years; while workers are free to specify (in self-management agreements) other issues to be so decided.

Referendums

The workers in the basic organisations of associated labour make decisions on the following questions by referendum:

(a) the adoption of the self-management agreement constituting the basic organisation and the self-management agreements on association in a work organisation, composite organisation, or business community;

(b) changes in the composition or organisation of the basic organisation;

(c) the adoption of the by-laws of the basic organisation and of the work organisation or composite organisation with which it is associated, the outlines of the plan of the basic organisation, and rules concerning the principles and scales for distribution of resources for workers' personal incomes and joint consumption;

(d) the renouncement of their rights to returns on pooled resources; and

(e) the adoption of other self-management agreements as established by law.

In addition to these statutorily established matters for which a referendum is mandatory, workers may identify other questions to be so decided by internal self-management rules. Decisions by referendum are binding when adopted by a majority of the workers in the basic organisation.

There have been significantly more referendums since the recent constitutional changes than was the case earlier (see table 1). In 1969 one or more referendums were conducted in only about 10 per cent of the undertakings that had elected workers' councils and in only 5 per cent of the undertakings without such councils, whereas by 1976 only 48 per cent of organisations of associated labour had not held referendums. However, in view of the importance of the referendum as a form of direct decision-making, this proportion was still high.

Table 1. Referendums in undertakings (1969 and 1970) and in organisations of associated labour (1976)

Number of referendums held	Percentage of number of undertakings or organisations of associated labour		
	1969	1970	1976
None	90.9	93.7	48.0
One	8.2	5.7	27.6
Two or more	0.9	0.6	24.4
Total number of undertakings or organisations of associated labour	*8 114*	*7 741*	*9 036*

Source: Savezni zavod za statistiku: *Samoupravni društveno-ekonomski razvoj Jugoslavije 1947–1977*, Statistčki Prika 2 (Belgrade, 1978), p. 42.

Meetings

The matters to be decided on by workers at their meetings are not laid down by law but are determined by the workers themselves through internal self-management rules. The Associated Labour Law only provides that at meetings workers are to raise issues, make proposals and give opinions, and to agree on decisions and draw up general instructions for their delegates. Within a basic organisation of associated labour some types of decisions may also be taken by meetings of the workers in smaller units, such as workshops. For example, the workers in such units may adopt decisions on the distribution of resources for personal income as well as the utilisation of resources for joint consumption and other questions, if so provided in the by-laws of the basic organisation in conformity with the law.

Before decisions are reached by referendum or workers' general meetings or other means at the disposal of workers for expressing their personal views, preliminary discussions are held at special meetings called by the workers' council. Such discussions are organised, for example, for the purpose of discussing proposed decisions put forward by the workers' council on the conclusion of credit contracts for investment outlays or other types of contracts and self-management agreements providing for the procurement of major resources for the expansion of the organisation; or in relation to decisions concerning long-term investment of accumulated resources.

These procedures may raise a question concerning the time consumed by such preliminary discussions and meetings, particularly since meetings appear to be held more frequently than referendums. A study of 19,000 organisations of associated labour[9] showed that in 1976 about 95 per cent of them had held meetings; most of the remaining 5 per cent were organisations that had just come into being or were in the process of being constituted. Thirty-five per cent of the organisations concerned had held ten or more meetings while 19 per cent had held from four to five. In the majority of cases (71 per cent of the organisations concerned) meetings were held during working hours.[10]

The types of questions most often discussed appear to relate to the conclusion of self-management agreements and the adoption of by-laws and rules, followed by questions concerning planning and programming of the organisation's activities.

Workers' councils

All work organisations and composite organisations, as well as basic organisations of associated labour that have more than 30 members, are required by law to elect a workers' council to manage their affairs. In basic organisations which have fewer than 30 members, the workers' general meeting acts as the workers' council.

The workers' council has wide powers. In basic organisations it draws up and adopts by-laws and other self-management rules concerning relations in the organisation; establishes draft outlines for the basic organisation's plan and draft elements for the conclusion of self-management agreements on the outlines of the plans of other organisations and communities with which the basic organisation is associated. The workers' council decides on business policy and measures for the implementation of the organisation's policy and plan. It decides on credit transactions related to day-to-day business, in line with the plan, and adopts balance sheets at annual and other intervals.

The workers' council also elects, appoints and discharges its executive committee[11] and the managerial organs of the organisation; issues them with guidelines and instructions and supervises their work; and keeps the workers informed on all questions concerning their decision-making and supervisory responsibilities in the organisation. It also makes arrangements relating to the basic organisation's role in respect of the programme for national defence and social self-protection. The workers' council may also place other affairs relating to the work of the organisation under its jurisdiction in accordance with the by-laws of the organisation.

In a work organisation the workers' council exercises similar powers, within the framework of the self-management agreement on association by which the work organisation is constituted. In work communities the

47

workers in some cases also elect a workers' council which operates in conformity with the self-management agreement concluded with the organisations for which they perform specific services.

As regards the composition of workers' councils, the law provides that the various groups in an organisation within which a council functions shall be suitably represented. Thus in the workers' council of a basic organisation there must be delegates of staff engaged in all parts of the work, each part being represented by at least one delegate and the number of delegates from each part being in proportion to the number of workers in that part of the work. For instance, in the Železarna steelworks of Jesenice, the composition of the workers' council of the basic organisation of associated labour in the plate rolling mill is as follows:

	Number of delegates
Administrative staff	2
First shift of the rolling mill	2
Second shift ,, ,, ,, ,,	2
Third ,, ,, ,, ,,	2
First shift of the adjustment department	3
Second shift ,, ,, ,, ,,	3
Third ,, ,, ,, ,,	3
Shipping department	2
	19

The workers' council thus reflects the composition of the basic organisation as a whole. Similarly, in the workers' council of a work organisation, every basic organisation and work community operating within the organisation must be represented by at least one delegate, and delegates are elected in proportion to the number of workers in each of these constituent parts of the work organisation. The same principle applies to the composition of the workers' council in composite organisations, within which all work organisations of which it is formed must be proportionately represented.

Delegates to the workers' council of a basic organisation are elected by the workers in that organisation directly by secret ballot. The term of office may not be longer than two years. The same person may not be elected to the workers' council for more than two consecutive terms. This ruling is designed to ensure both a measure of continuity and the participation of the workers on the widest possible scale in the work of the workers' council. Workers who have been appointed by the workers' council to posts of special managerial or supervisory responsibility, such as the manager, the chairman or ordinary members of the board of management, heads of sections, and so forth, are not entitled to be elected to membership of the workers' council. This principle also applies to elections to the workers' council in a work organisation, in respect of which the law provides that none of the personnel holding managerial responsibilities in the basic organisations and work communities which make up the work organisation may be elected to its workers' council.

The members of the workers' council are answerable to the workers in the organisations which have elected them and they may be recalled on the initiative of the trade union if their discharge of their representative functions is not found satisfactory by the workers concerned.

As has already been indicated, the delegates to a workers' council are responsible for upholding the views of the organs that elected them and following their general instructions. Delegates are required to keep the workers in those organs informed about what they and the council are doing and to ask for further instructions as required when new subjects are discussed. If a delegate fails to act in conformity with instructions, the workers may decide that the delegate has lost their confidence and elect another.

All decisions of workers' councils are taken by majority vote.

The workers' councils of basic, work and composite organisations of associated labour may form one or more committees and entrust to them the performance of specific executive duties, as determined by the by-laws of these organisations. The members of the committees are elected by the workers' council from among its members and the ranks of workers generally, to the exclusion of those that are not eligible to the workers' council. They are elected for a two-year term and may not be elected for more than two consecutive terms to the same committee.

This provision, as in the case of the workers' council itself, is designed to ensure a measure of continuity by allowing the renewal of membership for two consecutive terms, while at the same time providing for some rotation of membership in order to enable a large number of workers to participate in the work of self-management bodies. In practice, it has been found that workers' councils are renewed by one-third of their membership every two years, and it also appears to be common for experienced and trusted workers to be re-elected after waiting a two-year period out of office.

This practice may make for a certain élitism in the membership of the self-management bodies. It has in fact been observed that, by and large, the more highly skilled workers and those with a good educational background are more frequently elected to membership of those bodies than are workers with lower qualifications, as indicated in table 2. Since

Table 2. Vocational and general or technical educational qualifications of members of central[1] workers' councils, 1960–70
(in percentages)

Qualifications	Year		
	1960	1965	1970
Manual workers	76.2	73.8	67.6
Highly skilled	15.1	16.7	17.2
Skilled	40.5	37.8	33.7
Semi-skilled	13.4	10.8	9.0
Unskilled	7.2	8.0	7.4
Trainees	0.0	0.5	0.3
Non-manual workers	23.8	26.2	32.4
With higher and advanced technical education	4.2	5.9	10.1
With secondary technical education	12.0	13.0	15.9
With lower technical education	7.6	7.3	6.4
	100.0	100.0	100.0
Total membership of councils	**156 300**	**149 404**	**135 204**

[1] A "central" workers' council is one for a work organisation as a whole, not for a part of a work organisation such as a plant or a work unit.

Source: Neca Jovanov: "Strikes and self-management", in Josip Obradovic and William N. Dunn (eds.): *Workers' self-management and organizational power in Yugoslavia* (University Center for International Studies, University of Pittsburg, 1978), p. 343, table 16.1.

the success of the organisation largely depends on the competence of the workers' council in handling business matters, it would seem that on the whole the workers prefer to entrust these matters to the more experienced and better educated members of the workforce.

Other factors relating to the composition of the workers' councils and their committees are reported in data collected by the Federal Bureau of Statistics for 1976, showing the proportion of women, young people and members of the League of Communists on such committees in various types of organisations of associated labour (table 3). The invariably high proportion of members of the League of Communists is especially noteworthy.[12]

Despite the wide powers conferred on the workers' councils by the Constitution and by statute, some observers feel that they are at present losing their predominant position as the most influential organs of workers' management. On the one hand, under recent legislation, a

Table 3. Delegates to workers' councils and committee members, 1979

Item	BOAL	Work organisation without BOAL	Work organisation with BOAL	Composite organisation	Work communities
Delegates to workers' councils	247 586	200 666	71 845	9 149	52 216
Percentages of—					
Women	*26.4*	*40.3*	*23.1*	*14.5*	*47.5*
Young people	*14.2*	*12.5*	*10.0*	*7.0*	*13.3*
Members of LCY	*37.9*	*38.2*	*47.4*	*58.9*	*42.7*
No. of committees	6 985	3 871	1 692	146	1 139
Committee members	66 544	34 910	22 320	2 680	9 798
Percentages of—					
Women	*21.4*	*32.7*	*19.7*	*13.7*	*41.0*
Young people	*11.9*	*10.2*	*7.7*	*5.6*	*11.3*
Members of LCY	*38.9*	*39.7*	*49.2*	*67.1*	*44.4*
Three main forms of organisations of associated labour, plus work communities:					
Absolute numbers	17 370	12 550	3 183	230	3 962
Percentages	*46.6*	*33.7*	*8.5*	*0.6*	*10.6*

Key: BOAL = basic organisation(s) of associated labour.
LCY = League of Communists of Yugoslavia.
Source: Federal Institute of Statistics, Belgrade, preliminary data, 1981.

number of fundamental issues formerly dealt with by the workers' councils are now referred to the workers directly (at meetings or by referendum). Decisions of workers' councils have sometimes been overruled by meetings.[13] On the other hand, where complex operating decisions have to be made or questions decided that are not of direct concern to the members of the workers' council, it has been noted that the council tends simply to approve the proposals made and decisions taken by the managerial organs. The need to combat the temptation to transfer decisions to the "technostructure" in self-managing organisations has been repeatedly emphasised by the highest authorities in the country.[14] But whatever may be the weaknesses in its functioning in practice, the workers' council is still legally entrusted with decision-making authority on many matters of business policy of vital importance to the organisation, and on the conclusion of self-management agreements (which must, however, be adopted by referendum) and the constitution of the managerial organs.

Managerial organs

As has already been indicated, organisations of associated labour are free by law to establish the type of managerial organ they choose, that is, an individual manager or a board of management, composed as a rule of from three to seven members. In practice, the majority of these organisations have preferred to have an individual manager: in 1976 there were some 30,000 individual general managers in organisations of associated labour (see table 4).

Whether it consists of an individual or a board, the managerial organ is appointed and relieved of duty by the workers' council. The appointment of a manager, or of the chairman and members of a management board, is carried out on the basis of a public competition announced by the workers' council and organised by a special selection committee composed of representatives of the workers, the trade unions and the socio-political community. Notice of competitions must be published in the official gazette and in one of the national daily newspapers. The committee selects one or more candidates from among the applicants and makes a recommendation to the workers' council, which may only appoint candidates proposed by the committee. (In practice, it is possible that a workers' council will not accept the committee's proposal, as happened in April 1979 when the workers' council of the Yugoslav air transport company, JAT, did not accept the committee's proposal to re-elect the existing general manager.) Candidates who are not satisfied with the decision of the workers' council may institute proceedings against the decision before the court of associated labour.

The term of office of managerial organs may be no longer than four years; however, the same person may be reappointed several times to the same function if the workers are satisfied with that person's performance.

In a basic organisation of associated labour the managerial organ carries out the day-to-day business management, co-ordinates the work, and makes proposals with regard to business policy and measures for its implementation. It may set up working parties, committees and other bodies to deal with specific questions and assist it in its duties. It issues orders to individual workers or groups of workers in connection with the work.

In the performance of its duties, the managerial organ is required to implement the decisions of the workers' council, the workers' general meeting and other bodies, and is responsible to the workers' council. It is, however, also responsible to society for the legality of the operations of

Table 4. Proportion of women, young people and members of the League of Communists of Yugoslavia among general managers of organisations of associated labour, 1976

| Area | Total | of which— | | | | | |
| | | Absolute numbers | | | Percentages | | |
		Women	Young people	Members of LCY	Women	Young people	Members of LCY
Bosnia and Herzegovina	3 897	169	63	3 425	4.3	1.6	87.9
Croatia	7 307	404	97	3 926	5.5	1.3	53.7
Macedonia	2 315	98	15	1 925	4.2	0.7	83.2
Montenegro	576	17	5	476	3.0	0.9	82.6
Serbia	11 722	589	116	9 343	5.0	1.0	79.7
Excluding autonomous provinces	7 091	387	76	5 751	5.5	1.1	81.1
Kosovo	1 003	23	15	806	2.3	1.5	80.4
Vojvodina	3 628	179	25	2 786	4.9	0.7	76.8
Slovenia	4 149	387	26	2 791	9.3	0.6	67.3
Yugoslavia	**29 966**	**1 664**	**322**	**21 886**	**5.6**	**1.1**	**73.0**
Underdeveloped areas	*7 791*	*307*	*98*	*6 632*	*3.9*	*1.3*	*85.1*
More developed areas	*22 175*	*1 357*	*224*	*15 254*	*6.1*	*1.0*	*68.8*

the organisation and for fulfilling the obligations of the organisation as laid down by law. The individual manager or the chairman of the management board participates in the proceedings of the workers' council, without the right to vote, and, if he considers that a decision adopted by that body or by any other self-management body is contrary to law or to the provisions of a general self-management rule binding on the organisation, he is required to bring this fact to the attention of the body concerned. If the unlawful decision is maintained despite his warning, he has the right to suspend its execution temporarily and to inform the competent organ of the socio-political community, which takes a final decision in the matter.

The managerial organ of a work organisation co-ordinates the work of the corresponding organs of the basic organisations operating within it, to the extent required in the interests of the work organisation as a whole and in conformity with the law as well as with the powers conferred on the work organisation by the workers in the basic organisations. In work organisations and composite organisations the managerial organ is appointed and relieved of duty, as in basic organisations, by the workers' council, under similar procedures.

Management is not an easy task in Yugoslavia. Managers can no longer rely on traditional hierarchical authority but must use their knowledge, political consciousness and understanding of people in doing their job. They are expected to run the organisations that elect them efficiently, to organise and co-ordinate the work and to propose business policy and measures for its implementation. They have to do all this within the limits of a developing economy and under the particular conditions of workers' management. In practice, this means that they are subjected to five particular forms of pressure. First, they must succeed in generating income over and above production costs, for if they do not, the workers will not be entitled to any personal income above the guaranteed minimum and the managers will be completely discredited. Secondly, they have to gain the confidence of the workers' council, to which they are always accountable and which may recall them at any time during their term of office. Thirdly, they have to carry out the decisions and conclusions adopted by workers in meetings and by referendums, as well as the decisions of the workers' council, which may occasionally run counter to a manager's own policies and views on the subjects in question. Fourthly, they are subject to close scrutiny by the socio-political organisations, which, while pursuing the same objectives of efficiency and development, may see them from a different point of view. And finally, managers have to take account of the plans and all decisions connected with them, and to comply with the array of regulations contained in the laws, in self-management agreements and rules, in social compacts and in other existing rules.

Such a challenging situation requires highly qualified managers and, in fact, the qualifications of managers of organisations of associated labour have steadily improved. From 1962 to 1976 the proportion of managers with higher education and expert training increased, in larger organisations, from 34 per cent to 78 per cent, and in smaller organisations, from 16 per cent to 76 per cent. Successful managers also tend to be reappointed for several terms. Thus, in both 1975 and 1977, out of some 30,000 managers, about 71 per cent had held their position for one or two terms, 23 per cent for from three to five terms, and 6 per cent for more than five terms (see table 5). In addition to this tendency towards longevity in management posts in the same organisation, there is also a certain amount of horizontal mobility among managers who move from one organisation to another. In 1975 more than half of the managers surveyed had over 20 years of service in managerial office.[15]

While it is normal for good managers to retain the confidence of the workers, there is undoubtedly a danger of élitism here, too, and, indeed

Table 5. Percentage distribution of general managers and chairmen of boards of management, by total length of service in such managerial office and by length of tenure of current managerial appointment, 1975 and 1977[1]

Year (and kind of organisation in the case of 1977)	Total length of service in managerial office, in years			Length of tenure of current managerial appointment, in years			Total No. of individuals concerned
	≤ 9	10–20	> 20	≤ 9	10–20	> 20	
1975 total	11.5	36.1	52.4	70.7	22.9	6.1	30 852
1977 total	76.2	18.5	5.3	71.7	22.2	6.1	27 949
Of this in—							
BOAL	85.2	11.7	3.1	69.6	24.3	6.1	12 642
Work organisations without BOAL	67.1	25.5	7.4	77.5	17.5	5.0	11 483
Work organisations with BOAL	68.3	24.2	7.5	62.5	29.4	8.1	2 291
Composite organisations	61.6	25.6	12.8	59.4	29.3	11.3	125
Work communities of BOAL	84.0	12.5	3.5	62.0	28.3	9.7	1 408

Key: BOAL = Basic organisation(s) of associated labour.
[1] *Samupravni društveno-ekonomski razvoj Jugoslavije, 1947–1977*, op. cit., p. 39.

this was a lively issue in Yugoslavia in the early 1970s. A conscious effort is none the less made to open the ranks of management to meritorious workers who are willing and able to accept the challenge. The spread of general education and specialised managerial training courses and the system of public competitions for managerial posts have stimulated self-development and opened up new opportunities to many rank-and-file workers.

It is noteworthy, for instance, that the situation as regards length of service of general managers of organisations of associated labour changed significantly in recent years. In 1977 more than three-quarters of those managers had less than ten years of service, as compared to 11.5 per cent in 1975, which indicated a considerable shift towards younger personnel. This probably reflects the massive appointment of managers of basic organisations of associated labour after such organisations were established on the new bases provided by the constitutional changes, since 85 per cent of the managers of basic organisations had less than ten years of tenure of managerial office.

Workers' management in organisations of special social interest

In organisations of associated labour that provide services of special social interest, such as education, health protection, social welfare, scientific and cultural services and other activities which are essential for the life and work of citizens and the development of the country, the same workers' management principles apply. However, the way in which the workers' management rights are exercised may, in these cases, be regulated by statute or by decisions of the assemblies of the socio-political community, with a view to ensuring that these activities are performed in harmony with the interests of the community. The decisions thus taken by outside authorities are adapted to the specific nature of the actitivites concerned, that is, the same regulations are not uniformly applied, for example, to organisations providing information services and those concerned with social welfare.

The main purpose of these special arrangements is to provide for participation in decision-making on the activities of those organisations by the consumers of the services they provide, the other organisations of associated labour concerned, the founders, the socio-political community and the socio-political organisations. This participation is most often ensured by the delegation of representatives of these various interests who sit on the workers' councils of the organisations of associated labour providing social services, that is, the self-managing communities of interest, where they have the right to take part in decision-making, on equal terms with the workers elected by the organisation itself, on all questions concerning the activities of the organisation, the intended use of resources, the appointment and dismissal of the managerial organs and other matters within the competence of the workers' council.

In some cases, for example with regard to organisations providing information services, special bodies representing the community have been established to examine programmes and plans for their activities and to make recommendations, which the workers' council is obliged to take into consideration in the establishment and implementation of the organisations' programme. This is the case in the weekly magazine *Nin*, of Belgrade, where, apart from the workers' management bodies and the editorial board, there is a particular organ, the editorial council, composed of delegates representing various socio-political organisations, the assembly of the socio-political community, the University of Belgrade and other institutions, together with a number of persons with outstanding qualifications in the cultural and research fields. However, no decisions taken by such bodies may interfere with the exercise by workers in those organisations of their self-management rights relating to their work, for example, the regulation of mutual relations, and the setting of principles and scales for earning, allocating and distributing income and for earning personal income.

MAKING AND IMPLEMENTATION OF DECISIONS UNDER WORKERS' MANAGEMENT

Under the workers' management system the ordinary workers' management role in relation to the making and implementation of decisions includes submission of proposals, drafting of decisions, adoption of decisions, and supervision of their implementation.

Proposals may be made by ordinary workers as well as by professional staff, a manager or a board of management, trade unions, and workers' supervisory commissions. When a workers' management body agrees that a proposal should be considered, a workers' meeting or the workers' council sets up a special working party or committee to study the matter and make fully argued recommendations. The exact procedure differs in different organisations and in relation to the type of proposal concerned; for example, on some subjects there are standing committees engaged in the preparation of draft decisions. It is required that at least two variations of a proposal should be put forward, with detailed explanations. However, this is not always done, and quite often it appears that only one decision is put forward for consideration.

Discussions are then organised to enable workers to state their views, make suggestions and come to an agreement. The final draft decision is then prepared, with the necessary explanations. The trade unions play an important role in these discussions and in the preparation of the final draft.

According to the subject of the decision, it may be adopted by the workers at a meeting, by referendum or through their representatives on the workers' council or other organs. Decisions are carried by a majority vote of all the workers at a meeting or in a referendum, or by a majority vote in the workers' council. Under article 497 of the Associated Labour Law, decisions of a workers' council must as a rule be taken by public vote; decisions to be taken by secret ballot are determined by by-laws.

The implementation of decisions is the responsibility of the workers' council and its committees as well as of the managerial organ and professional staff, who are answerable to the workers' council. Direct control by the workers over the operation of the workers' management organs is provided for through a system of full information. The organs of workers' management are required to furnish workers with regular, timely, truthful and complete information, understandable in content

57

and form, concerning the business of the organisation, its financial position, the earning and distribution of income, and all other matters of importance for the taking of management decisions. Decisions and conclusions reached and important statements made in meetings of the workers' council or other organs must be made public in an appropriate way in the form of excerpts from the minutes of such meetings, not later than seven days after the meeting has taken place. The workers' council and the managerial organ are required to permit all workers in the organisation to examine documents, files and reports, in order to acquaint themselves with the financial situation of the organisation and its business operations. The Associated Labour Law provides for the imposition of fines on organisations of associated labour if workers are not kept regularly informed on these matters, or if workers' requests for information concerning decisions of the workers' council or other organs are refused. An individual manager or other responsible party who submits inaccurate information or fails to inform workers in good time may also be fined. Workers have the right to look into the work of the workers' council, of the managerial organ, and of staff in positions of special authority or responsibility, and those organs or staff may not prevent them from doing so. At the same time, the workers' management organs are bound to take into account and respond to the workers' opinions and proposals, within their respective spheres of activity. Individual workers or groups of workers are thus afforded every opportunity of exercising direct supervision over the functioning of the workers' management organs and the operation of the organisation. They may also propose to the supervisory organ, described below, that it should investigate a specific occurrence or take certain measures.

Direct control of the general operation of the organisation as a whole and of its elected organs is also exercised by the workers through the workers' meetings to which those organs report. Another means whereby workers can exercise their right of supervision is through the trade unions, as will be seen subsequently.

Supervision is exercised by the workers indirectly through their elected organs, that is mainly through the workers' council, which directly supervises the activities of its own executive committee, of the managerial organ and of the professional services. It is the responsibility of the workers' council to issue guidelines and instructions to those organs and services for the elimination of any irregularities, and it may revoke or suspend measures taken by its executive committee. These powers are exercised by the workers' councils of basic, work and composite organisations of associated labour, each at its own level.

In addition to these methods of supervising and controlling the implementation of decisions taken in management organs, the

Constitution of 1974 and the Associated Labour Law introduced a new supervisory organ, the "organ of self-management workers' control", or workers' supervisory commission, to safeguard workers' management rights and the principle of social ownership of resources by co-ordinating and improving the supervision by the workers themselves of the functioning of workers' management in organisations of associated labour. By making it easier for workers to draw attention to weaknesses and irregularities that may appear in the functioning of the workers' management system in organisations of associated labour, these provisions aim to counter negative or destructive trends which may arise, and to strengthen the system from within.

Workers' supervisory commissions are formed in basic and work organisations, composite organisations, co-operatives, banks and other financial organisations, insurance communities, self-managing communities of interest and other self-managing organisations and communities. A work community may also set up such a commission if it so desires.

The members of a workers' supervisory commission in a basic organisation or a work community are elected by the workers, by direct and secret ballot. Members of the workers' council and of its executive committee, as well as workers holding positions which make them ineligible to the workers' council, may not be elected to the workers' supervisory commission. In an organisation engaged in production at least three-quarters of the members of the commission must be production workers, while in an organisation providing public or social services or in a work community the composition of the commission reflects the occupational structure in that organisation or community. Members may not be elected for more than two consecutive terms, and their term of office may not exceed two years.

In a basic organisation the workers' supervisory commission supervises—

(a) the implementation of the by-laws and of the provisions of other internal self-management rules and of agreements and social compacts to which the organisation is a party;

(b) the implementation of decisions made by the workers and by the workers' management organs, and the conformity of those decisions with workers' management rights, obligations and interests;

(c) the performance of workers' work obligations and management functions, and of the functions of the organs of the basic organisation;

(d) the responsible use of social resources;

(e) the application of the principle of income distribution according to work done;

(*f*) the protection of the workers' rights and mutual relations in associated labour;

(*g*) the information of workers on matters of concern for decision-making, and supervision of the functioning of the organisation; and

(*h*) in general, the full exercise of the workers' management rights, the fulfilment of their duties under the workers' management system and the defence of their interests.

In a work organisation or composite organisation, the commission exercises this supervision at the level of the organisation as a whole, and not in its component parts. The workers' supervisory commission operates independently. It is not a decision-making body. Its function is to examine and reach a conclusion with regard to observed irregularities, to suggest remedies and to submit its conclusions and recommendations to the organs and services that are authorised to take remedial action, as well as to inform the workers, organs or services involved in the activities where the problems were observed. It is required to inform the workers' general meeting on issues which the meeting is competent to decide, and also in cases in which the managerial organ, the workers' council or other authorised organs or services fail to take appropriate action to do away with established shortcomings. The commission reports to the workers on its proceedings and recommendations. It is directly responsible to the workers' general meeting. It co-operates closely with the workers' council, which is required to act on its recommendations and to notify it of any established irregularities, and of the action taken or the attitude adopted in regard to them. In the event of a disagreement between these two bodies, a final decision on the matter is taken by the workers at their meeting.

Should the workers' council or the general meeting fail to take steps to eliminate observed shortcomings, the workers' supervisory commission may notify the social attorney of self-management, the court of associated labour, or other competent supervisory organ (see Chapter 5). These authorities may propose to the assembly of the socio-political community to suspend the execution of a decision or other measure of the workers' council that violates the workers' management rights or the principle of social ownership, or may take temporary measures of social protection against an organisation of associated labour in which workers' management is substantially disturbed or social interests harmed, or if the organisation fails to comply with its obligations as laid down by law. A workers' supervisory commission uses its right to turn to the organs of the socio-political community only when all the possibilities of taking measures to eliminate observed shortcomings in an organisation of associated labour under the self-management system have been exhausted.

The manager or board of management of an organisation of associated labour is obliged to provide the workers' supervisory commission with all documents, files and reports that are essential to the performance of its supervisory duties. The managerial organ is also bound to provide the administrative or professional services required by the commission, and must eliminate any irregularities pointed out by the commission in the sphere of activities within its scope. The managerial organ may not assign tasks to the workers' supervisory commission, which acts independently, but it may suggest that the commission should investigate specific occurrences or operations.

Because of the likelihood that workers performing these functions of worker's supervision may offend individuals or groups in the organisation, the Associated Labour Law goes to considerable lengths to provide for the protection of the members of the workers' supervisory commission from any kind of victimisation as a result of the conscientious performance of their supervisory duties. Thus, managers or workers in positions of authority and responsibility who call a worker to account for behaviour in a supervisory capacity, or who use their influence to place such a worker in an unfavourable position, commit a major violation of workers' management rights and work obligations. Punitive measures are also provided for in cases in which workers' supervisory commissions or any of their members are refused access to documents or information or otherwise hindered in the exercise of their supervisory functions.

Only limited experience of the operation of these workers' supervisory commissions has been acquired as yet, but they have succeeded in uncovering and remedying a certain number of irregular practices and of violations of the principles of workers' management. For example, in 1976, at the suggestion of the trade union and self-management organs, the workers' supervisory commission in the "Mehanotehnika" organisation of associated labour at Izola looked into the work and business dealings of that organisation and discovered numerous weak points. The commission compiled a detailed and substantiated report on the situation in the organisation and put forward proposals for action to eliminate the irregularities it had discovered. One of the consequences was that new appointments were made to a number of administrative posts. To a growing extent the commissions are now concentrating on attempting to anticipate unsatisfactory developments by drawing attention to potential dangers in good time and urging the competent organs to take preventive action. In the "Lasta" automobile work organisation, for example, the workers' supervisory commission came to the conclusion that there were numerous problems. It informed the workers and their management organs of this discovery, and as a result steps were taken to eliminate these weaknesses.

Most of the questions with which these bodies deal fall into three main groups. The first concerns matters relating to work discipline and work obligations, violations of workers' management rights in the field of labour relations, distribution of resources for personal incomes, allocation of housing, overtime pay, safety at work, waste in production, checks on sick leave and other such matters. The second group includes questions of financial and business operations, especially as regards control of business results, the utilisation of income and resources, the carrying out of production plans, violation of good business standards, economic offences, unjustified business trips within the country and abroad, and so forth. The third group comprises questions relating to the application of statutory regulations and self-management agreements and social compacts, checks on the implementation of decisions of the workers' meetings and other bodies, the fulfilment of contracts, and similar legal matters.

In 1976 the commissions were active, that is, intervened in various cases, in more than 15,000 organisations of associated labour out of more than 22,000 that were surveyed. About 115,000 reports were delivered to various organs in the organisations of associated labour and to outside agencies. More than 85 per cent of the findings were taken into consideration, while only 8.5 per cent of them were rejected outright. Most of the interventions by the commissions were made in basic organisations of associated labour (52 per cent), and in work organisations without basic organisations (32 per cent).

Some weaknesses have been noted in the functioning of this new institution, such as a certain superficiality in carrying out supervisory duties, failure to react in good time to established shortcomings or arbitrary conduct, and officiousness or a tendency to usurp the functions and authority of other organs in the organisation.

It may be mentioned that the elected members of the workers' supervisory commission are not remunerated or compensated in any way for carrying out these functions; in this they differ from the members of various supervisory services that are normal components of organisations of associated labour, such as those concerned with the internal control of financial operations, the quality control of goods and services, occupational safety or security. All those services work independently, but co-operate closely with the workers' supervisory commissions.

Diagram 1. Management structure of organisations of associated labour

Composite organisations of associated labour

Work organisations

Basic organisations of associated labour

Managerial organ (General manager)

Administrative support

Managerial organ (General manager or board of management)

Administrative support

Managerial organ (General manager or board of management)

Administrative support

Committees

Committees

Labour relations committee

Committee for national defence and social self-protection

Other committees

Workers' council

Executive committee of workers' council

Workers' council

Executive committee of workers' council

Workers' council

Executive committee of workers' council

Committee for national defence and social self-protection

Committee for national defence and social self-protection

Bureau of information and documentary services

Disciplinary commission

Disciplinary commission

Workers' meetings

Disciplinary commission

Workers' supervisory commission

Workers' supervisory commission

Workers' supervisory commission

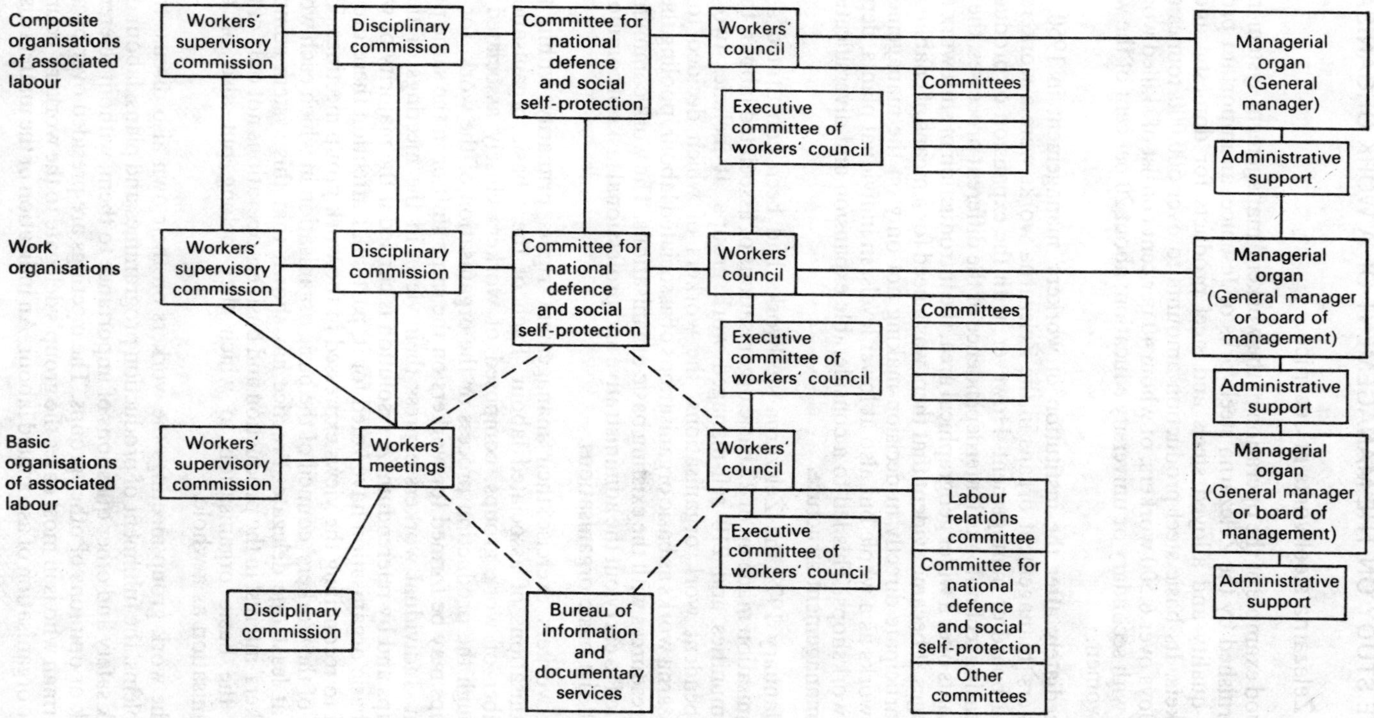

CASE STUDY ON THE MANAGEMENT OF A WORK ORGANISATION

The Železarna steelworks at Jesenice

A good example of the operation of the workers' management system in practice is furnished by the Železarna steelworks of Jesenice, an important producer of high-quality and alloyed steels and steel products for domestic and foreign markets. Its basic steel production amounts to over 500,000 tonnes a year. It employs over 6,500 workers, of whom 40 per cent consist of skilled workers and staff with secondary or university education; about 20 per cent of the workforce are women.

Immediately after the institution of workers' management in 1950, the only workers' management organs in the Železarna works were a workers' council and a board of management. However, with the expansion of production, the increasing technological interdependence of the different processes, the dispersal of plants over a wider geographical area, the introduction of shift work and other changes, it became evident that there was a need for a means of enabling workers to participate directly in decision-making not only on the management of the steelworks as a whole but also at lower levels, in individual plants, departments and workshops. This led to a considerable expansion and diversification of the self-management structure.

By January 1977 the Železarna steelworks had been constituted as a work organisation made up of 22 basic organisations of associated labour, three work communities and 210 self-managed work groups. It includes two formerly independent work organisations, the workers of which decided to join the Železarna works as basic organisations of associated labour, pooling their labour and resources with the existing basic organisations. The work communities were formed to carry out the administrative and professional tasks of common interest to all the basic organisations.

The workers exercise their management rights primarily within the basic organisations of associated labour. Each of these basic organisations has a number of work groups, composed of workers closely associated at work through the production process or the organisation of the work; for example, groups may be formed for workers on the same shift or in the same part of the plant. Individual workers express their views in the meetings of these work groups and by referendum. A resolution is carried if the majority of workers in the basic organisation have voted for it; particular attention therefore has to be paid to reconciling the views expressed in the work group meetings. This is the task of the workers' council of the basic organisation in which each work group has at least one delegate. Practice has shown that this system stimulates the workers' interest in the production and business operations not only of the group and the basic organisation to which they belong but also of the work organisation as a whole.

At the work group meetings the workers on their own also discuss their work problems, the fulfilment of production programmes and plans, labour discipline, work safety and other questions of importance to them, without reference to the work or opinions of other groups. The meetings are presided over by an elected chairman who is in most cases the group's delegate to the workers' council of the basic organisation of associated labour. An indication of the matters discussed at these meetings is given by the following list of subjects dealt with in the 13 meetings held by one work group in 1976:

(a) regular monthly discussions of production results;

(b) discussion of conditions to be met for setting up new basic organisations of associated labour;

(c) an action programme for making economies;

(d) relations with self-managing communities of interest engaged in the production of goods;

(e) distribution of resources allocated by the basic organisation of associated labour for joint consumption;

(f) the social compact on the allocation of income in 1976;

(g) the self-management agreement on social self-protection in the basic organisation;

(h) discussion of new requirements in the general system of payments;

(i) reclassification of some jobs within the basic organisation;

(j) subscription to a public loan for new roads;

(k) decisions of the second session of the conference of the Železarna works branch of the League of Communists;

(l) aid to the victims of an earthquake in the Soca river basin;

(m) grievances within the factory;

(n) social assistance to some of the workers;

(o) the self-management agreement on the basic principles for the 1977 plan;

(p) the self-management agreements on the basic principles for the development plans of self-managing communities of interest in the public services from 1976 to 1980;

(q) discussion and adoption of the self-management agreement on association of labour and resources in the basic organisation, and of its fundamental by-laws; and

(r) discussion and adoption of the plan for 1977.

The delegates of the work groups to the workers' council of each basic organisation of associated labour are responsible to those groups and must keep the workers informed of the work of the workers' council; they must also transmit the views and proposals of their work group to the council, but they act independently in the process of give and take necessary to reach a decision acceptable to all groups.

The workers' council elects an executive committee, a committee for national defence and social self-protection, and other committees such as an economic committee, a labour relations committee, a committee for personnel policy and social standards, and a general affairs and information committee. In some cases, other special committees have been set up, for example for work safety or technical innovations. These bodies have no right to take decisions except within the limits of programmes and guidelines laid down by the workers' council or general meetings, but they prepare the background papers for decisions of the workers' council and ensure that those decisions are carried out.

In 1976 the workers' councils of the basic organisations of associated labour in the Železarna works, and those of the self-managing work groups, met on an average once every two months, but many of them met regularly every month.

All the 25 basic organisations and work communities in the Železarna works are linked by common interests in the production process, in particular by a unified system of income earning and allocation. They therefore elect joint self-management organs to exercise their collective rights, discharge their collective obligations, meet their common needs and promote their joint interests. Each of the basic organisations of associated labour is represented on the workers' council of the steelworks as a whole by at least two delegates, elected by direct and secret ballot. On all important matters of common concern, particularly with regard to financial obligations, the central council takes a decision only after all the workers' councils of the basic organisations have taken their own decisions on the issue. A specific feature of the decision-making process in the Železarna workers' council is that it may not take a decision on any matter on which decisions are normally made by a workers' meeting or by referendum unless it has the consent of the delegates of each and every basic organisation. Decisions on other questions are carried by a majority vote of those present.

Each basic organisation elects one delegate to the joint workers' supervisory commission of the Železarna works as a whole. This body has wide powers, particularly in supervising the use of associated resources and allocation of income among the basic organisations. Its programme of action includes the submission of periodical reports on matters such as representation and advertising costs, the use of official cars, the justification of business trips, as well as general business operations and the carrying out of the social plan. In 1976 this body, on the initiative of the work groups, other self-management organs and its own members, investigated and submitted reports on the following matters:

(a) grievances;

(b) housing problems;

(c) financial management and functioning of canteens;

(d) the self-management agreement on the establishment of an "Innovator of the Year" prize (thus exercising control over the proper implementation of a self-management agreement);

(e) work safety, with special reference to serious accidents; and

(f) labour discipline and workers' attitudes to work.

The steelworks is run by a five-member board of management with collective responsibility. It is composed of a chairman, a vice-chairman and one member for each of the following sectors: financial matters; development and production; and personnel and welfare matters. A member of the board of management of the Železarna works is specifically assigned to the tasks of business management of the work communities, which do not have individual managers. Members of the board are appointed by the workers' council for a four-year term.

The Železarna works has pooled its labour and resources with other work organisations in a composite organisation of associated labour, the Slovenske Železarne (Slovenian Steelworks). The workers' council of the Železarna works elects from its members eight delegates to sit on the workers' council of the composite organisation.

As explained in Chapters 1 and 5, the delegate system links the workers in basic organisations of associated labour directly to the socio-political communities. In this particular case, each basic organisation in the Železarna works elects its own delegation to the assembly of the commune, for a four-year term. The number of delegates depends on the size of the basic organisation and the composition of the delegation reflects the structure of the organisation's workforce. Each basic organisation and work community occupies one seat in the chamber of associated labour of the assembly of the commune, except the three smallest ones, which have a joint delegate, and which are thus obliged to co-ordinate their views before meetings of the delegate conference. The members of the delegation participate in meetings of the assembly in rotation, in order to avoid any alienation of delegates from their constituents and to ensure that all members of the delegation bear a fair share of the responsibilities involved.

Delegations to self-managing communities of interest are elected by the basic organisations in a similar way, for a two-year term. At present, the basic organisations elect separate delegations for three different areas of public service, namely child care, education and science; health care, old age and disability insurance and employment; and culture and physical education. The delegations elected by the basic organisations meet in three separate delegation conferences, in which they co-ordinate their views and elect from among their number the delegates to attend each assembly, who are chosen in function of their knowledge of and interest in the subjects to be discussed. These delegations play an important part in transmitting proposals from the basic organisations to the assemblies of self-management communities of interest and in keeping the workers informed of discussions and decisions taken there, particularly in connection with the elaboration of self-management agreements on the basic principles of the plan for a self-managing community of interest. The draft plan prepared by the executive organs of the respective communities is discussed and amended and eventually adopted by the assemblies of the work groups of the basic organisations of associated labour.

Recognising the importance of full and accurate information for workers' management, the Železarna steelworks set up a few years ago a centre for management research and information. The centre collects and prepares material of common concern for the self-management organs of the basic organisations and for their delegations, and also keeps on file the minutes of the meetings of all the self-management organs and work groups and the resolutions adopted by them. It acts as an information link between the workers and their self-management organs and the business managing organs, professional services, socio-political organisations and self-managing communities of interest. The centre publishes a weekly newspaper which is distributed free to all active workers, retired workers, and other members of the community; it carries information about all events taking place in the Commune of Jesenice. The centre also carries out research work and training activities for delegates and members of workers' management organs.

The trade union organisation is also present and active in the Železarna works. There is a trade union in every basic organisation of associated labour and work community, with an executive committee on which every work group is represented by at least one member. They are autonomous organisations, but they take into consideration in their activities the directives issued by the Conference of Trade Unions and the joint executive committee of the Železarna works trade unions. The 13 members of the joint executive committee of the Železarna works trade unions head committees for the following questions: self-management and economic affairs; supervisory staff; leisure time and excur-

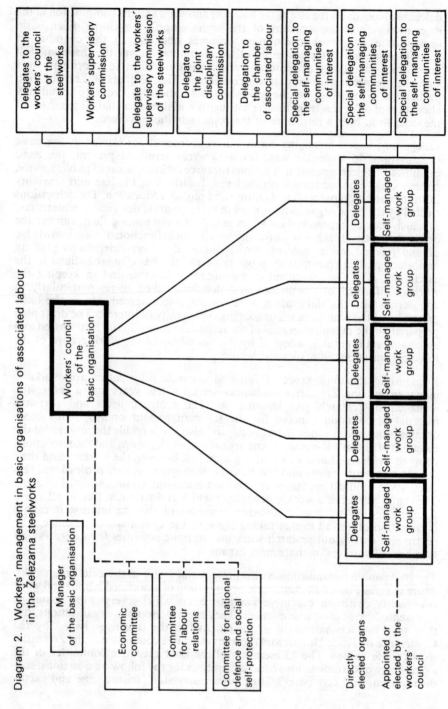

Diagram 2. Workers' management in basic organisations of associated labour in the Železarna steelworks

sions; recreation and sports; education and culture; and "workers' control" (the workers' supervisory commission). Trade union activities touch on every aspect of the operation of the steelworks and the welfare of its workers.

The League of Communists, with 800 members, and the Union of Socialist Youth, with 2,050 members, are also influential in the works.

RESPONSIBILITY FOR THE PERFORMANCE
OF WORKERS' MANAGEMENT FUNCTIONS

One of the basic premises of the workers' management system, laid down in the Constitution, is the equality of rights, obligations and responsibilities of workers in organisations of associated labour.[16] The workers, who are directly in charge of managing socially owned resources and means of production, are responsible to one another and to the community as a whole, and they may be held responsible—morally, politically, socially and, sometimes, financially—for failing to carry out their workers' management functions and obligations.

The constitutional provisions in this respect establish, first, that persons entrusted with workers' management, public, or other social functions shall perform those functions on the basis and within the framework of the Constitution, laws, or by-laws, and authority legally granted to them, and shall be responsible for their execution; that in performing these functions, they shall be subject to social control; that all workers are personally responsible for the conscientious performance of their workers' management functions; and that the elected or appointed bearers of workers' management, public or other social functions are personally responsible for their performance; that such persons may be recalled or replaced, and that they have the right to resign and to explain their actions; that they may be dismissed and that their re-election may be limited; that the work of all organs of authority and workers' management and that of persons entrusted with workers' management, public or other social functions must be conducted publicly; that the responsibility of the members of an executive organ, the individual manager and the members of a managerial body depends on the degree of influence they exert on the adoption or implementation of a particular decision; and that the conditions and procedures for discharging that responsibility are established by law and by self-management by-laws and rules.

Responsibility for the performance of workers' management functions is regulated by the Associated Labour Law, 1976, while the duties of the bearers of workers' management functions, the kinds of responsibility for breach of duty and the procedures for establishing liability are regulated in detail by the by-laws of the basic organisations and by the self-management agreement on association in a work organisation or composite organisation of associated labour, in accordance with the law.

According to the Associated Labour Law, delegates elected to the workers' council are directly responsible to the workers who elected them; they are bound to act in conformity with the instructions given by the latter and must keep them informed about their activities and the proceedings of the workers' council on which they serve. Should the delegates fail to perform satisfactorily, or to follow the instructions they have received, the workers may recall them. Delegates to the workers' council of a work organisation or a composite organisation are responsible to the workers' councils of the basic organisations which elected them, and the latter workers' councils are obliged to inform their constituents if such a delegate fails to follow instructions. The workers' councils of the basic organisations may propose the institution of proceedings for the delegate's recall. Members of the workers' councils bear personal and financial responsibility for any decisions they may adopt which go beyond the scope of their authority or are taken against the warning of the competent supervisory organs (e.g. the managerial organ, the executive committee, the workers' supervisory commission, the social attorney of self-management or the Social Accountancy Office.). Should such a decision be harmful to the organisation, the managerial organ is obliged to stay execution of it and to institute proceedings before the Court of Associated Labour. The Law does not specify in what way members of a workers' council may be held personally and financially responsible for such decisions.

Members of the executive committee of a workers' council are responsible to the workers' council that appointed them and to the workers as a whole in the organisation in which they perform their functions. They are responsible for the execution of decisions taken by the workers' council or by the workers themselves at a meeting or by referendum; they are also responsible for providing the workers' council and the workers with complete and accurate information. The workers or the workers' council may recall the executive committee or any of its members, if they are not satisfied with its activities. Members of an executive committee are financially liable for losses caused by the execution of a decision made on its proposal if, in making such a proposal, they concealed information or knowingly gave inaccurate information to the workers' council or the workers. It is provided that the workers' council of a basic organisation may rescind a rule or suspend a measure that was made by its executive committee, if it considers that the committee had overstepped its authority or violated a general workers' management by-law, or failed to carry out established policy or to implement the decisions of the workers' council or of the workers.

The Associated Labour Law also lays down the responsibility of a separate organ, formed by the workers' council of an organisation of associated labour, for the safeguarding of business secrets. This organ is responsible for keeping such secrets and specifying which workers may be authorised to have knowledge of them or to disclose them in certain circumstances.

Similarly, responsibility both to the workers' council and to the workers as a whole for the conscientious performance of his or her functions, for the business results of the organisation and for organising and co-ordinating its work is an integral part of the rights and obligations of the general manager or the chairman of a board of management. The workers' council of the organisation ascertains the responsibility of the managerial organ in relation to the above-mentioned matters, and the latter may institute proceedings before the court of associated labour if it considers that the facts concerning its responsibility were erroneously or incompletely established. A conclusion of the workers' council or a decision of the court of associated labour establishing the responsibility of the managerial organ provides the basis for instituting proceedings for its dismissal.

The above-mentioned provisions of the Associated Labour Law pertaining to the financial liability of the members of an executive committee also apply to an individual manager and to the members of managerial boards.

Workers who are entrusted with special authority, such as deputy and assistant managers or heads of individual departments, fall into a special category; like the managerial organs, however, their direct responsibility is to the workers' council.

The question of responsibility is different for individual executives or groups of executives in a basic organisation that are not considered to be managerial organs but that perform specific duties which fall within the sphere of activity of the managerial organ and carry out their functions under its authority in accordance with the by-laws of the organisation. These individuals or bodies are responsible to the managerial organ for the performance of such duties, and to the workers' council within the limits of the authority granted.

Members of workers' supervisory commissions in basic organisations and work organisations of associated labour are directly responsible to the workers who elected them. In other types of organisations, where such commissions are formed on the basis of elected delegations, the members are also responsible to the workers in the basic organisations or communities associated in the organisation concerned, and may be recalled by them. The recall of members of a workers' supervisory commission is carried out at the suggestion of the trade union.

The rights, obligations and responsibilities of members of a workers' supervisory commission are determined by by-laws or other general workers' management rules, in accordance with the law.

The conclusion of self-management agreements and social compacts entails very specific obligations and responsibilities on the signatory parties for the execution of such agreements. According to the Associated Labour Law, parties to a social compact, for example, are obliged to take the necessary measures for its implementation; and they may be held socially and politically responsible for the non-performance of obligations stemming from the compact. From the day of its conclusion, the parties to a self-management agreement take on the obligations and responsibilities as well as the rights specified in the agreement, unless it provides otherwise.

Parties to a self-management agreement who fail to fulfil their financial obligations, undertaken on the conclusion of the agreement, are liable for any losses that this failure may cause to the other parties to the agreement. If in such an event the agreement provides for indemnity in monetary form, and if the non-fulfilment of obligations has resulted in losses exceeding the amount of the indemnity, the aggrieved parties have the right to damages in excess of the amount of the indemnity provided for.

Delegates to the assemblies of the self-managing communities of interest are responsible for carrying out their duties in conformity with the general instructions given by the members of the community who elected them.

Delegates to the assemblies of the socio-political communities likewise follow the general instructions given by their self-managing organisations and communities, but express their views and vote independently. They are responsible both to the workers who elected them and to the delegations from which they were chosen, and they must keep both informed about their work.

Delegates to local community bodies are responsible for the discharge of their duties to the working people and citizens who elected them.

The notion of responsibility thus permeates all functions and activities throughout the workers' management system. In view of the large number of workers who participate in workers' management activities and hold office of one type or another in the workers' management system, it is hardly surprising that socio-political bodies have in recent times placed special emphasis on the importance of developing a sense of responsibility among working people throughout society as a whole.[17]

INFORMATION AND TRAINING OF
WORKERS AND DELEGATES

In a system where workers are called upon to assume such a wide range of responsibilities, including the organisation of production, the management of undertakings, and the distribution of income, it is evident that the training and information of workers and delegates is of the highest importance.[18] Indeed, the success of the whole workers' management system depends to a great extent on the degree to which workers are qualified to assume such complex and responsible duties and the maintenance of adequate arrangements for keeping them informed on all questions concerning the work of their organisations and on social and economic affairs in general.

This is particularly true in the light of the considerable differences which exist between groups of workers with regard to their level of qualification for management decision-making and capacity to understand socio-economic developments on a larger scale. There are still organisations of associated labour in which the general level of education among the workers is relatively low, the skill structures unfavourable and workers' management consciousness poorly developed. In such cases there is a danger that lack of knowledge and preparation for workers' management among the mass of the workers may allow individuals and groups in positions of technocratic and bureaucratic strength to dominate the decision-making process.

It was recognised from the very beginning that an extensive system of training for workers' management was absolutely essential to its success. In a predominantly agricultural society, such as Yugoslavia was at the time of the introduction of workers' management, people tend to cling to values of stability and authoritarian methods of control, whereas workers' management required a new outlook reflecting creative initiative and a willingness to assume responsibilities and risks on a footing of general equality. Thus, in addition to raising the level of literacy and general education for the population as a whole to fit them for the tasks of workers' management, basic ideological and political training was required, to enable the people to understand the aims and values of the system. As time went on and as the complexities of workers' management, both in the work organisation and in the wider framework of society as a whole became more apparent, an increasing degree of special emphasis was given to socio-economic education of a more technical nature.[19]

Training for workers' management was carried out first and foremost through the entire education system, from elementary school to university. Every worker is thus made aware of his role as worker and as manager in the workers' management system and in the community. The

73

training process continues in the workplace, through various agencies such as the "workers' and people's universities", "self-managers' clubs", political schools, and educational centres in organisations of associated labour, and at seminars, conferences and other specially organised meetings.

One of the first steps taken immediately after the liberation of the country was the formation of people's and workers' universities as centres of educational activity for the entire population. Their importance was particularly great in the years immediately following the Second World War, when mass education and the elimination of illiteracy were matters of very high priority. Numerous cultural centres were accordingly built in all parts of the country, and played a particularly important role in the countryside and villages. The "people's universities" are open to all citizens, and provide general education. "Workers' universities" provide vocational training. They have made a great contribution to building up the vocational qualifications of the younger working class and to its successful integration into the economy in the postwar period of reconstruction and in the building of the new Yugoslavia.

Workers' and people's universities carry out their educational activity through seminars and courses for general, socio-economic, and vocational education. Between 1973 and 1977 the number of seminars and courses grew by 16 per cent and the number of participants by 17 per cent, as shown in table 6.

The mass media also contribute to workers' training through newspaper articles, special publications, and educational programmes on radio and television. The trade unions are also particularly active in this field.[20]

Training for workers' management is thus a mass programme, designed to reach the broadest possible audience among the population. It has been estimated that about a million workers take part in various training activities every year. The programme also constitutes an attempt to relate general orientation to occurrences in real life and to the practical problems that confront workers as managers. The third characteristic of the programme is that it is constant, a steady effort to qualify workers for the complex and continually evolving responsibilities of workers' management.

As a factor in making real decision-making by workers possible, equal importance is attached to ensuring that workers are adequately informed. As a matter of everyday practice, existing means of keeping workers, delegates and members of delegations informed are continually being improved and new means found. Information is disseminated through factory newspapers or bulletins, notice boards and posters, by word of mouth in workshops, and through work brigades, shifts or other

Table 6. Activities of people's and workers universities, and number of participants in them, 1964–79

Kinds of seminars and courses, and No. of participants	Year			
	1964	1973	1977	1979
General education	4 956	8 153	8 076	5 427
Participants	149 416	217 211	229 728	153 117
Socio-economic education	5 067	3 809	5 984	6 406
Participants	211 464	262 963	303 846	320 123
Vocational training	3 451	3 489	4 049	6 081
Participants	118 209	124 491	171 920	232 481

Source: *Statistički bilteni SZS*, 1979, No. 1203.

groups.[21] It is widely recognised by managers and members of workers' councils and other workers' management organs that full information is the essential factor in the smooth functioning of those organs, of workers' meetings and, in general, of the entire workers' management system. The trade unions, the League of Communists and other socio-political organisations play an important part in the effort to comply with the constitutional obligation to keep workers informed, and to overcome shortcomings in this regard which may be due to lack of funds, or, occasionally, to conscious attempts to avoid informing workers about the real situation of their organisation. As has been indicated above, the various self-management organs and services within organisations of associated labour have a statutory obligation to keep the workers informed, regularly and fully, on a wide range of questions relating to the work of the organisation, the disposal of its resources, and the activities of the self-management organs and the implementation of their decisions. The workers' council and the managerial organ of a basic organisation are also required by law to inform workers of any relevant warnings or findings and decisions of the social attorney of self-management or of other competent authorities responsible for supervising the legality of the operation of an organisation of associated labour. Organs of the socio-political community or the trade unions may also request that decisions they have taken should be brought to the workers' attention.

JOINT VENTURES: WORKERS' MANAGEMENT AND FOREIGN INVESTMENT WITHIN THE COUNTRY

Joint ventures based on foreign investment in Yugoslav organisations of associated labour represent one of the more recent institutions of the

Yugoslav socio-economic system and a specific form of business and financial linkage of the domestic economy and foreign partners.

The originality of the legal arrangements for foreign investment in Yugoslavia, as established by the federal authorities in 1967, lies in the fact that they comply with the modern tendencies and requirements of production and technological integration on an international scale while fully guaranteeing the status of the workers and their organisations under the workers' management system. As a means of linking the domestic economy with foreign capital the setting up of a joint-stock company of the traditional type is not acceptable in Yugoslavia: to quote Edvard Kardelj, in view of the contemporary integration of the world economy, traditional stockholder relations would lead "to ever greater domination of the capitalist elements in the Yugoslav economic system and, consequently, to economic dependence and subordination to the economic exploitation of foreign capital".[22]

Under the Yugoslav Constitution of 1974 an organisation of associated labour has the right to make use of foreign resources in its operations under conditions and limitations determined by statute. The Constitution also guarantees that the rights of foreign investors with regard to resources invested in an organisation of associated labour in Yugoslavia may not be curtailed by laws or regulations once the contract establishing those rights has gone into effect. Regarding the socio-economic status of the workers and the achievement of workers' management in joint ventures, the Constitution establishes the principles that—

(a) the workers of an organisation of associated labour that makes use of foreign investments have the same socio-economic and management rights as do workers in organisations of associated labour that use the resources of other domestic organisations of associated labour in their operations; and

(b) foreign investors in an organisation of associated labour in Yugoslavia may participate in the income of that organisation only within the limits and under the conditions governing mutual relations among domestic organisations of associated labour.

According to existing Yugoslav law[23] and practice, joint ventures of domestic and foreign partners are based on the following principles and provisions.

The basic aim of joint ventures based on foreign investment in domestic organisations of associated labour is to play a more extensive and lasting part in the international division of labour, obtain modern technology, increase exports, improve supplies of raw materials and intermediate goods to the domestic market, decrease imports of finished products, and improve the operations of Yugoslav organisations of associated labour. Foreign partners may invest resources in a Yugoslav organisation of associated labour in order to attain common business goals and to promote common business interests. Such an investment is accompanied by a sharing of the risks involved and by the right to a share of the income accruing from the joint operation. As a rule, foreign investment is long-term. The relations that stem from the investment of foreign resources are agreed upon for the time required to attain the intended common business goals.

The mutual relations of the parties in a joint venture are determined by a written foreign investment contract entered into by a domestic organisation of associated labour. (The contracting Yugoslav organisation is normally a basic organisation of associated labour, but it is laid down by law that work and composite organisations may conclude such contracts as well, in conformity with their self-management agreements on association.) An investment contract may not be concluded in the fields of insurance, commerce, or "social activities". (The latter limitation does not apply, however, to the field of scientific research. In exceptional cases the Federal Executive Council, with the agreement of the competent authorities at the republican and provincial levels, may make provision for an organisation of associated labour to conclude a contract on investment in specific social activities if the investment will contribute to the development of the activities in question.) Foreign investment in the field of banking is governed by federal law.

An investment contract may not be contrary to the social plan of Yugoslavia, to the social compacts concluded by the domestic organisation of associated labour, or to the self-management agreements which it has concluded or to which it has acceded. The contract regulates in particular—

(a) the investment goals and the conditions, purpose and use of the investment;

(b) the total value of the investment;

(c) the way of determining the part of the income of the domestic organisation in which the foreign partner shall be entitled to share;

(d) the principles and means of calculating the share of the foreign partner in the income of the domestic organisation;

(e) the conditions, method and deadlines for payment of the part of the income to which the foreign partner is entitled;

(f) the conditions, method and deadlines for reimbursing the investment;

(g) the respective liabilities of the co-signers when business losses are incurred, as well as in other situations; and

(h) the way of settling disputes between the parties.

77

The total value of the resources invested by a foreign party in any one domestic organisation on the basis of an investment contract must be less than the total value of resources invested by domestic organisations of associated labour. (Exceptions are allowed only in cases in which foreign investment will be of special value, as specified in a law passed by the Federal Assembly, for the development of a given branch of economic activity.) On the other hand, the Federal Executive Council recently adopted a rule to the effect that a foreign investment in a domestic organisation of associated labour must amount to at least 10 per cent of the total value of the joint project, and not less than 5 million Yugoslav dinars.

In joint ventures in Yugoslavia there is so-called "decision-making by mutual consent" on the part of foreign partners and domestic organisations of associated labour through a joint managerial body. The investment contract lays down the procedure for forming this joint body and appointing its officers, as well as its method of operation. By law, the joint managerial body must be set up within the basic organisation which disposes of the invested resources and carries out the joint operations, and which must itself be represented on that body. If several basic organisations dispose of the invested resources, they decide jointly on their representatives on the joint managerial body and determine in which basic organisation it is to be set up. When another domestic organisation of associated labour joins a foreign partner in investing resources in a domestic organisation of associated labour in order to carry out a joint project, the domestic investing organisation must also be represented on the joint managerial body. The foreign partners may not have a greater number of representatives than those chosen by the domestic organisations of associated labour.

Yugoslav legislation contains only general provisions concerning the officers of the joint managerial body, which in practice is most often known as "the business board". This body attends to the execution of the provisions of the investment contract and may decide on questions relating to the organisation of work and business operations, the increase of labour productivity, and other questions with regard to the joint venture, as long as decision-making on these questions does not fall within the inalienable rights of the workers, based on the right to work with socially owned resources. (Such rights include, for example, management of the work and affairs of the organisation, regulation of mutual labour relations, decision-making on income that workers generate when labour and resources are pooled in various ways, and decisions regarding the earning of personal incomes.) The joint managerial body is also authorised to submit proposals and opinions to the organs of the domestic organisation of associated labour on all questions that are of importance to the joint operation. An organ of the domestic organisation (e.g. the workers' council, the board of management or the manager) that receives such proposals or opinions is bound to consider them and to inform the joint managerial body of its views.

A foreign partner shares in the income accruing from a joint venture in proportion to the contribution its investment has made to generating that income. The foreign partner's right to share in the income generated by the joint operation ceases when the value of its investment is returned together with an amount corresponding to profits earned while its right to share in income was still in effect, or when the period established by the investment contract expires, regardless of the amount of the return on the investment. The investment contract may not provide for the permanent participation of a foreign partner in the income of a domestic organisation of associated labour generated by a joint venture.

A domestic organisation of associated labour in which foreign resources are invested is bound to keep separate accounts in its ledgers of the income from the joint venture if the investment contract provides for the participation of the foreign investor in the income. In a domestic organisation of associated labour in which a foreign party invests resources which give it the right to participate in the income flowing from the joint operation, the investment contract guarantees, according to the workers' contribution to the generation of the income of the basic organisation of associated labour and within the limits of that income, resources for—

(a) personal incomes and joint consumption in conformity with the principles and rules valid for all organisations of associated labour;

(b) the payment of debts incurred in earning the income from the joint operation; and

(c) introducing technological improvements.

After the allocation of the above-mentioned resources, the income resulting from a joint venture is allotted to—

(1) the foreign partner, as a share of the income earned by the joint operation; and

(2) the domestic organisation of associated labour.

Investment contracts may entitle foreign partners to the return of the value of their investment or the return of specific objects that constituted their investment in a domestic organisation of associated labour. The domestic organisation of associated labour and the foreign partner establish in the investment contract the maximum amount due to the foreign partner for income earned on the investment. The foreign partner's liability for obligations stemming from the joint operation is limited to the amount of the investment, unless a greater liability was accepted in the contract. Foreign investors have the right to transfer their income from joint operations abroad, in conformity with the law on foreign currency affairs and credit relations abroad and the law on foreign investment. (Foreign investors may also use these resources to increase their investment in the joint operation, or may conclude other investment contracts with other domestic organisations of associated labour, or may dispose of the resources in some other lawful manner in Yugoslavia.)

The investment contract, as well as changes, additions, or extensions concerning it, are subject to approval by the Federal Committee for Energy and Industry.

Disputes that arise between a domestic organisation of associated labour and a foreign partner over an investment contract are settled by the competent court in Yugoslavia, unless the investment contract provides that such disputes shall be settled by the Foreign Trade Court of the Yugoslav Chamber of Economy or by some other domestic or foreign arbitrating body.

An investment contract may be cancelled before the scheduled date of its expiry if losses have been incurred or if the joint goals established by the contract have not been achieved for several years of joint operation, or when one party to the contract fails to carry out essential obligations as specified by the contract, or when the conditions that existed at the time of its conclusion have substantially changed.

Since 1968, when, in conformity with Yugoslav legislation, foreign investments were first made in joint ventures for domestic production and business, more than 160 contracts have been signed with foreign companies, including Bayer (Federal Republic of Germany), Ciba-Geigy (Switzerland), Dunlop (United Kingdom) and Fiat (Italy).

Notes

[1] Statistics of these various types of organisation will be found in the last two lines of table 3.

[2] Associated Labour Law, Arts. 346–381.

[3] Associated Labour Law, Arts. 320–345.

[4] Associated Labour Law, Arts. 382–387.

[5] Associated Labour Law, Arts. 400–408.

[6] See pp. 52–54.

[7] "Report to the Eighth Congress by CTUY President, Mika Spiljak", in *Yugoslav Trade Unions* (Belgrade), Nov.–Dec. 1978, p. 3.

[8] See, for example, the report of the Eleventh Congress of the League of Communists of Yugoslavia (1978) and the Eighth Congress of the Confederation of Yugoslav Trade Unions, which adopted a resolution on the tasks of the Yugoslav trade unions in the struggle of the working class for the development of self-management socio-economic relations and the political system of socialist self-management. *Sindikati* (Belgrade), 1978, No. 8, pp. 35–88.

[9] Savezni zavod za statistiku: *Samoupravni društveno-ekonomski razvoj Jugoslavije, 1947-1977*, Statistički prikaz (Belgrade, 1978), p. 42.

[10] It was noted, however, by the members of the ILO mission to Yugoslavia, that, in general, meetings lasted only about one-and-a-half hours. They were conveniently scheduled at the end of the working day, and careful preparation enabled them to take decisions expeditiously.

[11] On the duties of the executive committee see p. 70.

[12] See pp. 159–165.

[13] The ILO mission were informed of some such cases, for example, in the Jugohemia trade and pharmaceutical corporation.

[14] See for example the following passage from Josip Broz Tito: "Sixty years of revolutionary struggle of the League of Communists of Yugoslavia", address delivered at the special meeting of the Central Committee of the LCY, 19 April 1979, in *Review of International Affairs* (Belgrade, Jugoslovenska Stvarnost), May 1979, p. 22: "With reference to self-management, I want to point out that there are many cases of disparity between norms and practice. There [is] also bureaucratic and technocratic opposition to the implementation of our self-management system. In places, concealing themselves behind alleged self-management forms, narrow groups are trying to pull strings, and are placing self-management organs, assemblies and delegations before accomplished facts. All [too] often criticism is levelled at unknown culprits rather than at those who sponsored such decisions, bypassing the self-management avenues."

[15] In two of the organisations visited in Zagreb by the ILO mission, the manager had been in office for more than 25 years.

[16] In recent times the principles and conditions of responsibility for management have been emphasised in a number of important political documents. At the Second Congress of Self-Managers in Yugoslavia (1971) the principles of responsibility were treated separately in a resolution on current political tasks and in another on strengthening responsibility in a workers' management society. In 1971 the Federal Assembly adopted a resolution on the responsibility of persons entrusted with workers' management and other social and public functions (*Službeni List*, No. 52/71). Statements concerning fundamental principles concerning responsibility were also included in the documents of the Tenth and Twelfth Congresses of the League of Communists of Yugoslavia (1974 and 1978), as well as in the documents of the Eighth Congress of the Confederation of Trade Unions (1978).

[17] See note 16 above.

[18] The role of information in the delegate system was one of the subjects discussed at the Third Congress of Self-Managers of Yugoslavia, held in Belgrade from 16 to 18 June 1981 (see *Yugoslav Trade Unions*, special issue, July 1981, p. 19).

[19] cf. Nikola Pastuovic: "Education and training for self-management", in Obradovic and Dunn, *Workers' self-management and organizational power in Yugoslavia*, op. cit., pp. 435–448.

[20] See pp. 170–171.

[21] In the Toz pencil factory it was noted by the ILO mission that information was provided directly by the manager at meetings as well as through bulletin boards, a periodical and an internal radio station.

[22] Edvard Kardelj: "Protivrečnosti društvene svojine u savremenoj socijalističkoj praksi", in *Teorija i praksa samoupravljanja u Jugoslaviji* (Belgrade, Radnička štampa, 1972), p. 81.

[23] The law on foreign investment in domestic organisations of associated labour, published in *Službeni List*, 7 Apr. 1973, and the regulations on determining the minimum amount of resources that foreign partners must invest in a domestic organisation of associated labour, published ibid., 11 Aug. 1978.

POSITION OF WORKERS AS SUCH
IN ASSOCIATED LABOUR

3

According to the Constitution, the entire social system in Yugoslavia is "based on the power of the working class and all working people and on relations among people as free and equal producers and creators whose labour serves exclusively for the satisfaction of their personal and common needs". From the beginning, and throughout its development, the workers' management system has sought to achieve the elimination of all forms of wage labour and a new and dominant status for the worker in all areas of social life. All forms of exploitation of one man's labour by another are forbidden. Labour is the only basis for material reward, since all other forms of profit making have been excluded. No one may gain material or other benefits, either directly or indirectly, from the exploitation of another's labour, or prevent or limit workers in any way from exercising their management rights to take decisions, on equal terms, on questions concerning their work and the conditions as well as the results of their labour. Associated workers have equal rights, obligations and responsibilities. In fulfilling their social functions, they are responsible to one another and to the community as a whole. They regulate relations within and between their organisations and communities of associated labour by self-management agreements, by-laws and other rules agreed upon and adopted jointly.

The constitutional rights of workers belong equally to all workers, whatever their occupation, qualification or social status. Within an organisation of associated labour engaged in economic activity, no distinction is made as to rights and obligations between those who work directly in the production process and the administrative, professional and managerial personnel. A differentiation between wage earners and salaried employees, found in the Fundamental Law of 1950, which introduced the workers' management system, was abandoned in later legislation. Workers who engage in professional, artistic or cultural activity on their own account are entitled, in principle, on the basis of their work, to the same socio-economic status, rights and obligations as workers in associated labour. The same is true for farmers and agricultural workers: those of them who decide to pool their labour in co-operative or other forms of association also enjoy the same rights, obligations and responsibilities as workers in organisations of associated labour.

Workers entering into associated labour in any of the above forms acquire the inalienable right to work with socially owned resources, for purposes of satisfying both their personal and social needs. This right can neither be renounced nor transferred to another, and it is incompatible with the obtaining of material benefits or other advantages that are not based on the labour of workers in associated labour. It endows the workers with the right to manage, on an equal footing with other workers, the work in an organisation of associated labour; to decide on the pooling of their labour and resources with other organisations; to decide on over-all income earned and its allocation among the associated organisations according to the work performed and the fulfilment of their obligations to the community; to allocate net income for personal and joint consumption, investments and reserves along lines laid down in self-management agreements; to earn personal income corresponding to the results of their labour and their personal contribution to the increased income of the organisation; and to regulate labour relations. In exercising these rights, workers are obliged to take into account the general social interests of the community and "to use the socially owned resources in a socially and economically reasonable way, and constantly to renew, expand and improve such resources".[1]

The right to work with socially owned resources may be distinguished from the right to work, as such, which is also constitutionally guaranteed to all citizens in Yugoslavia. Thus, while all are ensured the right to enter into associated labour on terms of equality and, by exercising their right to work with social resources, to earn an income on the basis of their work, the freedom to work independently is also guaranteed. All are free to choose their occupation, and every citizen has access under conditions of equality to all jobs and functions in society. Limiting or preventing the exercise of the right to work is contrary to the Constitution, while forced labour is prohibited. It goes without saying, however, that this consti-tutionally proclaimed right to work does not automatically guarantee that all citizens will find the work they desire whenever and wherever they wish. There are still regional disparities in levels of development within the Yugoslav economy, and although there is a constant expansion of work opportunities it is not yet possible to absorb the overflow of the labour force arising from the migration from rural to urban areas and the fast natural growth of population in the countryside since the Second

World War. Evidence of this is to be found in the migration of large numbers of Yugoslav workers, in recent years, to other European countries where jobs were available. It must be emphasised that there is no administrative system in Yugoslavia for the planned assignment of workers seeking work to the areas where their qualifications are required with an obligation to accept such assignments regardless of their place of permanent residence or their own wishes. The Constitution does state that those who do not wish to work and are capable of working are not entitled to the rights and protection that are based on labour; but the conception of social and economic policy that would make it possible theoretically to achieve full employment at the cost of endangering productivity, freedom to work and the principle of distribution according to labour is not accepted in the Yugoslav workers' management system. Reliance is rather placed on economic and political measures designed to stimulate economic activity and thus create more favourable conditions for the expansion of work opportunities.

LABOUR RELATIONS

In the light of the changes in the status of the worker that are inherent in associated labour, labour relations take on a special character under workers' management. There is no longer an employer empowered to take decisions relating to the workers by virtue of his status as owner, manager or state-appointed director of the undertaking. Indeed, as has been shown above, the right of the manager to hire and fire workers and assign jobs within the enterprise was abolished in the early 1950s, when the organs of self-management took over personnel management and labour relations matters. Under the present system, the workers in organisations of associated labour regulate such matters collectively by special rules adopted by mutual agreement, namely by self-management agreements on the mutual relations of workers in associated labour. These rules must be in conformity with constitutional principles, international standards embodied in the legislation of the federation and the republics and autonomous provinces, and other provisions of the law. In the case of self-managing communities of interest providing social services a similar procedure is followed, but certain aspects of labour relations and the rights and obligations of the workers in those communities may be governed by legislation.

Establishment of a labour relationship

A labour relationship in an organisation of associated labour may be established by any person who is 15 years of age or over and in good health and who meets the requirements laid down by the organisation concerned for a specific job. The establishment of a labour relationship takes place at the will of the workers' council or other competent self-management organ, in accordance with the requirements of the undertaking. When this organ confirms that there is a need to increase the number of workers for specific production jobs or other tasks, it determines the number of workers needed and the qualifications they require. The organisation is then required to advertise the vacancies or to hold a public competition; only in exceptional cases may this procedure be dispensed with. A public competition is also compulsory for the filling of vacancies occurring in posts of a managerial or administrative nature carrying special authority, including the post of general manager. As has already been mentioned, the incumbents of these posts are appointed for a period of four or five years, but they may be removed by the managerial organ or the workers' council which appointed them. If workers performing these functions are removed from their posts, or fail to be reappointed when a public competition takes place, they do not necessarily leave the organisation.

Selection from among the candidates who have answered an advertisement or entered for a public competition is carried out by the workers' council or by a committee appointed by it. It is considered that a labour relationship has been established when the responsible organ has made its choice and the worker concerned has submitted a written statement to the effect that he or she is familiar with, and accepts, the basic self-management rules concerning labour relations in the organisation. If the worker does not report for work, without a valid reason, on the appointed day, the labour relationship is considered not to have been established.

A labour relationship may be established for an indefinite period, or for a period specified in advance, in special circumstances laid down by law; only in exceptional cases is it possible for organisations to engage workers to carry out temporary or seasonal work.

Where workers are not occupied for the full statutory 42 hours per week on the work they are required to perform in the organisation, they are entitled to establish labour relationships with other organisations of associated labour in order to make up working time. It is also possible for workers who are fully occupied in one organisation or work community to work in another as well, under conditions determined by law.

Termination of a labour relationship

The termination of a labour relationship takes place in the following cases:

(a) if the workers themselves request the termination of their labour relationship in writing, or if they agree in writing with the competent organ that their relationship with the organisation should be terminated;

(b) if they refuse to work on a job offered to them which corresponds to their vocational qualifications or acquired skills, or if they refuse to undergo training in order to acquire skills required for another appropriate job.

Termination may also ensue in the following circumstances:

(a) if it is discovered that a worker failed to disclose relevant information, or supplied inaccurate information, at the time of the establishment of the labour relationship, where such information is essential to the performance of the work for which the worker was recruited; or

(b) if the worker does not fulfil his or her obligations at work, thus violating the interests of other workers and of the organisation as a whole.

Worker-trainees who have established a labour relationship with a basic organisation for an unspecified length of time will have that relationship terminated if on completion of their training they fail to pass the vocational examination.

If it is established that a worker's labour is no longer needed owing to economic difficulties resulting from the irresponsible attitude of some workers towards their work, the workers' council may decide to terminate the labour relationship of the workers whose irresponsibility has occasioned the organisation's difficulties. On the other hand, workers' labour relationships may not be terminated when structural changes or technological and other advancements which lead to higher productivity have made them redundant: in such cases the organisation is obliged to take measures to provide for the vocational training or retraining of redundant workers and their assignment to new jobs, in co-operation with the self-managing community of interest which is responsible for employment in the area.

Workers who are found incapable of doing the jobs or tasks entrusted to them, or who for a prolonged period of time have failed to achieve the normal results, may have their labour relationship terminated if they refuse to accept jobs or assignments corresponding to their working abilities. In such a case the facts are established by a commission appointed by the workers' council from among workers who have at least the same level of qualifications as the worker whose ability is under examination.

Worker's labour relationships are also terminated by law if, for example, they refuse to make written statements of acceptance of the self-management agreement on association of workers in a basic organisation; if it has been established in a manner specified by law that they are totally unfit for work; if they meet the requirements for an old-age pension, unless otherwise specified by law; if under the law or a legally binding decision of a court or other competent organ they are forbidden to perform specific jobs or work tasks; if they have been absent from work for more than six months while serving a prison term; and in some other specified cases. Only in cases and under conditions determined by law must or may workers in a basic organisation be temporarily removed from their jobs.

A decision to terminate workers' labour relationships in a basic organisation and the reasons for rendering such a decision must be served on the workers in writing, along with instructions regarding their right to lodge a complaint.

Rights and obligations of workers as such

The rights and obligations of the workers as such are defined partly in the Associated Labour Law and other statutes and partly by the self-management agreements entered into by workers in organisations of associated labour. Thus, workers are legally bound to carry out the work entrusted to them conscientiously and diligently, to make every effort to improve their knowledge and skills and to abide by the established rules of work discipline. They have the right, under the law, to be assigned to jobs which correspond to their qualifications and acquired skills; only in exceptional cases may they be assigned to jobs requiring lower qualifications, on a temporary or a permanent basis, with their consent. The conditions and cases in which workers from one organisation of associated labour may be assigned to work in another are laid down in self-management agreements drawn up by the organisations concerned.

Under the workers' management system, workers' remuneration is not determined by market forces or by collective bargaining between an employer and a trade union, nor can it be determined by the State nor by any agency other than the basic organisation of associated labour itself. The Yugoslav Constitution guarantees that it is the workers in the basic organisation who determine the principles and scales for the allocation of the organisation's income, including those applying to the distribution of resources for personal income. The State may intervene only if such intervention is necessary to correct decisions on the allocation of income which violate the principle of distribution according to work done, or which are deemed seriously to disturb the performance of the national economy.

As laid down by law, the basis for the personal income to which workers in associated labour are entitled is the income earned by the basic organisation whose work and affairs they themselves manage. A worker's personal income is determined in accordance with the principles of distribution according to work done, the increase in productivity in the basic organisation in which the work is done, and the solidarity of workers in associated labour. The amount of workers' personal incomes therefore depends on the results of their work and on their individual contributions to the increase of the income of their basic organisation as a whole. This system gives workers a direct material incentive to increase the organisation's income by raising productivity, modernising the production process, improving the organisation of work, pooling labour and resources for more efficient operation, and other means, since the better results achieved are reflected in their personal incomes and consequently in their standard of living. The principles and scales governing the calculation of a worker's personal income are based on the quantity and quality of the work done, taking into account the complexity of the job, efficiency in the utilisation of tools and other instruments of labour, savings in labour, utilisation of working time, responsibility and the conditions under which the work is performed, as well as the increase in the income of the basic organisation. Workers who make a special contribution to the organisation's increased income through innovations or other forms of creativity in their work are entitled to special rewards, under conditions laid down in general workers' management rules in conformity with the law. Workers are also entitled to compensation for personal income not earned owing to public holidays, annual vacations, sick leave, attendance at vocational training or other educational courses to which they are assigned, and in some other cases of absence from work.

All workers are guaranteed, in return for their labour, a level of income sufficient to ensure their material and social welfare and security. By law, the amount of guaranteed personal income is determined by the workers in a basic organisation by general workers' management rules on the lines laid down in self-management agreements concluded with other basic organisations and in social compacts to which they are a party. The level of guaranteed personal income is determined in accordance with the general level of productivity of labour and the general social and economic conditions prevailing in the region, community or economic sector in which the worker is engaged. However, the amount of guaranteed personal income fixed by a general self-management decision of a basic organisation may exceed that laid down by law or provided for in a social compact. From the net income earned by their basic organisation, workers are first required to set aside resources for their personal incomes up to the amount of guaranteed personal income. If it is not possible to pay this amount from the net income of the organisation the difference is made up by a withdrawal from its reserves, or from the joint reserve of the work organisation or other organisation of associated labour within which the basic organisation operates, in conformity with the self-management agreement on association. Resources from the joint reserve fund formed for the territory of a socio-political community are also used to pay guaranteed personal incomes, as determined in accordance with the provisions of self-management agreements and by law.

In the course of the year, workers provisionally determine and pay out personal income as advance payment for periods of time, not exceeding one month, determined by self-management rules. With each advance payment the workers receive a pay slip indicating how it has been calculated and specifying all items and factors taken into account. The final accounting of the personal income of every worker in a basic organisation is carried out when the organisation's annual balance sheet is drawn up.

Under the workers' management system workers who establish a labour relationship with a basic organisation accept responsibility for carrying out their work obligations and abiding by the work rules established by self-management decisions. They may be held accountable for violating work discipline or work obligations, or for not abiding by decisions adopted in the organisation in which they work, and they are subject to disciplinary sanctions, including fines. Major violations of a worker's obligations are, for example, non-fulfilment or unconscientious, tardy or negligent fulfilment of work and other obligations; violation of provisions concerning safety measures against fire, explosion, or other natural disasters; unlawful disposal of social resources; supplying inaccurate information if it has an essential bearing on decision-making in basic organisations; providing of inaccurate information by workers in positions of special responsibility which mislead workers in regard to the exercise of their management rights. By law, disciplinary measures that may be imposed for these and other violations of work obligations and discipline include a warning, a public warning, and assignment to another job for a specified period. A fine may be imposed only for specific major violations, such as non-fulfilment of a job or task or its performance in a negligent, irregular or tardy manner, if the result is to jeopardise the life and security of other workers or endanger material goods of major value; provocation of brawls or disorders in a basic organisation; abuse of position or exceeding given authority; and providing inaccurate information misleading workers about their rights. Only in exceptional cases laid down by law may the termination of a labour relationship be imposed as a disciplinary measure, for example in cases of unjustified absence from work for at least five consecutive days.

The determination of violations of work obligations or discipline and the imposition of penalties falls under the authority of the disciplinary commission in the basic organisation, which is composed of an uneven number of members, including the chairman, elected by the workers in the same way as the workers' council is elected, and for a term of office fixed by a self-management rule. A specified number, not exceeding one-fourth of the total number of members of the disciplinary commission, may be persons from outside the basic organisation, elected by the workers from a list drawn up by the chamber of associated labour of the commune on the proposal of the trade union. Proceedings are instituted at the request of the workers' council, the manager or the chairman of the management board, the workers' supervisory commission, the social attorney of self-management, the trade unions or the competent organ of the socio-political community. The worker must be heard by the disciplinary commission and must be given an opportunity to defend himself. The trade union must be notified of the institution of proceedings before the disciplinary commission, since it plays an important role in protecting the workers' interests. Workers or the initiators of proceedings against them have a statutory right to file a complaint concerning decisions of the disciplinary commission and the workers' council may confirm, alter, or annul such a decision.

Conflicts and their resolution

It is not claimed that workers' management will eliminate all sources of social conflict, nor establish an ideal harmony. The power conflict between management, as the owner of the means of production, and organised wage-earning labour no longer exists, but discrepancies in the interpretation of existing provisions or disagreement over economic issues can always arise: indeed the goal and meaning of workers' management is, in the words of Edvard Kardelj, "that working people should resolve as democratically as possible the contradictions that objectively exist and always reappear in the development of social relations and man's social consciousness".[2] The system encourages the confrontation of ideas and the voicing of criticism, and is designed to provide a democratic means of reconciling interests and resolving the majority of social conflicts and contradictions. While collective agreements between management and unions are no longer concluded, certain forms of negotiation, consultation and concertation continue to take place within the organs of workers' management and among the various forms of organisations of associated labour and the socio-political communities.

Work stoppages are not an uncommon occurrence in Yugoslavia. No complete statistics on work stoppages are available, but in recent years several studies have analysed the causes and characteristics of work stoppages under the workers' management system.[3] According to these studies, it would appear that the basic causes of disputes lie in inequalities in the earning and distribution of income, and the existence of economic and social differences and differentiations that are not based on distribution of income according to work done. As a result of such conditions, disputes may arise between different parts of organisations of associated labour, or between the workers and the organs of management in an organisation. When these disputes cannot be settled by ordinary workers' management procedures, they may lead to work stoppages or strikes.

The causes of conflicts, in other words, lie in the relatively poor development of workers' management in certain cases, as a result of which the workers are unable to secure and safeguard their elementary socio-economic rights and interests; these conditions occur mainly where the workers' management rights have been usurped, or where the workers are unable to express themselves to the extent required to exert the necessary influence on decisions. It has been noted, for example, that the vast majority of work stoppages are initiated by production workers, who tend to be less well represented than other workers on workers' management bodies.[4]

Failure to provide workers with adequate information on the situation in their organisation and the real conditions and possibilities for overcoming difficulties that directly affect them is also one of the causes and immediate motives for conflicts and disputes. "Exclusiveness" in the work of the management organs and the absence of regular and direct communication with workers also undoubtedly contribute to such conflicts.[5] In some cases, however, a work stoppage has been precipitated by the publication of data on the distribution of income, revealing the privileged position of supervisory and administrative personnel as compared with that of production workers. An analysis carried out recently by the Self-Management Research Centre of the Trade Union Federation of the Republic of Slovenia tends to prove that in most cases conflicts materialised through the misinformation or the misunderstanding of workers regarding the reasons for decisions taken by their management organs and the consequences of these decisions on their personal incomes.[6] The work stoppage was used as a means of attempting to redress a situation in which they felt that the wrong decisions had been taken or in which the interests of the majority of the workers had not been given their due weight in decision-making.

Work stoppages in Yugoslavia are generally short, most of them lasting only a few hours or, at most, a full working day.[7] The reluctance of workers to use the strike weapon and the wildcat nature of such action, which constitutes most often a protest against the decisions of their own elected management organs, undoubtedly facilitate the rapid resolution of differences. Striking workers do not always enjoy the support of their trade union in such action, although the latter frequently endeavours to reach a solution that will satisfy the workers' demands.

Until recently, there were no set rules governing the settlement of disputes under the system of workers' management in associated labour. There were, however, examples of cases in which organisations of associated labour had attempted to lay down conditions and procedures for the settlement of disputes, including work stoppages, through internal self-management rules.[8]

The Second Congress of Self-Managers of Yugoslavia (1971) proposed the "self-management resolution of conflict situations and work stoppages", which required:

(a) that the organisations of associated labour, associations of producers and councils of work communities should work out, and adopt through worker's management rules, methods and procedures for arriving at self-management and social agreements for the effective adjustment of conflicts of interest within organisations of associated labour, between such organisations and between organisations of associated labour and the socio-political communities;

(b) that the appropriate trade union organisations and organs should initiate and carry out these activities and should establish their competence in the matter through self-management rules and social enactments precisely defining their responsibility for the efficient settlement of disputes by workers' management methods; and

(c) that the trade unions should take the initiative and assist in the discovery of workers' management methods of guaranteeing internal order, the regular functioning of the police force and the protection of social property in the event of disputes.[9]

In recent Yugoslav labour and legal theory, based on the principles of the Constitution of 1974,[10] two kinds of disputes are distinguished in associated labour under workers' management: disputes that are settled by regular workers' management procedures; and disputes that it has not been possible to settle by regular means.

In the case of a dispute which it has not been possible to settle by regular means, two basic situations are distinguished:

(a) if the dispute arose among the workers in particular parts of an organisation of associated labour or between the workers and an organ of the organisation, the trade union institutes proceedings before the management organ in the organisation;

(b) if the dispute arose between the workers in an organisation of associated labour and an organ of a socio-political community, the trade union institutes proceedings before the competent organ of management in the organisation of associated labour and the appropriate organ of the socio-political community.

In both cases, the trade union institutes proceedings either at the request of the workers or on its own initiative, attempting to arrive, together with the competent organs, at a basis for settlement of the dispute and at specific measures to be taken.

The workers' council is bound, at the request of the workers, immediately to institute proceedings, terminate them quickly, and inform the workers of its decisions.

If the character of the dispute is such that it could lead to disruptions in work and in workers' management or cause major losses, the workers are bound to inform the trade union, other socio-political organisations, and the assembly of the socio-political community. It is also laid down that the workers select their delegates who, with the representatives of the trade union and other socio-political organisations and the assembly of the socio-political community, form a joint committee for settling the dispute. A settlement achieved by means that are not in conformity with these provisions is deemed to constitute a breach of work obligations or to be contrary to workers' management.

If the workers or the trade union are not satisfied with the course and manner of settling a dispute, the trade union requests the assembly of the appropriate socio-political community to consider the workers' claims. If the assembly of the socio-political community considers that the request is justified, it may at the workers' request take various measures, namely dismiss the workers' council, appoint a new executive organ or business managing organ, and make new appointments to other posts held by workers with special authority and responsibilities, if the dispute has arisen as a result of the improper work or conduct of the persons currently occupying those posts.

Finally, if a dispute has arisen with an organ of the socio-political community, or for reasons relating to questions that are matters for decision by the workers either in meetings or by referendum, or which are decided by the workers' councils, the workers' council requests the assembly of the competent socio-political community to adopt appropriate regulations or measures within the framework of its jurisdiction.

CONDITIONS OF WORK AND SOCIAL WELFARE

The Constitution guarantees the workers' rights to working conditions that ensure their physical and moral integrity and security. Basic standards are laid down by law, but the actual conditions are determined by the workers in the basic organisations of associated labour in relation to the nature and requirements of the work. Thus, the law provided that working time may not in general exceed 42 hours a week, although in certain specified cases and for a limited period, longer hours may be worked if the nature of the work so requires, or in order to meet the demands of exceptional circumstances. It is also possible, under conditions determined by law, to shorten working time. Workers are entitled to daily and weekly breaks and to paid annual vacations of not less than 18 working days. The working week is at least five days. The distribution of working time and breaks is regulated by the workers in the basic organisations of associated labour. During work breaks, the workers have the right to a hot meal which is usually served in the organisation's own canteen. The cost of these meals is met from the resources set aside for joint consumption.

In the majority of organisations of associated labour, holiday centres in tourist areas have been established where workers can spend their annual holidays with their families, or go for a period of convalescence. The trade unions take an active part in organising and providing for workers' holidays, as part of their concern for the constant improvement of working conditions and the provision of welfare facilities.

Occupational safety in the widest sense is one of the most important components of social policy in Yugoslavia. Not only is it enforced through special inspection of workplaces by supervisory organs but it is also integrated into the decision-making process, so that, for example, an investment or other decision proposed by a self-management organ is evaluated from the point of view of its effect on the health and safety of workers and their general conditions of life and work before a decision is taken in the matter.

In theory and in practice, work safety is not limited to accident prevention and health protection in the workplace, but is understood as a systematic, comprehensive and multidisciplinary programme designed to develop, protect and strengthen workers' physical and psychological capabilities. All organisations of associated labour are obliged to adopt general self-management regulations with regard to the special measures for work safety required in different workplaces, such as, for example, regular medical checks for workers, or precautions with regard to dangerous materials or machinery, and to allocate powers and responsibilities within the organisation with respect to the application of these and all other aspects of work safety. Workers have the right to refuse to work if their life or health is endangered by the failure of the responsible parties to take the prescribed occupational safety measures. The law provides for special protection of pregnant women from heavy work, work hazards, overtime and night work, as well as providing for maternity leave and other special protection for mothers and children. Young workers are also ensured similar protection.

Workers are covered by systems of compulsory social insurance which are paid for partly by direct contributions from workers' personal incomes and partly by contributions from the resources of organisations of associated labour or other organisations or work communities. On the basis of this insurance, the workers are entitled to benefits in the event of illness, maternity, disability, unemployment, old age and other contingencies. The members of workers' families are also insured for health care, family pensions and other benefits.

The cost of medical care of all kinds and in every kind of medical institution for workers and their families is covered by self-managing communities of interest for health care and health insurance. Only a minor part of the expenses in a few specified instances—for example, for orthopaedic devices, medicine or health checks—is paid for out of the worker's own pocket. Financial compensation is paid to workers for days lost from work because of illness, starting from the first day of incapacity for work and for an unlimited time until they regain their health or a permanent disability is established. Compensation for the first 30 days of incapacity amounts to between 80 and 90 per cent of the personal income earned during the preceding year, and is paid directly by the organisation of associated labour in which the worker works. This is designed to encourage the organisations to take a direct interest in promoting the health and working capacity of the workers, through preventive health measures, improved safety at work, recreation and similar measures. Compensation beyond the initial 30 days falls within the responsibility of the self-managing communities of interest for health care and health insurance, and amounts to 90 per cent of the worker's personal income. In cases where incapacity for work results from certain causes laid down by law (i.e. if the incapacity is due to an occupational accident or disease, or to the donation of blood, skin transplants, or live tissue or an organ to another person) workers are entitled to full compensation at the level of their personal income for the past year. Compensation during maternity leave also amounts to 100 per cent of the personal income of the worker concerned.

Special care for mothers is provided for on a universal basis, regardless of whether or not the mother is employed, by a system which includes protection of mothers during pregnancy, childbirth and maternity, and also provides for contraception. Women workers have a statutory right to 180 days of maternity leave, of which 28 days must be taken before the expected date of confinement. After returning to work, women have the right to work half time until their child is 1 year old. With a medical certificate, a mother may take unpaid leave until her child is 3 years old. Such an absence from work none the less counts as time worked for pensions purposes, and the workers concerned may not be dismissed from their jobs. All workers, men and women alike, are entitled to a special allowance for infant care supplies. Working mothers and fathers also have the right to be absent from work if necessary to attend to the needs of children or other members of the family.

The compulsory social insurance system provides retirement pensions for all workers in Yugoslavia with an established work relationship, on reaching a certain age and subject to a certain number of years of service,[11] and insurance coverage for the families of deceased workers. The system is based on the principle of uniformity, all workers being entitled to the same pension rates irrespective of their previous rates of remuneration. The resources for the payment of pensions are collected and managed by the self-managing communities of interest for pension insurance. Thus, while the basic rights and conditions for earning a pension are regulated by statute, the practical application of the scheme is under the autonomous authority of the self-managing communities of interest. The organs of these self-managing communities of interest for pension insurance, formed on the delegation principle by the direct election of representatives of both workers and pensioners, themselves former workers, are in charge of the management of resources for financing pensions, and deal with such questions as the assessment of personal incomes for the establishment of a pension base, the appraisal of pension liabilities and the determination of the minimum level of pensions. They are also concerned with such aspects of the welfare of pensioners as holidays and recreation and the management of special resources for the construction of pensioners' housing. All decisions concerning pension rights are taken by these organs, and they have full legal powers for their enforcement.

In Yugoslavia all workers are automatically covered by disability insurance, which is distinct from both health insurance and retirement pension insurance, although the same principles apply to the financing and management of disability insurance as of pension insurance, and although the responsibility for all regulative functions concerning disability insurance lies with the self-managing communities of interest for pension insurance. Disability insurance is designed to provide financial compensation for workers in a state of partial or complete incapacity for work and to enable them to go on working as long as possible in order to ensure their social integration. A worker who because of an illness (occupational or other) or accident (at work or not) becomes temporarily or permanently incapable of working is entitled to a disability pension. The only condition for obtaining such a pension is that the worker must have worked for at least the five years immediately preceding the invalidity; the conditions for younger workers who have become invalids are more favourable. The amount of the disability pension depends on the personal income previously earned and on years

97

of service. Workers who become permanent invalids as a result of an accident at work or an occupational illness are entitled to a disability pension of an amount equal to that which they would receive under the most favourable conditions for a retirement pension. A worker who is physically injured to such an extent as to be unable to perform the ordinary acts of everyday life without the assistance of other persons is entitled to a supplementary allowance for special care and aid.

Special forms of disability pensions apply to workers who are partially disabled. This refers to workers able to work at the same or other jobs, with or without professional rehabilitation, full time or part time. Workers working half time are compensated for the remaining work time in proportion to the personal income they earn during their part-time work. This compensation is paid for out of the funds set aside for disability and pension insurance. Workers who are no longer able to continue in their previous job but may be able to work full time with adaptation of a workplace, professional rehabilitation, or a transfer to another job, earn the right to a personal income corresponding to their new jobs. If this personal income is less than the personal income the workers would have earned at their former jobs, they are entitled to the difference between their current personal income and the personal income of a worker doing the same job as they did previously, or a similar job. The right to occupational rehabilitation includes the workers' right to acquire completely new vocational training qualifications of a level at least as high as that of their previous qualifications, the right to specific forms of adaptation of working conditions, and appropriate orthopaedic aids.

The work organisation is required to keep disabled workers on, and to help them to prepare themselves for further work. A work organisation in which there are no appropriate jobs is obliged, together with the organisations of social security and employment, to find a disabled worker an appropriate job in another work organisation.

In the event of unemployment, workers are entitled to two kinds of protection, namely—

(a) assistance in finding work elsewhere and vocational guidance and training or education with a view to new employment; and

(b) financial compensation for the loss of income and other kinds of material assistance.

While provided for in the Constitution and by statute, unemployment compensation is governed and administered by self-management agreements constituting communities of interest for employment and unemployment insurance. Only workers who find themselves involuntarily unemployed through circumstances beyond their own control are entitled to the financial benefits provided for. Those whose labour relationship has been terminated through their own fault or by their own wishes do not have a right to claim financial compensation, unless the termination is due to the transfer of a worker's spouse to another place of residence, or to health reasons. The level of benefit varies in the different regions; in the Republic of Slovenia, for example, workers who have worked at least one year without a break, or 18 months with interruptions during the preceding two years, are entitled to an allowance during a period of unemployment. This allowance amounts to 60 per cent of the average monthly personal income earned by the worker during the last two years preceding unemployment, and it may not be less than the minimum guaranteed personal income in the Republic. The amount of any allowance paid for more than 12 months is automatically increased in accordance with increases in the cost of living during the preceding year. Workers in receipt of unemployment allowances also receive additional amounts in respect of the members of their immediate family.

In order to assist workers in finding new jobs, provision is made for vocational training in trades corresponding to expected labour requirements. Workers also receive financial compensation for expenses incurred during the period of training, including payment of transport expenses for themselves and their families to places where appropriate work is available.

Special assistance is also provided by the trade unions, in specific cases, to their members who are unemployed. Unemployed workers retain their status as trade union members.

Other social rights guaranteed to workers by law include permanent occupancy of socially owned housing allocated to them for their personal and family needs.

Education is also a right of all citizens. At least eight years of schooling is obligatory under the Constitution, and citizens have the right to acquire knowledge and vocational skills at all levels and in all kinds of educational and training institutions on a footing of equality. Decisions with regard to the opening, financing and operating of schools and other institutions for the education and vocational training of citizens are made collectively through the association of the consumers and providers of these services in self-managing communities of interest for education.

SOCIO-ECONOMIC STATUS OF WOMEN

Women enjoy the constitutional workers' management rights assigned to all workers, and they participate on a basis of equality in decision-making and in dealing with problems of general social development as well as with the vital questions of special importance to them.

Women workers participate in the adoption of decisions concerning the basic questions of work and life which fall within the competence of the organs of workers' management in organisations of associated labour. Many of these questions are regulated by by-laws and other internal rules that are in conformity with the principles and standards laid down in the labour and social legislation of the federation and of the individual republics, and that are adopted by the workers' councils or by the workers directly through referendums and at meetings. The action taken on particular questions, especially the provision of facilities and benefits of particular interest to women, depends of course to a great extent on the financial and other resources available to the particular organisation of associated labour in which the women work.

As delegates of the workers' management bodies in the assemblies of the communes, provinces, republics and federation, women take the initiative in relation to general and particular economic, labour, social and other problems of interest to the workers or to particular categories of workers. This was the case, for example, in the discussions on the draft regulations on labour relations, social insurance, marriage and the family. Thus women workers exercise effective influence over general economic and social policy, particularly with regard to the adoption of the short-term and long-term plans for the economic and social development of the country. After a preliminary debate in which the representatives of the self-management bodies of the organisations of associated labour and socio-political organisations participated, the Federal Assembly adopted, on 30 March 1978, a resolution on the basic directions of social activity for the advancement of the socio-economic status and role of women in socialist self-management society.[12]

The results of a comparative study of the record of women's employment and their membership of workers' councils[13] in the past few decades show that in 1952, out of the total number of workers employed in productive activity, approximately 24 per cent were women, while only 13 per cent of the members of workers' councils were women. Ten years later, in 1962, the proportion of women in the total number of workers so employed had increased to about 29 per cent, and in the workers' councils to around 17 per cent. From that time on, the number of women elected to the workers' councils grew along with the constant increase in the number of women employed, but the participation of women in the organs of management of the economy did not keep pace with these increases. The situation prevailing in the social activities sector was more favourable in this regard. According to the results of the elections for workers' councils in 1976, women comprised 21 per cent of the total number of elected delegates, and 17.4 per cent of the number of workers elected to the executive committees of the workers' councils. The proportions of women elected to the workers' councils of composite organisations of associated labour (11.3 per cent) and to their executive committees (10.1 per cent) were the lowest. On the other hand, the proportion of women in administrative work in the work communities for the performance of common services of a financial, commercial, legal or other nature (41 per cent) was considerably greater than the proportion of women among production workers (34 per cent).

The proportion of women elected as general managers in economic organisations and social service institutions grew from 2 per cent in 1962 to 7 per cent in 1976. Women appear to be more frequently chosen for this function in smaller organisations (10 per cent) and considerably less often in medium-sized and large enterprises and institutions (4 per cent). According to recent statistical research, in composite organisations of associated labour out of 52 managers only one was a woman; in work organisations containing basic organisations, out of 1,904 managers 30 were women; in basic organisations of associated labour, out of 12,962 managers 484 were women; and in work organisations not comprising basic organisations (these are primarily smaller enterprises and institutions), out of 13,124 managers 1,125 were women. The situation in this regard differs greatly from one economic or social sector of activity to another. In industry, for example, out of a total of 5,939 managers 105 were women; in commerce and hotel and restaurant management, out of 3,904 managers 94 were women; in schools, out of 4,847 principals 478 were women; in cultural-educational institutions, out of 456 directors 150 were women; and in health care facilities, out of 1,623 managers 294 were women. There are differences between regions as well: for example, in Slovenia, the most highly developed republic, 10 per cent of the total number of managers are women, while in Montenegro, one of the least developed republics, only 1 per cent are women.

The election of women to socio-political functions has been slow to develop. In the elections to the Federal Assembly held in 1974, 13.6 per cent of the elected delegates were women; in the republican assemblies, 16.8 per cent were women, and in the provincial assemblies 20.9 per cent.

In the commune assemblies, however, only 15.2 per cent of the total number of delegates were women, and in the executive organs of the commune assemblies women delegates comprised 4.5 per cent of the total. In the assemblies and councils of the local communities, the representation of women increased from 3.1 per cent in 1969 to 7.2 per cent in 1977.

Women remain very much in the minority in the highest bodies of the socio-political organisations as well. In the Central Committee of the League of Communists of Yugoslavia 11 per cent of the members are women, whereas women comprise approximately 21 per cent of the

League's total membership; whereas women make up about half of the total membership of the Socialist Alliance of Working People, in its Federal Conference only 16 per cent of the members are women. In the Council of the Yugoslav Confederation of Trade Unions, 22.9 per cent of the members are women, and that proportion more or less corresponds to the proportion of women in the total trade union membership.

The still inadequate representation of women in workers' management bodies and in public socio-political life reflects a situation influenced by the socio-economic and cultural heritage of the past and traditional patriarchal and conservative conceptions about the place and role of women in society, which are still current in some social settings. Despite the progress that has been made since the Second World War, the causes of the present situation are directly linked to the in some ways primitive socio-economic and material conditions in which working women live and work, to the general standard of living and, of course, to economic conditions and possibilities in the organisations of associated labour themselves and in the country as a whole at the current level of development. The general, vocational and socio-economic education of women and their training for the performance of responsible management and other social functions also remains a problem that cannot be neglected. However, through the development of new social relations in production and distribution on the basis of workers' management, serious efforts are being made to facilitate the further integration of women into different types of activities, to increase their influence in various areas of social life, and gradually to arrive at radical solutions to their practical problems.

Notes

[1] Associated Labour Law, Art. 13.

[2] Edvard Kardelj: *Pravci razvoja političkog sistema socijalističkog samoupravljanja* (Belgrade), p. 95; see also idem: "Sistem socijalističkog samoupravljanja u Jugoslaviji", in *Samoupravljanja u Jugoslaviji, 1950–1976* (Belgrade, Privredni pregled, 1977), pp. 16–17.

[3] For example, social conflicts and the socialist development of Yugoslavia were the main subjects of the Sixth Conference of the Yugoslav Association of Sociologists (Portoroz, 10–13 February 1972). The papers submitted to that meeting were published in three volumes, and extracts were also published in the journal *Sociologija*, No. 3, 1971. Special attention was given to conflicts in work organisations; see, for example, J. Zupanov: "Upravljanje industrijskim konfliktom u samoupravnom sistemu" (The management of industrial conflicts in the self-management system); S. Mozina: "Izvori konflikta u radnim organizacijama" (Sources of conflicts in work organisations); and S. Grozdanic: "Konfliktne situacije i nacin uredjivanja sporova u praksi radnickog samoupravljanja" (Conflict situations and the way of settling disputes in the practice of workers' self-management). The basic results of the research on work stoppages done by Neca Jovanov in the Yugoslav trade unions were published in his report to the First International Conference on Participation and Self-management (Dubrovnik, 13–17 December 1972), and in his book *Radnički*

Štrajkovi u SFRJ od 1958 to 1969 (The workers' strikes in SFRY from 1958 to 1969) (Belgrade, Zapis, 1979).

[4] See also Obradovic and Dunn (eds.): *Workers' self-management and organizational power in Yugoslavia*, op. cit., pp. 339–399.

[5] In a resolution of the Second Congress of Self-Managers of Yugoslavia (1971), the basic causes of conflicts and work stoppages in associated labour were identified as inadequately developed workers' management, inadequate guarantees for the system of income and distribution according to work done, and bureaucratic usurpation of workers' management rights. In a survey of recent studies of workers' participation in management in Yugoslavia carried out by W. J. Burt for the International Institute for Labour Studies and published in its *Bulletin* (Geneva), No. 9, 1972, the following points are listed (on p. 167) as the main reasons for strikes (or work stoppages): "restrictions on workers' rights, undeveloped self-management in particular undertakings, inadequate systems of determining and allocating enterprise net income (especially personal incomes), the general welfare and social position of groups of workers, the general conditions of business, the State's economic policies toward undertakings and their situations on the market, superfluous labour, inefficient systems of information, and inadequacies in the system of responsibility and the mechanism for the resolution of conflicts."

[6] cf. *Syndicats Yougoslaves*, No. 115, Sep.–Oct. 1978, pp. 5–7.

[7] Jovanov, op. cit., p. 363, table 16.15.

[8] Examples of the basic "rules of conduct" in cases in which conflicts arise in a work organisation are the by-laws of the Železarna steelworks of Jesenice and the Merkator commercial organisation in Ljubljana; see the study by S. Grozdanič: "Novije tendencije i pojave u praksi radničkog samoupravljanja", in *Teorija i praksa samoupravljanja u Jugoslaviji* (Belgrade, Radnička stampa, 1972), pp. 710–732.

[9] Resolution on "the building of self-management relations in a work community", in *Sindikati*, May 1971, pp. 500–502.

[10] Article 47. The basic principles for dispute settlement laid down in the Constitution are elaborated in the Associated Labour Law of 1976 and in the internal self-management regulations of the organisations of associated labour.

[11] Entitlement to retirement pensions is subject to the following conditions: (*a*) for a man, 65 years of age and 15 years of service, 60 years of age and 20 years of service, or 40 years of service regardless of age; and (*b*) for a woman, 60 years of age and 15 years of service, 55 years of age and 20 years of service, or 35 years of service regardless of age. Specified categories of insured persons who have worked for longer periods at jobs from which serious health hazards cannot be eliminated have the right to added years of service. This means that the actual time spent on the job by such beneficiaries is accounted for at greater length and the pensionable age limit is proportionately lowered (such jobs include the work of pilots, railway engine drivers, miners working under ground, certain jobs in metal works, and certain forms of public service). Workers who were active participants in the war of national liberation have similar more favourable conditions, as do the severely disabled.

[12] *Službeni List*, 7 Apr. 1978.

[13] Statistics concerning employment of women workers and their election to self-management organs are taken from Savezni zavod za statistiku, *Samoupravni društveno-ekonomski razvoj Jugoslaviji, 1947–1977*, op. cit.

INCOME AND PLANNING IN ORGANISATIONS OF ASSOCIATED LABOUR

4

The self-managing economic organisations in Yugoslavia function in a market economy, where the results of labour, in the form of commodities, are sold for a financial return known as income. All the basic principles and characteristic features of the workers' management system are brought to light in the relationships governing the creation, management and disposal of income, which are regulated in detail by the Associated Labour Law of 1976.

Some basic concepts relating to income which have already been mentioned may be briefly recalled. In the first place, the aim of production and other economic activities is to earn income by working with socially owned resources; income earned is used to meet individual and social needs, promote economic growth and raise the general standards of living. In a basic organisation of associated labour, income is the source and limit of all expenditure, as it is in society as a whole. Income earned by working with socially owned resources can be distributed and spent only in the manner laid down by the workers themselves in self-management agreements or social compacts or by mutually co-ordinated development plans. The income of basic organisations of associated labour engaged in production serves as a basis for linking those organisations among themselves and with organisations providing public and social services. Such services are no longer financed by the State but, instead, share in the income generated in production, in return for their contribution to the generation of that income.

In addition, as already noted, the right of workers in associated labour to dispose of the total income of their basic organisation enables them to control the trends of socio-economic development, and this fact makes it necessary to integrate the workers in associated labour to an increasing extent into the political decision-making process.

SOURCES OF INCOME

Broadly defined, the income of an organisation of associated labour is the difference between the amount earned by the sale of goods or services and the cost of production and the depreciation of fixed assets. Although the sale of goods and services is the principal means of earning income, a basic organisation's income is also derived from other sources, which include a share in income earned through the pooling of labour and resources with other organisations under a joint programme; income earned by the free exchange of labour with non-economic organisations in self-managing communities of interest; and various subsidies, compensatory allowances, bonuses, grants and so forth received under statutory provisions, contractual arrangements or self-management agreements.

Sale of goods and services

The sale of goods and services on the national or international market is, quantitatively, the most widespread way of earning income. Under the laws of market competition—Yugoslavia exports about one-quarter of its products and imports about one-third of the goods it consumes—the general rule of economic life is that the capacity to produce depends on the capacity to sell, as in other market economies, although there are still some sectors which enjoy special protection.

Pooling of labour and material resources

Income derived from a share in jointly earned income is in a more original category; indeed, this is one of the innovations introduced into the economic system in Yugoslavia by the Associated Labour Law. The pooling of labour and material resources for carrying out a joint production programme is one of the basic forms of income earning to which special attention is paid. Decisions to undertake joint programmes are made freely, by the workers themselves, in their own immediate and long-term interests, and are set forth in self-management agreements. The Associated Labour Law seeks to encourage basic organisations to explore on a broader scale the possibilities of such linkages between organisations with a view to strengthening the productive resources of the economy as well as reaching a higher level of socialisation in production and in Yugoslav life in general.

Respecting the freedom of workers in basic organisations to decide on the contents of such agreements, the law seeks to preserve the principle of the distribution of income according to work done as well as that of the equal status of the parties to such an agreement. Thus, when organisations pool labour and resources for the joint production and sale of goods and services and thereby earn joint income, this income is divided on the basis of jointly established rules and is allocated by each of the organisations in accordance with its contribution to the joint revenue. (This is the case, for example, where several basic organisations are associated in the joint production of a product, each being responsible for a different phase. For example, one forest management and wood processing work organisation is made up of three basic organisations of associated labour, each covering a different phase of production, one for forest management, one for the mechanical processing of timber and one for the final processing. The final product of the first organisation is the raw material for the second, whose final product is the raw material for the third, which produces building timber and household furniture. The market value of the finished product of the third basic organisation of associated labour contains the expended resources and invested labour not only of the third but of the other two as well.) When a joint production programme is undertaken—and this is obligatory in some cases, such as when the entire output of one organisation is sold to another, or where production organisations are tributary to trade organisations—the organisations concerned draw up a self-management agreement that regulates the conditions for pooling their labour and material resources, the principles and scales governing the distribution of their joint gross income, the co-ordination of production plans and other questions of common interest, relationships with third parties and the circumstances in which the agreement may be broken. The agreement may also establish internal compensation funds or other means of giving concrete expression to the solidarity and equal status of the partners in joint production. By law, all parties must be on a footing of equality with regard to the sharing of joint revenue, which is distributed proportionately to the contribution each organisation makes to its creation. Organisations that contribute labour share in the income earned, along with those that invest funds or provide other services. Joint gross income may be related to the market prices for goods and services exchanged or to internally agreed prices (which must, however, respect market prices).

Joint investment programmes

Similar general principles apply to the distribution of joint income,[1] in cases in which, under a joint investment programme, one basic organisation provides funds for another that produces goods or services. In those instances, from the income earned by the organisation which uses the funds, part must be allocated first for workers' incomes and joint consumption in that organisation, up to the amount determined by the relevant self-management agreement. The remaining part of the income earned is shared between the two organisations that are parties to the agreement. Thus the investing organisation obtains a return on its investment, while at the same time the organisation which used the funds is also entitled to a share in the increased income created by its labour, over and above the share for workers' personal incomes and joint consumption.

On reimbursement to the investing organisation, the sum invested must immediately be returned to its investment fund, while the part of joint income accruing to the investing organisation is included in its over-all income to be distributed in the same way as income earned in any other manner (and therefore cannot be entirely allocated to the personal incomes of workers).

Free exchange of labour

The system of the free exchange of labour as a basis for income earning is another original aspect of the notion of income in Yugoslavia. In accordance with the same general principles as in the case of joint production programmes, the equality of rights of each of the parties participating in the exchange of labour is guaranteed. Workers in organisations of associated labour providing essential social services—education, health services, social welfare, and so on—have the right to share in the income earned by workers in the basic organisations engaged in economic activities with which they are associated, in proportion to the contribution made by their labour to the generation of value added in production, the rise in the output of labour generally and the develop-ment of society as a whole.[2] This notion of the mutual interdependence of production and of the development of social services is given concrete expression, as explained above, in the mechanism for the exchange of labour and sharing of income established in the self-managing communi-ties of interest, in which providers and consumers of the services concerned take decisions jointly on matters of common concern, including the generation and distribution of income.

Subsidies, etc.

Bonuses, subsidies, compensatory allowances, grants, and so forth are, as elsewhere, instruments of economic and social policy used where necessary in the interests of society as a whole—for example, bonuses for the production of staple foods such as milk or meat, or for some exports; subsidies for the use of artificial fertilisers; financial compensation for the sale of products at prices fixed below their market level for social reasons;

grants to railways and other public services, as well as other enterprises of general social importance, that operate at a loss. Any conflicts or disagreements that may arise with regard to such particular sources of income, where various regional interests or those of particular organisations do not coincide, are settled as far as possible by self-management agreements between the organisations concerned, or social compacts entered into by the communes, provinces and republics with the participation of those organisations.

ALLOCATION OF GROSS INCOME

The income of a basic organisation serves to cover all its outgoings in respect of consumption, investment, reserves and social obligations (see diagram 3). National income being the aggregate of the incomes of the basic organisations, the allocation of income—that is, the determination of the uses to which it shall be put—is of considerable importance to the entire economic system, and is therefore dealt with in some detail in the Constitution, the Associated Labour Law and other relevant legislation, as well as in self-management agreements and social compacts. The Constitution establishes the right of workers in basic organisations of associated labour to decide on the disposal of the total income earned, subject to discharging their responsibilities towards other workers and towards the community as a whole. The socio-political communities and other organisations of associated labour or work communities may also have a say in the allocation of a basic organisation's income, but only in circumstances laid down by law or by self-management agreements or contractual arrangements. The first phase in the allocation of gross income concerns its distribution among certain items of general social need, contractual and other obligations, and the part which remains as the net income of the basic organisations. The Associated Labour Law distinguishes 12 different items to which income is allocated at this stage. They can be divided into four categories, as follows:

(1) Obligations for the satisfaction of the general needs of society as a whole, that is, for the public service, the army, the judiciary and so forth; contributions towards the satisfaction of collective social needs, for example, to the organisations that provide educational, cultural, scientific or health services, or which ensure workers' social security (in so far as the latter services are not paid for directly by the workers from their personal income). In this category may also be included social obligations in the form of fines for economic offences, expenses incurred in administrative or court proceedings, and other expenses arising from statutory obligations.

(2) Contractual obligations relating, for example, to the payment of

financial, legal, accounting and other services provided by work communities, insurance premiums on social property, and membership fees or other contributions to chambers of economy or general associations of organisations of associated labour, including also fees for economic services provided by other organisations.

(3) Expenditures on certain items which, while not forming part of the basic organisation's activity, are useful and necessary both for the organisation and for society as a whole. In this category fall the expenditure on conservation, protection and improvement of the working and living environment, and expenditure on national defence and social self-protection, in fulfilment of the basic organisation's responsibilities in this regard.

(4) The net income of the basic organisation—that is, the part of its gross income on the disposal of which workers decide freely in their basic organisations of associated labour, taking into account the social character[3] of income and planned development goals.

The aim behind the relevant provisions of the Law is to establish a direct link in the allocation of income between the organisation's own needs and those of the community, or in other words between the various parts of the social structure—organisations of associated labour engaged in production, organisations in the spheres of health, education, culture, science and the arts, and institutions such as the public service, the judiciary, the army, and so forth. The allocation of some parts of income for particular non-economic purposes does not result from one-sided decisions taken by the persons concerned outside organisations of associated labour engaged in production, but is achieved through joint decisions. The assemblies of the socio-political communities share in these decisions only to the extent necessary to ensure that the allocations from the income of organisations engaged in production remain within reasonable limits, so that development possibilities are not endangered. As regards the satisfaction of the more general needs of society as a whole indicated in the first category above, the decisions concerning the allocation of income are made directly by the assemblies of the socio-political communities, though, again, within limits provided for in development plans so as not to discourage economic expansion. It is laid down in Article 113 of the Associated Labour Law that as a rule, in order to gain an insight into the possibilities of basic organisations and their development needs, the workers in all basic organisations shall be called upon simultaneously once a year to express their views on proposals for the determination of obligations concerning the satisfaction of general and collective needs. This provision is aimed at preventing unrealistic decisions from being taken by individual organisations in regard to those

Diagram 3. Distribution of the income of a basic organisation of associated labour

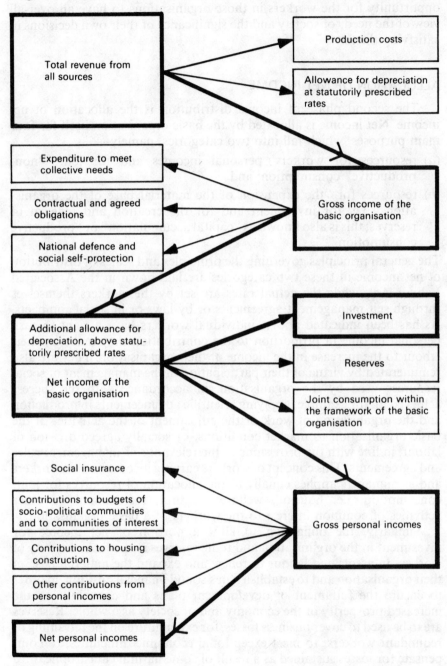

items in the allocation of income, while at the same time providing an opportunity for the workers in those organisations to have an over-all view of the needs of society and the significance of their own decisions in satisfying them.

ALLOCATION OF NET INCOME

The second phase of income distribution is the allocation of net income. Net income is allocated by the basic organisation itself for four main purposes, which fall into two categories, namely—

(a) resources for workers' personal incomes and for joint "non-productive" consumption; and

(b) resources for "the expansion of the material base of the organis-ation", i.e. for investment and for the creation and renewal of reserves; this is also known as "capital accumulation" or "productive consumption".

The general principles governing the principles and scales of distribution of net income in these two categories are laid down in the Associated Labour Act, while the actual rates are set by the workers themselves through self-management agreements or by-laws or in social compacts. As has been indicated above, individual workers have a right to earn personal income in proportion to the contribution they make by their labour to the increase in the income of their organisation. They are also remunerated by virtue of their participation in the management of social resources used by the organisation, in accordance with the success achieved in, for example, applying scientific advancements in production and the organisation of work or the adjustment of the activities of the basic organisation to market conditions, or socially agreed division of labour, in line with the provisions of the relevant self-management rules and agreements. This concept of workers earning income both as workers and as managers applies equally to the allocation of resources for joint consumption, i.e. housing, welfare, cultural, recreational or other activities of common interest to the workers of a basic organisation.

Similarly, the obligation to allot a portion of net income for investment in the organisation and to its reserves stems from the duty of workers in associated labour to renew and expand the material base of their organisation and to establish it in a sound financial position, in order to ensure the fulfilment of development plans and contribute to the increased prosperity of the economy and of society as a whole: Reserves are to be used to cover business losses, for expenditure on the retraining of redundant workers, to meet exceptional economic difficulties, to com-pensate for losses sustained as a result of some natural catastrophe or to meet specified obligations laid down by law. The scales of allocation for these purposes are determined by self-management agreements and social compacts, taking into account the nature of the activities of the organisations concerned and the role they play in the maintenance and development of society as a whole, as well as the development aims that have been collectively determined by the organisations concerned.

The principles and scales regulating the allocation of net income are in fact determined at four different levels. General self-management rules or agreements in this respect are adopted at the level of the basic organisation itself, at the level of a work organisation consisting of several basic organisations, at the level of a group of organisations in one branch of economie activity or in a large "reproduction complex",[4] and, finally, social compacts adopted at the level of the commune, province or republic also play a role in determining these matters.

Only the principles and scales decided on in the general self-management rules adopted by the workers in a basic organisation are directly applied to the allocation of net income; but the decisions of the basic organisations in that respect are co-ordinated with those of other basic organisations in the work organisation to which they belong, or at the wider level of the economic sector or reproductive complex, through the self-management agreements adopted at those levels. The agreements establish common principles and scales for the basic organisations concerned. By law, the principles adopted by the workers in a basic organisation must be in conformity with, and may not be contrary to, those laid down in self-management agreements at those other levels. Should the decisions of a basic organisation be out of line with those of other basic organisations in a work organisation, the competent organ of the socio-political community may order the necessary measures to guarantee the protection of workers' management rights and social property. If a basic organisation adopts a by-law that is contrary to an agreement concluded between it and other basic organisations operating outside the work organisation to which it belongs, or contrary to a social compact concluded by it or to which it has acceded, proceedings may be instituted before the court of associated labour.

The part of income that results from exceptionally favourable circumstances, such as natural or market conditions, or certain types of economic policy measures, may be used for the development of the basic organisation or other organisations of associated labour in which it has accrued, unless it is specifically provided by law that it should be used for the development of the commune, republic or autonomous province concerned.

The final stage in the distribution of net income is the allocation of resources for personal incomes. As indicated in the preceding chapter, the principles and scales for the remuneration of workers are set by the basic organisations of associated labour in conformity with the general principles established by the Associated Labour Law, such as the principles that remuneration is based solely on the income earned by the organisation, and that workers are remunerated according to work done and according to their contribution, both by their labour and by their work as managers, to the increase of the organisation's income. Personal incomes are also calculated, in accordance with the principle of solidarity, in proportion to the increase in productivity of the individual worker concerned, and of the workers in other basic organisations with which a worker's own basic organisation is associated; and the same principle of solidarity applies to that part of resources allocated to joint consumption, to provide social assistance and other services of particular concern to workers in lower income brackets. It was also noted above that provision is made for the allocation of special awards for workers who have made a personal contribution to increased income of the organisation by innovations, rationalisation or other forms of creativity; and that all workers are entitled to a guaranteed personal income of a level sufficient to ensure their material welfare and social security.

The Associated Labour Law provides that the workers in a basic organisation are to determine the principles and scales for the distribution of funds for personal incomes, and that if they fail to do so only the statutorily guaranteed personal incomes may be paid. This provision is designed to bring the workers organised in associated labour face to face with their responsibilities in this respect, and to avoid arbitrary or last-minute decision-making in these matters that might be influenced by group self-interest or the demands of certain categories of workers. The decisions taken by the basic organisation with regard to the distribution of resources for personal incomes must, as explained above, be in line with the relevant provisions of the self-management agreement concluded within the work organisation, and may not be contrary to other self-management agreements or social compacts to which the basic organis-ation is a party.

At the end of a year, when the final tally of each worker's personal income is drawn up, the law provides that all must receive written pay slips showing, in addition to their net personal income, all the principles and scales for the calculation of the organisation's income and the amount appropriated from that income and allocated for the satisfaction of collective needs such as education and health care, for the general needs of society, and for joint consumption in common with other workers in the basic organisation. Considerable importance is attached to this method of calculating income per worker in relation to the distribution of the total income of the organisation as a means of keeping workers aware of their responsibilities within the organisation, and more generally to society as a whole.

Indeed, all the provisions concerning relationships based on income and the disposal of income and social resources are aimed at widening the horizon of the workers beyond their short-term individual or group self-interest, and promoting a better understanding, throughout society, of the interdependence of its parts. This provides an incentive for workers to take an interest in the activity of their basic organisation and its relations with other organisations of associated labour, in order to generate more income from which their personal income is derived; and by participating in decisions concerning the allocation of income to collective social needs they may gain a broader view of those needs at the level of the commune, the republic and the federation as a whole.

CASE STUDY ON THE ALLOCATION OF INCOME

The TOZ pencil factory in Zagreb

The following case study of the self-management system of distribution of income in the TOZ pencil and school and office supplies factory in Zagreb shows how the system operates in practice.

TOZ was founded in 1937 for the production of pencils; it has undergone a considerable expansion and diversification of production since the end of the Second World War, and produces at present a wide assortment of writing materials, including some 260 kinds of finished goods and 1,600 semi-finished products. In 1979 TOZ had 748 workers, with an additional 300 persons involved in some form of co-operative employment. Fifty-seven per cent of its workers are women. Since 1952 it has developed a flourishing export trade. The firm has constantly adapted its products and its production techniques to modern technology and has attained a relatively high level of labour productivity. An extensive training programme has contributed to this result. TOZ also has a well developed system for the information of workers, and organises special education and training for their management functions. The trade unions, the League of Communists, the Socialist Alliance of Working People, the Union of Socialist Youth and other socio-political organisations are all active within the organisation.

TOZ has a long tradition of workers' management, dating back to the formation of the first workers' council in 1950. As early as 1958, self-managing economic units were formed within the organisation and by 1961 income was computed and distributed at the level of those units. TOZ was one of the first organisations to implement the principles of the constitutional amendments of 1971 and the new Constitution of 1974. It is composed of six (previously four) basic organisations of associated labour and one work community (previously three, two of which were recently converted into basic organisations of associated labour). Relations among the constituent organisations are regulated by a self-management agreement on association adopted in 1972.

The method of distributing income and of evaluating personal incomes of workers has gradually evolved through the different phases of the development of workers' management. The present system is based on a self-management agreement on the distribution of income that was adopted by the workers in 1976, on the basis of the corresponding social compact of the Socialist Republic of Croatia and self-management agreement of the chemical industry group of Croatia. The workers of TOZ participated both directly and through their delegates in the drafting and adoption of these agreements. They were, for example, particularly active in regard to the ranking of jobs, incentives, provisions concerning resources for joint consumption, and other such matters. The trade union was also active in discussing these questions. Proposals made in the workers' meetings were transmitted to meetings held in all the other basic organisations of associated labour for consideration, and through this procedure some of the proposals, as regards the ranking of jobs for instance, were adopted on the basis of a comparison of job posts in the whole work organisation. Among the most significant changes introduced as a result of the demands of the workers and of their management organs, the following may be mentioned:

(1) The workers in the basic organisation of associated labour for the production of ball-point pens proposed that certain tool manufacturing and maintenance jobs should be given a ranking of 10 per cent more points than other jobs because of the complexity of the work. This proposal was adopted, after being submitted to workers' meetings in the other basic organisations of associated labour and work communities for comparison with other jobs in the work organisation.

(2) A proposal by the trade union that the ranking of the lowest-ranked jobs should be raised by 10 per cent was adopted, as was a proposal of the workers' council of the basic organisation of associated labour for the production of ball-point pens that cleaning jobs should be given a higher ranking.

(3) At a panel discussion on the changes in incentives, the workers of the basic organisation of associated labour for development suggested that they should be given incentives for attaining the plan targets for new assortments, on the ground that their influence was more directly related to the adoption of new products than to over-all output. This proposal was adopted.

(4) On the other hand, a proposal made by the workers of the work community for common administrative and expert services that work posts in accountancy should be given a higher ranking on the ground that the workload had increased, was refused by the meetings of other workers, who argued that a solution could be found by increasing the staff of the work community in question.

Through their delegates the workers in TOZ also initiated certain changes, which were afterwards adopted, in the draft of the social compact on the generation and distribution of income in the Socialist Republic of Croatia. The original draft limited the possibilities of income distribution in the basic organisations of associated labour to the plans of their economic groups (in the case of TOZ, this was the chemical industry group). This provision did not satisfy the basic organisations in TOZ, which managed to have amendments introduced into the social compact that provide for the exchange of assistance between basic organisations of associated labour for the payment of personal incomes, on condition that payments to the reserves of the entire work organisation are guaranteed.

The self-management agreement on the distribution of income regulates in detail the determination of common scales for the allocation of income and the distribution of resources for personal incomes among the basic organisations of associated labour and work communities. Through the same agreement the workers also regulate such essentials as the prices for goods and services, interest rates to be paid on credit for investments, export and import terms and so forth. These decisions are determined partly by external factors such as national economic policy and market conditions and partly by conditions within the work organisation.

Under the agreement the workers at TOZ undertake—

(a) jointly to do their utmost to generate income;

(b) to pool labour and resources so as to ensure their efficient utilisation in the production process;

(c) to co-operate continually with one another in business operations;

(d) to improve the organisation of work and business management;

(e) to co-ordinate the development programmes of the basic organisations;

(f) to co-ordinate research work;

(g) to prevent the possible emergence of unfair competition;

(h) to create and use a system of mutual information on business results, the distribution of income and personal incomes; and

(i) to prepare and carry out development programmes that will ensure the attainment of the goals of the work organisation in the spheres of economic and social development.

The income of a basic organisation is the part of its total revenue that remains after the workers have allocated resources to cover production costs and depreciation at the rates established by law. That income is earned through the sale of goods and services on domestic and foreign markets and exchanges with other basic organisations in TOZ. The workers in the basic organisations of TOZ periodically discuss and compare general conditions affecting the generation of income and the economic position of each basic organisation. It is on the basis of such discussions that they adopt decisions on which the size of the income of each basic organisation largely depends; thus, starting from the planned income of the work organisation as a whole, the workers endeavour to establish realistic and equitable economic relations among various basic organisations. This is also part of the process of adopting the joint plan of the work organisation and the plans of each basic organisation.

Under the terms of the agreement part of the gross income of the basic organisations must be allocated (as shown in table 7) to the organisations that contribute to the satisfaction of collective needs in the spheres of education, scientific and cultural activities, health care, social insurance and similar activities; for the satisfaction of general social needs such as national defence and the protection of the working and living environment; and certain other obligations of common interest to the basic organisations and work communities of TOZ. Proposals regarding the amount of allocations for general social needs are made by the basic organisations, in relation to their respective incomes, through their delegates to the assemblies of the socio-political communities, and decisions are taken by the Assembly of the Republic of Croatia or by the assemblies of the City of Zagreb and of the commune in Zagreb, where TOZ is located.

Table 7. Charges on the gross income of the basic organisation of associated labour for the production of ordinary and India ink in the TOZ work organisation, according to the final balance sheet for 1978

Item	Dinars
Gross income of the basic organisation	*12 557 874*
Obligations to the self-managing community of interest for education	244 749
Obligations to the self-managing community of interest for science and culture	29 214
Obligations to the self-managing community of interest for health care and social welfare	15 713
Obligations to other social activities	32 540
Expenditure for retirement pension and disability insurance	198 913
Expenditure for unemployment insurance	27 812
Commune levies	11 125
Republican levies	520 758
Obligations to the work community	1 294 096
Membership fees	18 899
Insurance premiums	154 008
Depreciation charges in excess of minimum rates	621 178
Payment for banking services	131 473
Other expenses incurred in meeting obligations laid down by law	42 728
Net income of the basic organisation	*9 214 668*

The net income of a basic organisation is distributed as shown in table 8 among four items—gross personal incomes, joint consumption, reserves and the business operations fund, which is largely invested (see diagram 4).

In determining the amount to be allocated to personal incomes, the basis used is the planned amount of personal income per worker for the current year in the economic group to which TOZ belongs, i.e. the chemical industry group. Because of the difficult working conditions in the industry, the planned personal income in this group may be increased by 18 per cent over the average personal income of workers in Croatia generally. Under the TOZ agreement this increase ranges, for example, from 3 to 15 per cent for work in shifts, 1 to 15 per cent for air pollution, 1 to 20 per cent for work with dangerous chemicals and 1 to 10 per cent for work in places affected by noise and vibration. Besides these factors relating to working conditions, the amount allocated to personal incomes depends on the amount of income generated per worker; if the index of income generated per worker of a basic organisation in relation to the planned income per worker for its group reaches a certain level, the gross personal incomes are increased according to a scale laid down in the agreement. Correctional factors are applied to the amounts so arrived at corresponding to the degree of utilisation of resources in the basic organisation in relation to the degree of actual and planned utilisation of resources in the chemical industry group in the Socialist Republic of Croatia. The determination of the total amount allocated for personal incomes

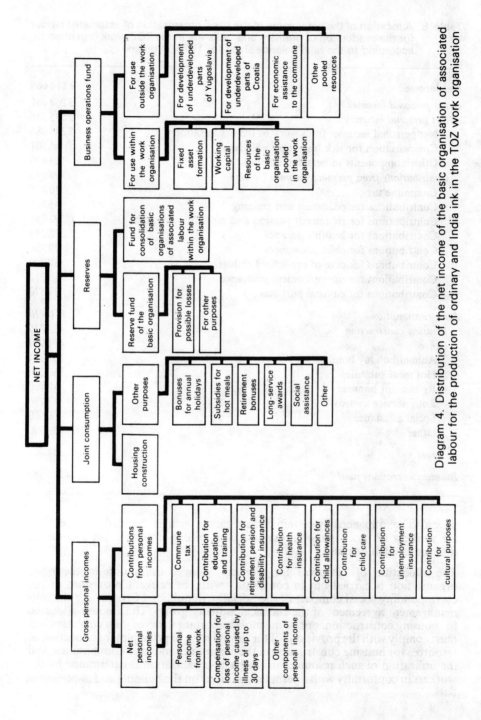

Diagram 4. Distribution of the net income of the basic organisation of associated labour for the production of ordinary and India ink in the TOZ work organisation

119

Table 8. Allocation of the net income of the basic organisation of associated labour for the production of ordinary and India ink in the TOZ work organisation, according to the final balance sheet for 1978 (in dinars)

Net income	**9 214 668**
Gross personal incomes	*3 264 469*
Net personal incomes	*2 555 556*
Net personal incomes from work in the organisation	2 385 085
Compensation for sick leave up to 30 days	56 501
Other components of personal incomes	113 970
Contributions from personal incomes (levies)	*708 913*
Commune tax	30 221
Contributions for education and training	45 720
Contributions for retirement pension and disability insurance	297 761
Contributions for health insurance	222 249
Contributions for child allowances	29 281
Contributions for care of pre-school children	38 799
Contributions for unemployment insurance	15 312
Contributions for cultural purposes	29 570
Joint consumption	*870 710*
Housing construction	*459 710*
Other	*411 000*
Annual holiday bonuses	137 614
Hot meal subsidies	166 200
Retirement bonuses	17 700
Long service awards	13 296
Social assistance	6 600
Other	69 590
Reserves	*314 000*
Business operations fund	*4 765 489*

may also be influenced by certain circumstances such as the need for incentives for workers with occupational qualifications of importance to production, or that are in high demand.

The allocation of resources for workers' joint consumption in the basic organisation is carried out in conformity with the relevant provisions of the corresponding social compact of the Socialist Republic of Croatia and the self-management agreement of the chemical industry group. The amount allocated for housing construction, one of the most important items of joint consumption, must comply with the provisions of the law relating to principles for allocation of resources for housing construction in the communes and local communities, and the utilisation of such resources in the basic organisation is determined by the workers in conformity with internal regulations on the building and allotment of flats.

The workers decide on the amount to be allocated to other items of joint consumption on the basis of the income earned by the basic organisations and the average net monthly personal income paid per worker of the city of Zagreb. For example, bonuses for annual holidays are allocated at a rate of up to 60 per cent of average monthly personal income paid; bonuses on the occasion of normal retirement, early retirement or disability at the rate of up to three times average monthly personal income; and length-of-service awards, assistance from solidarity funds to workers in emergencies, and other such items at the rate of from one to three times average monthly personal income. The distribution of resources for joint consumption is determined in advance for the following year, and the amounts spent are reported at the end of the year in the final balance sheet of the basic organisation.

The allocation of resources for investment is made by workers in the basic organisation, in keeping with their constitutional responsibility to renew and expand the material base of their own labour and that of society as a whole. Such resources may be pooled with those of other basic organisations within TOZ or outside of it, with a view to creating increased income.

The workers determine the principles and scales of allocation of resources to the reserves of the basic organisations in accordance with the provisions of the corresponding law, while their utilisation is regulated by the self-management agreement on the distribution of income. The agreement provides for the use of reserves to cover business losses, the difference between losses incurred and insurance compensation, loans to the working capital fund for the requirements of everyday business, payment of personal incomes if the work organisation temporarily does not have the resources for this purpose at its disposal, loans to other organisations, contributions to the joint reserve fund, and certain other uses. Decisions on the use of reserves are adopted by the workers' management organs in the basic organisations.

A basic organisation of associated labour in TOZ that operates at a loss is required to adopt a rehabilitation programme within a set time. Operating at a loss occurs when a basic organisation does not earn sufficient income to cover its obligations concerning common and general needs and to pay the workers their personal income in the form of advance payments. The rehabilitation programme must aim at the elimination of the causes for business losses as well as setting time-limits and specifying the means of compensating for such losses. The basic organisations are required to set aside 30 per cent of their reserves for a rehabilitation fund. If after a year of operation under a rehabilitation programme the workers in the basic organisation concerned have not been able to eliminate the causes of business losses, they then appoint new managerial workers, as prescribed by law. Basic organisations that are not able to pay the agreed guaranteed personal income to their workers may call upon the other basic organisations in TOZ for appropriate aid, in proportion to their economic strength; however, if this inability to reward workers is due to bad management, the organisation is obliged to undertake a rehabilitation programme, as when operating at a loss.

In making decisions on the distribution of resources for personal incomes, the workers try to ensure that the share of each individual in those resources will correspond to the scope, quality and prompt performance of the individual's work. The basic rate for personal income for each job is obtained by the addition of points assigned on the basis of an analytic evaluation of the job. The complexity of the work, the knowledge and skill required and the worker's capability account for 42 per cent of the value of the job; responsibility, 23 per cent; effort, 15 per cent; and working conditions, 20 per cent. For each of these factors there is a specific method of evaluation. In addition to the basic rate, the worker is entitled to increased personal income calculated according to the length of service. This increase ranges from 1 per cent of the basic rate for three to four years of service to 12 per cent for more than 14 years of work. Every worker is also entitled to a special incentive payment for working the full number of working hours during the month.

The self-management agreement on the distribution of income also regulates in great detail the method of calculating personal incomes for time-rated workers, which are determined on the basis of the completion of assignments. There are also special scales for determining the individual worker's share in the distribution of personal income related to the average income earned per worker as compared with the average income earned in the preceding year; the value of the stock of unfinished and semi-finished goods in relation to the established norms; the fulfilment of the monthly production plan, or sales plan, of the different basic organisations concerned; the amount of exports; the utilisation of production capacity; accuracy in accounting, and other factors. These common scales apply in all the basic organisations and work communities of TOZ.

Workers also receive special rewards for innovative and creative work, the sum being calculated in relation to the savings resulting from innovations or the value of the patent of an invention. Other elements of personal income provided for in the agreement include reimbursement of workers' transport costs in so far as they exceed 5 per cent of the average net personal income earned in Zagreb in the preceding year, and meal allowances amounting up to 10 per cent of the said average; and increased income for night work, work on state holidays, and work outside the plant.

Workers' personal incomes are computed and paid in advance monthly, on a provisional basis, and adjustments are paid every three months when the final balance sheet is drawn up for that period. A monthly balance sheet based on the accounting data of business results is prepared by the office for plans and analysis of the work organisation for each of the basic organisations and communities. This serves as a basis for the calculation by the workers' council of each basic organisation of the value of the points for payment in that month. These decisions are announced publicly, and the central office then computes the personal income of each individual according to the above-mentioned scales. The personal income is based on a work list, where each worker's output is recorded, or the number of hours worked if the worker is paid time rates. The accuracy of the work list is checked by a special commission which adds particulars of lateness, unpaid leave, sick leave or unjustified absences, after which the list is signed by the responsible managerial staff and sent to the accounting office. The list of workers whose personal incomes were decreased because of failure to complete their allotted assignments or work time is published; every worker has the right to raise objections to the recorded data, which must then be rechecked before the personal income of the workers is finally computed.

Every month the commission singles out the workers who have the highest performance rates in their work units and who have at the same time put in the full complement of working hours and maintained a high quality of work. These workers are entitled to special financial rewards and special honours such as a banner for outstanding work, which they keep at their work station throughout the month, as well as publication of their picture and interviews in the factory newspaper. Workers who are designated as the best workers for two or more consecutive months may have their rewards increased up to five times the basic rate.

In clerical work, appropriate formulas have been devised to compute rewards for work of above average value. For example, the value of points may be increased if the appointed tasks are carried out properly in spite of absences for sickness, or decreased if time targets for a task are not met.

Workers receive a detailed pay slip listing all the elements of their personal income (see table 9). The management organs carry out a careful analysis of personal incomes paid, checking the accuracy of computed contributions, and analysing the reasons which led to particularly high or low individual incomes. The findings are reported and discussed every month at a special meeting of all managerial, expert and administrative workers, and the appropriate measures then taken.

During 1978 the workers were also granted the following supplements from the resources for joint consumption:

(a) a holiday bonus amounting to 94 dinars for each day of vacation;
(b) a supplement for hot meals of 21.04 dinars per meal, which in this case amounts to 80 per cent of the price of a meal;
(c) an allowance for transport to and from work in as far as the itinerary exceeds two fare zones, up to a maximum of 240 dinars a month;
(d) a lump-sum housing credit of 200,000 dinars;
(e) a lump-sum home improvement loan of 50,000 dinars;
(f) a severance payment of 14,601 dinars on retirement;
(g) awards for years of service with the work organisation (for example, for 20 years, 12,000 dinars) given every five years;
(h) supplements of 800 dinars a year to pensioners with low pensions; and
(i) various social assistance payments to workers with low incomes—assistance in the event of a death in a worker's immediate family, for children's education, and so forth.

In 1977, on the occasion of the 40th anniversary of TOZ, awards of an average of 2,320 dinars were given to members of the collective.

The effects of the implementation of the self-management agreement on the distribution of income and personal incomes at the TOZ works are under continuous appraisal. At the same time efforts are constantly being made to improve the system of income distribution. In April 1977, on the basis of the common principles and scales contained in the self-management agreement and in conformity with Articles 127 to 129 of the Associated Labour Law, the workers of TOZ adjusted the distribution of resources for personal incomes in accordance with important factors in business success such as labour productivity, profitability, reduction of various costs, introduction of new product lines, efficient production, marketing accuracy, optimal management of stocks and utilisation of capacity and so forth. As a result, the organisation achieved the following business record in 1978:

123

Table 9. Pay slip of a skilled worker engaged in the production of plastic castings in the TOZ work organisation, August 1978

1. Points per hour	19.70
2. Standard number of points per month (for 184 hours)	3 624.80
3. Points earned on the basis of output	3 914.78
4. Bonus for working the full number of hours	141.80
5. Total number of points (lines 3 and 4)	4 056.58
6. Value of one point in dinars	1.70
7. Gross personal income on the basis of work done, in dinars (1.7 times line 5)	6 896.19
8. Years of work (12 per cent of line 7)	827.54
9. Total gross personal income in dinars (lines 7 and 8)	7 723.73
10. Contributions and dues	2 525.66
11. Net personal income in dinars	5 198.07
12. Housing credit charge	150.12
13. Total pay	5 047.95

1. Total revenue for 1978 amounted to 537 million dinars, 102 per cent of the planned figure and an increase of 30 per cent over the previous year.

2. Costs were 33 per cent higher than in the previous year. However, this was entirely the result of increases in the price of raw materials, foreign currency rates and the price of services, above all transport. In such cases the workers generally adopt a plan for the reduction of expenses and a stabilisation programme, as preventive measures with a view to decreasing otherwise unavoidable costs due to factors beyond their control.

3. Income increased by 24 per cent; income per worker in 1978 was 280,477 dinars, which was 40 per cent more than the planned income per worker for this economic group.

4. The amount allocated to cover general, joint and other needs increased by 39 per cent.

5. The part of the net income of the organisation that was allocated to gross personal incomes increased by 33 per cent, to investment and reserves by 16 per cent, and to joint consumption by 13 per cent. The net income of the organisation was allocated as follows:

	Per cent
Investment and reserves	40.5
Housing construction	11.0
Net personal incomes	48.5

Allocations to reserves are within the limits of the legally established rates and are pooled in the joint reserve fund.

The average net personal income was 6,313 dinars, determined on the basis of income and labour productivity, the planned development goals of TOZ and its basic organisations of associated labour and the principles and scales of the self-management agreement for its economic group. Although according to that agreement and the amount of income generated it would have been possible to pay a higher average personal income, the workers decided on the amount in accordance with the development plans of the organisation and a policy of achieving stable personal incomes.

Great attention was paid to the formation of resources for personal incomes on the basis of rationalisation, innovation, and other forms of creativity. The work rules provide for a series of financial and moral incentives for the workers, and consistent recourse to such incentives is one of the essential factors in the growth of labour productivity. For instance, after the introduction of a change in technology in the manufacture of ink cartridges a decrease in the number of rejects brought a saving of 560,000 dinars for a year's production. The change of technology was the result of an innovation made by a worker at TOZ, who was awarded 30,000 dinars for this improvement.

Labour productivity increased by 11 per cent in 1978 over 1977, as a result of the mechanisation of production, the development of a system of rationalisation, good working conditions, and constant improvement of the organisation of business operations.

Exports were increased in 1978 by 25 per cent with respect to 1977. Besides boosting exports, the workers at TOZ took numerous measures to ensure an adequate supply of materials. They now produce some of the materials that were previously imported, and have been successful to some extent in inducing their domestic suppliers also to produce materials themselves instead of importing them.

The resources for accumulation, according to the average utilised resources, increased three times with respect to the economy in Zagreb.

For a number of years, liquidity in this organisation has reached a level of absolute solvency, without any kind of borrowing; in its giro account it always has a credit balance of 10 to 40 million dinars.

PLANNING

As has already been indicated, social and economic planning is an important element of the workers' management system. Its aims and organisation have evolved as workers' management developed. It will be recalled that the essential features of the short initial period of central planning and administrative management of the economy, from 1945 to 1950, were the dominant role of state enterprises, state budgeting and federal investment funds in which reserves were accumulated to be distributed in accordance with planned objectives. Yugoslavia then turned to a new planning method, in line with the progressive decentralisation of decision-making, the decline in the power of the State and the strengthening of the institutions of workers' management. Since then, the main issue has been how to create a coherent economic and social system which would make the idea and practice of workers' management compatible with a national economic plan and a market economy. A fully satisfactory planning system has been slow to develop; indeed, in the late 1960s and early 1970s political and economic problems almost brought to a standstill any systematic attempt to develop an efficient national planning framework. But with the introduction of new concepts of workers' management, based on associated labour, by the Constitution of 1974 and the Associated Labour Law, the planning process has also been reorganised as an integral part of the system. The new planning system, as outlined in the Social Planning Law of 1976[5] is a system in transition, and as such contains some ambiguities, particularly with respect to its practical functioning. The major features of the system were used in the preparation of the medium-term plan for 1975–80, and it was more fully applied in the preparation of the 1980–85 development plan.

Essential principles

The Yugoslav planning system forms part of a series of measures designed to strengthen the role of workers and self-managing organisations in the supervision and direction of economic development. Planning is regarded not as a means of enabling the Government to regulate a market economy but as an instrument for establishing and promoting relations among self-managing organisations and other agencies. It provides a framework for discussions and negotiations not between representatives of industry and the Government, but among workers in organisations of associated labour both in production and in other activities and other representatives of social interests in the socio-political communities. The main aim is to reach a wide social consensus on the direction of economic and social development and the means of achieving agreed aims.

The Social Planning Law pays more attention to the ideological aspect of planning as a means of developing social cohesion under the workers' management system than it does to the technical means of attaining that end or the operation of the plan in practice. Planning techniques are as yet not fully developed; the basic idea, however, is that instead of relying on market forecasts to obtain a general direction and co-ordination of production decisions, that is to be achieved by explicit, voluntary contracts—self-management agreements and social compacts—entered into freely by self-managing organisations in production and social services and by all other representatives of social interests within the socio-political communities. These agreements and compacts, reached by formal negotiating procedures, are the major instruments for achieving social consensus. They specify the objectives of the plan, the instruments of economic policy and all organisational arrangements; for example, long-term decisions as to the rate and structure of investments, financing arrangements, specialisation among the constituent republics of the federation, regional and social development, are specified in long-term agreements and social compacts. These documents are legally binding on the signatory parties.

The essential principles on which the planning system is based under workers' management are as follows:

(a) planning begins in the basic organisations of associated labour, and micro-planning and macro-planning are closely integrated;

(b) the income plans of basic organisations of associated labour are the basic building blocks of economic and social plans at the regional and national levels;

(c) there is pooling of labour and resources on joint projects, and joint planning; and

(d) workers participate actively in all phases of the planning process in their basic organisations of associated labour and at other levels through their delegates to assemblies of socio-political communities.

In Yugoslav society the basic plan is the aggregate of the plans of basic organisations of associated labour; all plans of other organisations are to be prepared in such a way as to yield a projection of economic and social development consistent with the interests, income and resources of basic organisations of associated labour. For example, the plans for education, housing, scientific, health and other organisations of associated labour have to be consistent with the planned resources of the basic organisations, on the basis of which they are in fact financed, and the same applies to the plans of local, republican and federal socio-political communities. The adoption of plans for which resources will not be available is forbidden by the Constitution.

In accordance with the principle of joint planning, basic organisations of associated labour are required to plan their future development in close contact with other organisations; this means that all related production, sales, investment, research and development activities should be co-ordinated among the organisations themselves. Contractual arrangements for future contingencies, through self-management agreements reached by the organisations concerned without state intervention, are thus substituted for pure market transactions. The fundamental principle of pooling of labour and resources fits consistently into this system of joint planning, for if self-managing organisations are to co-ordinate their economic activities on a long-term basis, in their own best interests, they will presumably be motivated to pool their resources under agreed rules for sharing income, making joint investments, following agreed marketing policies, procuring joint supplies of raw materials and so forth.

Finally, since the plan defines the main future activities of each organisation, all workers are involved in the determination of its content, and vote on its adoption. The Social Planning Law lays down in detail the procedures for the approval of plans, whether workers participate directly, as in their basic organisations, or indirectly through their delegates in the case of local community, republican or federal plans.

Planning procedures

Since Yugoslav society is very decentralised, it was necessary to establish formal procedures for elaborating the plan contracts among self-managing and hence largely autonomous organisations, while at the same time preserving the fundamental role of workers and self-managing organisations in the planning of economic and social development. The structure of the Yugoslav planning system is very complex: the Social Planning Law envisages a very large number of planning agencies, including—

(a) the organisations of associated labour (basic organisations, work organisations and composite organisations);

(b) self-management associations of various kinds (such as self-managing communities of interest in the field of social services, and banks, insurance communities and other financial institutions; and

(c) the socio-political communities (communes, republics, autonomous provinces and the federation).

Each of these agencies is under an obligation to draw up its own medium-term (five-year) plan and annual plans within that framework. Other organisations are also involved in the planning process, in an advisory or negotiating capacity; for example, the trade unions are particularly active in the negotiation of self-management agreements, while general industry and trade associations and chambers of the economy provide a forum where members exchange information on intended future activities. There are also planning and statistical bureaux at the local, republican and federal levels, which carry out the technical function of preparing detailed plans. Planning is thus an all-pervasive activity encompassing virtually all existing social institutions and agencies.

The entire planning system operates on the principles of simultaneity and continuity. The Assembly of the Socialist Federal Republic determines the period for which plans of various organisations and communities are to be made, as well as the time-limits for their preparation, on the basis of proposals made by the Federal Executive Council after consultations with the executive councils of the republics and provinces. The Federal Executive Council determines the compulsory uniform methodology and minimum compulsory uniform indicators, or targets, that must be used in the preparation, of the plans of the self-managing organisations and socio-political communities; this is done in co-operation with the competent authorities of the republics and provinces and in consultation with the Confederation of Trade Unions and the Chamber of the Economy of Yugoslavia. The self-managing organisations and socio-political communities are thus obliged to prepare plans simultaneously, in close co-operation and co-ordination. Moreover, once the plans have been adopted and are in operation, all participants in social planning have to monitor progress made in the implementation of the medium-range plans, which must be reviewed at least once a year. They have to set targets and assignments for the forth-coming year and make any adjustments that may be required in order to ensure the fulfilment of the plan.

Under the Social Planning Law the medium-term plan, for five years, is the basic obligatory plan; every organisation participating in the planning process has to prepare a medium-term plan, which the annual plans are designed to implement. Both types of plans have to be based on self-management agreements (in the case of self-managing organisations and associations) and on social compacts (in the case of local, republican and federal socio-political communities). Long-range plans, covering a period of ten years, are not obligatory, and for their preparation the formal procedure of drawing up self-management agreements is not required.

The planning procedure laid down in the Law comprises two stages. At the first stage self-management agreements and social compacts are concluded setting forth the basic outlines and principles on which the plan is to be based, and at the second stage the actual plans are drawn up by the self-managing organisations and socio-political communities.

The appropriate organs of self-managing organisations and communities and the competent authorities of socio-political communities are required to initiate, organise and guide the preparation of the self-management agreements and social compacts on their outline plans. Those organs must submit proposals that will make the individual plans compatible with vital common or social needs, interests and goals. They have to arrange for any necessary expert study of requirements and prospects for the development of the organisations and communities concerned, and they must prepare and publish the corresponding statistical material and documents and ensure that the organisations and communities concerned are fully informed. They may call upon in-dependent, specialised and research institutions to take part in this process. The elements of the outline plan for every work organisation, composite organisation of associated labour or other self-managing organisation or community are prepared by the basic organisations of associated labour connected with it. The workers of the basic organisations, on the proposal of the workers' council or other competent self-management body, decide on those elements, which must take account of rules and decisions adopted by the competent authorities of the socio-political communities. In a self-managing community of interest the outline plans are also drawn up by its component organisations. On the proposal of its executive body the assembly of each socio-political community decides on the preparation of outline plans, and schedules the planning exercise, in agreement with the trade unions, the chamber of the economy and the Socialist Alliance of Working People. Basic plans are drawn up by the competent bodies at the communal level, while plans of republics and provinces are prepared by the competent bodies of the communes, of regional communities and of self-managing organisations and communities located on their territory.

Once those agreements on outlines have been concluded, the elaboration of the actual plans begins. Basic organisations of associated labour prepare their plans independently, though they must incorporate obligations stemming from the self-management agreements and social compacts on the plan outlines and from relevant decisions of the socio-political communities. The plan of the basic organisation of associated labour is promulgated by the workers' council after it has been accepted by the majority of the workers by referendum. In a work organisation composed of two or more basic organisations of associated labour, the latter participate on equal terms in the preparation of the plan, after having accepted the relevant self-management agreement on plan outlines. Similarly in a composite organisation the plan is drawn up by all its component organisations on the basis of the self-management agreement on plan outlines which they have concluded. In the self-managing communities of interest plans are prepared and adopted by the assemblies, in which the organisations providing services and those that consume them have equal representation. In the socio-political communities, the draft plan is prepared by the executive body of the assembly and adopted by the latter. It encompasses obligations for the self-managing organisations and communities and socio-political communities at other levels within its territory. If those organisations and communities feel that the obligations and targets set in the draft plan are not in conformity with those established by the self-management agreement or social compact on the outlines of the plan, or those laid down by law, they are entitled to raise an objection in the assembly of the socio-political community concerned.

Planning is thus a two-directional process. In the pre-planning stages information, time-tables and general guidelines on economic policy are passed down from the federal level to the bodies concerned at lower levels, whereas the elaboration of actual plans proceeds from the bottom upwards. The self-managing organisations first prepare their own development plans, covering production, marketing, investments, financial activities, the number of workers required, and other matters; those plans are then co-ordinated and consolidated through local or republican chambers of the economy and industry and trade associations, or by direct mutual consultation. Self-managing organisations then negotiate directly with suppliers of social and public services (education, health and welfare, housing, energy, credit and so forth) for the future long-term provision of those services on the basis of the "free exchange of labour" as already described. The plans of those diverse organisations are then consolidated within local communities, making a comprehensive social development plan for each; and those social development plans are then consolidated among communes and regional associations of communes, and within each republic, the republican plans being consolidated in the social plan for Yugoslavia as a whole. As can be seen, the actual planning takes place mainly in the basic organisations of associated labour, while the organisations and communities at higher levels carry out functions of consolidation and information in the planning process.

This system of planning, encompassing a very wide spectrum of organisations, is based on the assumption that plans will become virtually self-implementing since they are drawn up by the organisations and people concerned and not by a central bureaucracy, and their contents, specified in self-management agreements and social compacts, are thus compatible with the interests of the signatory parties. The plans at each level focus on the solution of problems which market mechanisms alone fail to solve, such as capital mobility, the supply of semi-finished goods, regional specialisation, promotion of exports or import substitution. The concepts of joint planning and pooling of labour and resources are seen as instruments for the solution of such problems, self-managing organisations being expected to plan joint activities in order to achieve additional economic benefits which are to be shared by explicitly planned joint income-sharing arrangements. As has already been noted, this system of market planning by contractual arrangements is believed to constitute a new approach to the plan-versus-market dilemma.

Plan contents

The plan of a basic organisation of associated labour sets forth the mutual rights, obligations and responsibilities of the workers who have drawn it up. The plan covers—

(*a*) the pooling of labour and resources in the basic organisation (in conformity with the self-management agreement by which it was constituted);

131

(b) the programming and organisation of production; operating costs; the sale of products and services; the export and import of goods; research and the introduction of new techniques and new technology; the organisation of work and the utilisation of facilities; the productivity of labour and business performance;

(c) the earning and distribution of income; the main elements of prices and the conditions under which purchases and sales are conducted and services rendered; utilisation and conditions of credit; the pooling of labour and resources with other organisations and communities for income purposes; principles and standards for the distribution of income and its allocation for personal incomes, joint consumption, investment and reserves;

(d) education and vocational training of workers;

(e) the pooling of labour and resources with other organisations of associated labour with a view to securing favourable conditions for production with regard to such matters as the supply of raw materials and energy, or the maintenance, expansion and utilisation of facilities;

(f) joint consumption and the relevant expenditure, for example on housing, hot meals, medical care, children's nurseries, rest and recreation facilities, organised in the basic organisation of associated labour or in the work organisation, the local community, or in other self-managing organisations or communities;

(g) obligations towards other organisations or communities with which it is associated for income purposes and for the satisfaction of social and public needs;

(h) funding and other arrangements in the sphere of social self-protection and national defence:

(i) the protection of the human environment; and

(j) the creation of material, financial and other reserves.

The plan of a work organisation includes the same elements. If a work organisation is composed of two or more basic organisations of associated labour, its plan is based on their self-management agreement on basic principles, as well as on their plans. The same is true *mutatis mutandis* for the plans of composite organisations and other forms of association of labour and resources. The plan of a self-managing community of interests includes specific assignments and targets corresponding to the aims set forth in the agreement by which it was constituted; the extent to which and the means by which common requirements will be satisfied, and the quality of services to be rendered; the pooling of labour and resources for specific purposes; and the rights, obligations and responsibilities involved in the satisfaction of common requirements. Workers who associate their labour and social resources in collective farms, and those who pool their labour and private assets in co-operatives also make self-management agreements on the basic principles of plans and draw up plans for the forthcoming five-year period.

The plans of local communities, which are based on the self-management agreements concluded by the basic organisations of associated labour and other self-managing organisations and communities located on their territory, set forth objectives in the spheres of housing, public services, children's institutions, welfare and medical protection, education, culture, consumer protection, protection of the human environment, social self-protection, national defence and other areas of life and work. Any self-managing organisations or communities that fail to formulate their own plans are incorporated into the social plan of the local community in the manner prescribed by the communal assembly.

At higher levels the plans of the socio-political communities pursue the general objectives of developing workers' management and guaranteeing the full equality of the various peoples of Yugoslavia and its republics and provinces. They also co-ordinate economic and social development and aim to achieve a fuller development of the means of production and a higher standard of services in the social, cultural and other fields. They have to take account of the laws of the market, and at the same time seek to diminish differences in conditions of work and level of income in different sectors of the economy. In particular the plans—

(a) specify the common interests and aims of the socio-economic development of the socio-political communities, as set forth in the agreements on basic principles;

(b) provide for the pooling of labour and resources where necessary, the development of production forces, and for a steady increase in the standard of living;

(c) promote education and cultural activities as well as activities in the fields of science and technology;

(d) identify the conditions, possibilities and requirements for the development of the federation and its various regions and areas; and

(e) prescribe the means for the protection of the human environment and reinforcement of the defence and self-protection of the country.

Such a plan also lays down specific assignments for other organs and organisations functioning within the ambit of the socio-political community.

The social plan of a commune identifies the needs of the working people in relation to their work and other aspects of their lives, and sets targets of socio-economic development for the commune on the basis of these common requirements. It fosters the development of public services, housing construction and area and urban planning, and incorporates the obligations entered into by the commune through the self-management agreements and social compacts laying down the basic principles of the plans of the republic, province, and region to which it belongs. The plans made at the regional level incorporate similar obligations. The social plan of a republic or autonomous province includes, in addition to the above-mentioned elements, provisions concerning the formation and distribution of the gross national product and income; the co-ordination of the work of groups that are interdependent in respect of income and investment; the expansion of the material resources for development of the economy by the development of agriculture, transport, energy production and other elements of its infrastructure; regional and area development; and obligations laid down in self-management agreements and social compacts, particularly as regards the co-ordination of policy on development, economic relations with foreign countries, credit and monetary policies, and the financing of more rapid development of the less developed republics and provinces.

Planning at the federal level

The social plan for Yugoslavia as a whole is enacted by the federal Assembly after the assemblies of the republics and autonomous provinces have consented to it. Great importance is attached to that enactment, the preparation of which is a complex process. On the proposal of the Federal Executive Council, the federal Assembly sets the date by which the Council has to submit the draft of the social plan to the Assembly, and lays down the main economic policies to be followed in the medium-term plan. The Council then draws up a time-table for the preparation of the social compacts on the basic principles of the plan and the preparation of the draft plan itself, in consultation with the executive councils of the republics and provinces. The Confederation of Trade Unions and the Chamber of the Economy of Yugoslavia also participate in the drawing up of the time-table.

The social compacts setting forth the basic principles for the plan establish the common interests to be promoted and the targets to be attained in the planning period as well as the economic policies to be followed by the federation, the republics and the provinces. They also specify certain obligations to be assumed by the republics and the provinces and the self-managing organisations and communities, the competent organs of which are consulted in the preparation of the plan outline. The Federal Executive Council is responsible for the preparation of the social compacts on the plan outline, under the supervision of the federal Assembly, and the compacts are signed on behalf of the federation, the republics and the provinces, after approval by their respective assemblies and by the self-managing organisations and communities to which specific assignments are given after they have been approved by their self-management bodies.

The outline of the social plan itself is prepared by the Federal Executive Council and submitted to the federal Assembly together with an analysis of past developments and of prospects for the planning period as well as other relevant analyses and documents. Before submitting the draft plan to the Assembly, the Executive Council has to reconcile the differing points of view of the republics and provinces in order to formulate common economic policies. If no agreement can be reached among these parties by the date on which the draft must be submitted, the Federal Executive Council is obliged to report to the Assembly on the reasons for the failure to reach an agreement and may request the Presidency of the federation to adopt legislation providing for temporary measures pending a solution of the remaining questions.

During the time when the plan is in effect, the Federal Executive Council may if necessary suggest that changes and supplements be introduced or that the targets be adjusted to new conditions: in such cases the procedure is the same as for the drawing up of the original plan. The competent bodies of the federation and of the republics and provinces are responsible for making the necessary regulations and taking economic and other measures to ensure the fulfilment of the plan, while the respective executive councils must keep a constant watch over its implementation. On 31 May each year the Federal Executive Council must report to the Assembly on the implementation of the medium-range plan, give an estimate of development possibilities for the forthcoming year and suggest any new measures which may be necessary to ensure the fulfilment of the plan. A draft resolution covering such measures is submitted to the Assembly each year at the end of October. The executive councils of the republics and provinces actively participate in the preparation of this resolution, which reconciles their different views, as in the preparation of the original plan. Planning is thus in effect a continuing operation performed by responsible bodies at all levels.

The social plan of Yugoslavia covers all the elements already referred to, from the point of view of the national economy. It aims to stimulate and co-ordinate development on a basis of equality in all the constitutent parts of the federation, and especially to carry out the constitutional obligations of the federation regarding the more rapid development of the less developed republics and of the autonomous province of Kosovo. The objective of the plan is to establish stable conditions for the business activity of organisations of associated labour on the Yugoslav market and good economic relations on international markets, and to stimulate the sense of mutual responsibility of the republics and provinces for the prevention of economic and other disturbances that would hinder the development of Yugoslavia. It also provides for the development of the Yugoslav People's Army and the attainment of other common goals in the field of national defence and security, and for other action to develop self-management throughout society. The social plan encompasses the duties and tasks of the republics, provinces, regions and self-managing organisations and communities, as laid down in the social compacts and self-management agreements on the basis of the plan, and lays specific obligations on those bodies in conformity with the legislation enacted by the federal Assembly.

Practical problems

As a result of the introduction of workers' management, the main planning problems in Yugoslavia lie no longer in the collection and use of adequate and accurate data for the technical preparation of balanced and consistent national plans based on statistical forecasts but in the extensive negotiations, exchanges of information and conciliation of interests required to reach a consensus on objectives and targets of economic policy. The federation cannot force a republic into a certain scheme, nor can a republic impose its objectives on local communities and self-managing organisations; unless those planning agents actually agree and sign self-management agreements and social compacts, there can be no effective plan. In fact, during the preparation of the 1975–80 national development plan the republics failed to reach agreement on the development of certain sectors and on inter-republican specialisation, with the result that although the plan was formally completed and approved, it was practically without effect in those respects in which agreement among republics and autonomous provinces had not been reached.

Although planning in Yugoslavia is more a social and political process than a technical matter of preparing economic projections, Yugoslav observers feel that sophisticated planning methodology could nevertheless be very useful, for example in the preparation of alternative plans and in the simulation of alternative effects upon each planning agent, thus allowing for a more rational method of reaching consensus on plan objectives and policy instruments. One of the weaknesses of the planning system pointed out by experts is the insufficient development of methodology and lack of experience in working according to plans, with the result that plans are sometimes inexpertly made, obligations are not carried out, and plan perspectives are shortened. It appears, however, that the number of basic and other organisations of associated labour that are without their own plans, and those in which plans exist only on paper, is constantly decreasing, while the sense of responsibility for carrying out mutual obligations and the general interest in planning are increasing.

Other weaknesses that have been noted in planning in practice include the tendency for workers in some organisations to leave the preparation of plans to small groups of experts or technical specialists, their own role being limited to the formal adoption of the plan by vote. Such practices are in contradiction to the concept of planning under workers' management, and every effort is being made by the trade unions to eliminate them and to involve workers more directly in the planning process.

Another difficulty that sometimes occurs is the relatively slow pace at which conflicting interests are reconciled in the process of concluding self-management agreements and social compacts. In practice, this slowness requires a long and patient process of persuasion and negotiation among the participating parties. This procedure may prompt some people to seek a "shorter" way, in the name of efficiency, with the result that a bureaucratic or technocratic agreement or plan or decision is sought instead of a self-management one. In other cases, agreements and compacts have been concluded in such a way that the true issue of conflicting interests is sidestepped completely: following the line of least resistance, only general, non-controversial questions are dealt with. This procedure is contrary to the very essence of planning under workers' management, and leaves room for other methods of decision-making.

Notes

[1] "Joint income means the income jointly earned by a basic organisation which in its operations makes use of the resources of other basic organisations, and by basic organisations which have pooled such resources and which are on that account entitled to a share in joint income" (Associated Labour Law, Art. 67, para. 3).

[2] Associated Labour Law, Art. 92.

[3] According to Edvard Kardelj, writing in *Slobodni udruženi rad* (Belgrade, Radnička Štampa, 1978), "the socio-economic essence of income" in Yugoslavia "stems primarily from the social character of the means of production and not only from the social division of labour. When it is said that income is 'social', this means that it belongs to all workers jointly and to each of them individually on the basis of labour with social resources".

[4] The workers of basic organisations of associated labour associated in a reproduction complex are mutually dependent and linked not only by their work and business interests but by relations that stem from the joint generation and distribution of income. Examples of such association are the agricultural combines, which are linked by a joint interest in income from the production, processing and marketing of agricultural products. The Plava Laguna composite organisation of associated labour at Poreč is a reproduction complex that generates joint income through work organisations for the production of agricultural products, for hotel and restaurant management and for tourism.

[5] *Službeni List*, 13 Feb. 1976, pp. 109–124.

WORKERS' MANAGEMENT IN THE ORGANISATION OF SOCIETY

5

FORMS OF ASSOCIATION AND CO-OPERATION OF ORGANISATIONS OF ASSOCIATED LABOUR

In attempting to establish a social system based on the independent status and equality of worker-managers, it has been necessary to find a means of striking a balance between the inequalities to which free market forces may give rise in the economic field and the tendency of the State to assume a strong regulatory role. While it is accepted that the State has an essential normative function to perform in providing a framework for the full development of workers' management in production and in society generally, an attempt has been made to keep political intervention at a level that will not impede the creative initiative and independent economic action that workers' management is intended to promote. At the same time, given the still limited resources of the economy and the inevitable conflicts of interest and rivalries among different regions, sectors of the economy and organisations of associated labour, as well as conflicts between individual and social needs, some form of control is still deemed necessary. A realistic solution to these problems has been sought in the institution and promotion of various forms of autonomous regulation of relations between organisations engaged in production, those supplying social and public services, and the socio-political communities, by means of self-management by-laws and agreements, social compacts and other forms of association and co-operation. These links, designed to strengthen the self-managing nature of Yugoslav society, are based on the following common principles, which are characteristic of all workers' management institutions:

(1) All forms of association and co-operation are voluntary, and based on the free expression of the will and interests of the workers in the organisations concerned. Decisions relating to such association are taken by referendum or by some other means of direct expression of the views of the workers in basic self-managing organisations and communities. Only in cases specified by law may such decisions be taken by self-management organs through delegates. The legal basis of association and co-operation

is the self-management agreement. Thus, the creation of such an association is founded on the workers' realisation of the advantages it offers through the rationalisation of production (division of labour and specialisation), increased productivity of labour, the guarantee of a stable position and good development prospects on the home and international markets, better use of available resources and means of production, and the generation of a larger income. Through such association workers extend the sphere of their activity and influence beyond the framework of their own organisation of associated labour and consolidate their position as managers, because they become less dependent on fluctuating market conditions and on external administrative interference in their work and business affairs. The material benefit from association, in the form of increased income, belongs to all the associated self-managing organisations, and they distribute it among themselves in proportion to each one's contribution to its creation.

(2) Lasting forms of association in business and production can only be based on the principle of equality of the organisations that form an association and on the respect of their basic self-management rights. Since the stronger partners, or external elements, may try to bring economic and political pressure to bear in order to impose unequal relations among the associated organisations—in fact this occurs in everyday practice—legal means and measures have been provided for in order to prevent such practices. The workers in associated labour whose interests have been infringed, the trade union organisation, the "social attorney of workers' management" and other workers' management institutions and organs may demand and obtain by court procedure the dissolution of an association that violates the principles of equality of the parties and voluntary participation. This is also true in cases in which association leads to the damaging of interests of third parties or institutions, that is, when such an association serves to create monopolistic positions on the market or gives rise to discriminatory practices.

(3) The self-managing character of such associations is reflected in the fact that under the law and the Constitution the workers themselves determine on their own what the aims of the associations shall be and what resources shall be allocated to them and make appropriate decisions in that respect. This is designed to avoid any state-imposed uniformity or other forms of external interference or coercion.

Some elements of compulsion are nevertheless provided for in specific cases by the Constitution and the Associated Labour Law. These provisions are regarded as being transitional, and represent an exception rather than the rule; they are, however, quite widely applied in practice. For example, under conditions specified by the Constitution, organisations of associated labour may be compelled by law to pool a part of their income in order to finance the construction of specific projects considered essential for planned economic development and growth. These provisions are used in practice for the financing of public works such as the construction and expansion of the electric power network and other sources of energy and the improvement of means of communication. However, workers in basic organisations of associated labour cannot permanently be deprived in this way of their rights in regard to the disposal of the social resources entrusted to them. It is also possible, as has already been mentioned, for the establishment of self-managing associations and communities set up to meet the essential needs of the population to be prescribed by law. This applies, for example, to the self-managing communities of interest in the field of social services, to business associations and communities through which the unity of operation of large public systems is ensured, particularly in the fields of energy supply and communications, and to various forms of association linking mutually interdependent organisations engaged in production, trade and services. The Government thus retains the power, in circumstances specified by the Constitution, to compel organisations of associated labour to pool their financial and other resources even though government agencies no longer have any right of disposal over investment resources and the organisations distribute their income in its entirety. This power is intended to safeguard a number of vital social interests without interfering with the course of development of the whole social system along workers' management lines; it is therefore carefully circumscribed by the Constitution as a guarantee against its excessive use or abuse by the assemblies of the socio-political communities.

The varieties of self-management association and co-operation fall into five main groups: various forms of business association; chambers of the economy and general associations for particular economic sectors; financial institutions; self-managing communities of interest; and forms of association with persons working with privately owned resources.

Business association

Mention has been made above of cases in which mutually interdependent organisations engaged in production and trade are under a constitutional obligation to pool their labour and other resources. Those provisions of the Constitution were designed to counter the inequalities which arose during the period when the decentralisation of management in the economy and the freer influence of the laws of the market enabled organisations engaged in the sale of goods and services, particularly on foreign markets, to attain a privileged position economically, in relation to organisations engaged in production. The intention behind the establishment of the new relationship between production and trade has been to substitute for the traditional commercial margin a participation of commercial organisations in joint revenue earned through the sale of commodities produced. The Constitution and the Associated Labour Law therefore provide for relations between organisations of associated labour in trade and in production to be based on methods of co-operation and the self-management association of labour and other resources, with shared risks and shared responsibility, and equal influence in the determination of business and development policy. In foreign and wholesale trade, such co-operation and association are compulsory and are subject to detailed statutory regulation. While the actual form of association may differ, relations between the associated organisations are always governed by self-management agreements. Production and trade are thus linked into a single aspect of long-term economic development.

The position of the consumer in relation to retail sales is protected on similar principles. The organisations of associated labour engaged in retail trade are duty bound to co-operate with organised consumers in local communities and special self-managing organisations of consumers, and to agree with them on the assortment and quality of goods produced, conditions of sale and marketing methods, the return of part of the income earned to consumers, and other relevant matters.

General rules have been laid down for two specific forms of business association, namely business communities and communities of associated labour for joint planning and business co-operation. A business community may be formed by a number of organisations of associated labour that have business links, even though they may belong to different branches of the same industry or to different industries or sectors of the economy. Their purpose is to co-ordinate production of certain commodities or services, to pursue the division of labour and the improvement of working conditions by agreed means, and to organise jointly the sale of products on foreign markets, scientific research, the training of supervisory staff and other similar activities. A business community is thus a relatively stable form of co-operation. It may represent the associated organisations in legal transactions with third parties, the said organisations being responsible for obligations thus contracted in their name. The joint managerial organ of the business community is formed on the delegation principle and its composition and powers and the method of its election and recall are determined by the self-management agreement constituting the community. Business communities represent a flexible form of self-management association and integration and, as such, have gained increasing significance, particularly in the light of the still low degree of economic, technological, organisational and managerial integration of various spheres of activity in the Yugoslav economy. In 1977, for example, business communities were formed for copper, agro-chemistry (artificial fertilisers), the leather and fur industry and the rubber industry. However, it has also appeared in practice that this and other similar forms of association may be abused for the development of monopolistic positions on the market, and discriminatory practices which threaten the maintenance of free and equal conditions on the market for all producers.[1]

Communities of associated labour for joint planning and business co-operation are similar in many ways to the business communities. Basic and other organisations of associated labour which are associated and mutually dependent through production, trade, or in other ways, their business communities, banking organisations, collective farms, and other forms of self-managing association of labour and resources, may associate in communities of this nature to further their joint interests. For example, the Community for Joint Planning and Business Co-operation of the "Dom" reproduction complex in Ljubljana includes an organisation of associated labour for the production and sale of articles for household purposes and an organisation for catering services. In such a community the members agree among themselves on their development policy, make joint plans, pool resources for carrying out projects of joint interest, decide on terms for the mutual exchange of labour and the regulation of their relations on the market, agree on conditions of joint sale of commodities on foreign markets, on investments abroad, and on foreign investments in the organisations which form the community concerned.

These communities do not, in general, have permanent, joint management organs or other bodies. They serve the purposes agreed upon by their members, who include all joint decisions in their respective plans and work programmes and co-ordinate their work with a view to the attainment of agreed goals. When necessary, however, the members of such a community may set up special joint organs, by means of a self-management agreement, to co-ordinate and supervise the execution of obligations and responsibilities established by agreement as well as to promote co-operation among the members. The members may also found an internal bank or special organisations for the achievement of tasks they have jointly set themselves.

Chambers of the economy and general associations for particular economic sectors

"Chambers of the economy" and "general associations" for particular sectors of industry and commerce provide assistance to their member organisations in the determination of development policy, the preparation of plans and the regulation of their socio-economic relations. and in the consideration and solution of other questions of joint interest. The object is to promote business activities; to co-ordinate individual, joint, and general social interests; and to secure the adoption of laws, the determination of economic policy, and the conclusion of social compacts and self-management agreements. These bodies are mostly associations of organisations of associated labour engaged in the production of goods or services, business communities and banking organisations. Organisations of associated labour providing social or public services may form associations for their field of activity or join other general associations. The members of these general associations appoint delegates to organs of management which handle the association's business. Decisions are taken jointly through a process of negotiation and by agreement, both in general associations and in the economic chambers.

At the national level, through the general associations for each sector of the economy, the organisations of associated labour and business communities are associated in the Chamber of the Economy of Yugoslavia. Similarly, all the banking organisations and the insurance communities are associated in this Chamber through their respective national associations. In all of the republics and provinces, republican and provincial chambers of the economy are formed, so that besides the Chamber of the Economy of Yugoslavia, there are six republican and two provincial chambers of the economy that function as self-managing organisations and communities. In some republics regional chambers of the economy have been founded for regions that have indicated the need for such bodies. The Chamber of the Economy of Yugoslavia is itself a self-managing organisation, which co-ordinates the activities of the chambers of the economy of the republics and autonomous provinces and co-operates with them. As the self-management system has developed, these chambers have been transformed from quasi-governmental agencies, hierarchically superior to the self-managing work organisations and with responsibility for the carrying out of state economic plans and policy, into self-managing associations which, besides fulfilling the functions of co-ordination and harmonisation of interests, make it possible for organisations of associated labour and their broader associations to participate in the determination and implementation of economic policy in the socio-political communities. The role of the chambers and of other general economic associations is particularly important in the planning and co-ordination of the development of individual sectors of the economy, and the initiation of agreements which determine the orientation of production and ensure joint scientific research, technological modernisation, and the training of expert supervisory staff for the particular sector—especially in view of the fact that no government agencies exist to carry out some of those functions. This fact also explains the elements of obligation and universality in the structure and activities of the chambers, although care is also taken to preserve their self-managing character.

Financial institutions

Banks and other financial institutions play a significant role in the Yugoslav economy, as in all market economies. Their organisation and functioning have, however, been adapted to the specific needs of the workers' management system through a series of constitutional amendments and statutory provisions adopted in recent years.

As has already been explained, investment funds, which in the early years of development of the workers' management system had remained in the hands of the State, were later transferred to the control of banks constituted on a self-managing basis. By concentrating the greater part of the investment capital available, those banks acquired a strong position and, indeed, became autonomous centres of economic power on which the organisations of associated labour depended for credit. The managerial organs of the banks were thus able to impose high interest rates and even to dictate the business policy of the production organisations, thus seriously interfering with their self-management rights. It became evident in the late 1960s that the workers in organisations of associated labour could not achieve real control over the expansion and modernisation of the economy unless the position of the banks was fundamentally changed so that they acquired the character of a joint service for the benefit of the organisations that pooled their financial resources in them. This new conception provided the grounds for constitutional reforms which established a system of commercial banking with the following general characteristics:

(1) The founders of the banking organisations are the basic and other organisations of associated labour, self-managing communities of interest, and other socio-legal entities. Neither the government nor individuals may be founders of such organisations; however, they may deposit their funds with banking organisations and use their services in the process of disposal of those funds.

(2) The banking organisations are integrated into the system of workers' management as a specific form of association of labour and resources and are not outside or above the system.

(3) The funds deposited with the banking organisations do not have the character of anonymous capital managed by expert banking staff, but remain under the control of the depositors and are managed jointly by

145

them. The income earned through the business dealings of the banking organisations also belongs to those who contributed funds, and they distribute this income among themselves according to principles laid down by self-management agreements, after payment of the bank's operating expenses.

(4) Every banking organisation is obliged to adopt long-term and medium-term programmes on which its lending and trading are based; the programmes themselves are based on a self-management agreement concluded by the members of the banking organisation after consultation of the workers in the basic organisations of associated labour involved.

(5) The affairs of a banking organisation are managed by its members. Decisions are taken both by votes in the associated organisations and communities and by their delegates to the management organ—assembly or council—of the banking organisation. Delegates are obliged to follow the instructions given them by their electors, but this does not preclude the possibility of democratic discussion; on the contrary, delegates are expected to engage in dialogue and to reach decisions by consensus, based on the co-ordination of views expressing the individual interests of the different parties and their common interests, so as to reach solutions that are satisfactory to all members of the banking organisation and to society as a whole.

The originality of this new banking system which is being developed in Yugoslavia is that, while the banks retain their role of gathering and concentrating in an organised manner the financial resources available for economic growth and development, and are responsible for allocating these resources in a socially and economically valid way for the improved satisfaction of social interests, it is at the same time possible for the workers themselves, in organisations of associated labour, to manage jointly the resources pooled in the banks on the basis of their inviolable right to dispose of the income they create. Thus, the banks are institutions through which the workers expand the scope of their management activity; and at the same time, they constitute machinery through which the workers further their common interests, on a basis of solidarity, and can thus ensure a higher degree of security for the activities of their organisations.

Several different types of banks exist, varying according to their status and scope of functions. They include "internal banks", "basic banks", "associated banks", specialised organisations and savings and loan organisations. About 120 "internal banks" had been founded in Yugoslavia by the beginning of 1979. Such banks represent the first stage in the transformation of the banking system by the gradual substitution for credit relations of a new social relationship based on participation in joint income and the joint bearing of risks. An internal bank is founded within a work organisation or composite organisation of associated labour, or within a broader entity composed of several organisations mutually linked in production and trade, that is, by economic transactions and in the process of the creation of income. The function of these banks is to enable organisations of associated labour to pool their resources and to facilitate and rationalise their operation by financial means. Within a work organisation there is no hierarchical, centralised authority for decision-making on the disposal of income; this is done by the workers in the basic organisations. However, they are bound to manage income in the light of the work and needs of all the basic organisations associated in the work organisation or community to which they belong, and in the interests of the organisation as a whole. This entails the establishment of an adequate institutional form for financial transactions. Internal banks meet this need, since they offer possibilities for the co-ordination of interests of the associated but relatively independent basic organisations of associated labour. For the association of labour and resources on a larger scale than that of an internal bank, the basic and other organisations of associated labour, self-managing communities of interest, internal banks and other legal entities may associate to form "basic banks" to conduct their banking affairs; while for the implementation of development plans which exceed the possibilities of a basic bank, the members of two or more basic banks may establish an "associated bank" or a banking consortium.[2]

An example of banking organisation is provided by Beobanka, the Belgrade basic bank. It is one of the largest banks in the Belgrade Association of Banks, and was recently rated as occupying the 93rd place among the 300 largest banks in the world. It has eight branches abroad (Frankfurt, London, Milan, Moscow, Paris, Prague, Warsaw and Washington, DC), and a workforce of about 11,000 persons in eight "operational" units, two "organisation" units, and nine expert services. The "operational" units are formed according to economic sectors for organisations of associated labour that are linked through the production process. For example, there are operational units for organisations of associated labour in the fields of industry and commerce; agriculture and food processing; transport; and other services. There is an "organisational" unit for housing construction, one for the development of social welfare and one for carrying out transactions with individual citizens (the organisational unit for savings). Expert services are formed according to the kinds of affairs dealt with at the bank—e.g. for foreign currency dealings, financial operations and business development. All the three kinds of departments mentioned (operational units, organisational units and expert services) are composed of a corresponding number of divisions. The organisational savings unit has the greatest number of divisions (13); it is followed by the operational unit for industrial organisations of associated labour with seven divisions and the expert service for development with five divisions (planning and analysis, credit, research, inter-bank relations and statistics). The board of management has eight members, all of whom, with the exception of the chairman, are heads of departments. The self-management organs of the bank (the assembly, the executive board, the council of bank depositors and the executive board of the council of operational units) are composed of representatives of the various parties that are associated in the bank. All of the members of these bodies are elected on the delegation principle and represent the organisations of associated labour associated in the bank and the citizens who deposit their savings with the bank.

Communities for the insurance of people and property against damage, injury or similar types of risk may be founded through self-management agreements by organisations of associated labour, self-managing communities of interest, socio-political communities and other entities. The basic purpose of a "community for property and life insurance", like that of other financial associations, is to decrease or eliminate the causes of such damages and to provide compensation for them should they occur. It operates not with the purpose of earning an income from the sale of insurance but as a mutual insurance community based on the principles of solidarity and reciprocity. The associated members manage all the work and business dealings of the community jointly through their elected delegates to the community's assembly. In this way, they retain control over that part of the income which they helped to create and which is allocated for the insurance of people and property. It may be noted that this system was developed, as in the case of banks, because the insurance organisations had grown into very powerful and relatively independent bodies handling enormous social resources.

The Dunav self-managed property and life insurance community in Belgrade may be cited as an example of these new associations. It is composed of five separate "risk communities", for life insurance, private citizen and industrial insurance, agricultural insurance, vehicle and liability insurance, and transport and credit insurance. The affairs of the insurance community as a whole and of its individual risk communities are directed by communities of insured parties. They may be of a general type (serving all the risk communities) or specialised (serving a particular risk community). Where the need appears, a community of insured parties may found branches as well. The assembly of the insurance community is composed of delegates directly elected by the insured parties. Thus, the affairs and resources of the insurance community are managed by those who benefit from insurance (both individuals and bodies corporate) whom they elect directly through the delegates to the assembly of the insurance community.

Self-managing communities of interest

Self-managing communities of interest are, as has already been indicated, a relatively new and complex form of associating the labour and resources of organisations of associated labour in the economic field and those providing social and public services. They are based on the principle that the workers in associated labour and other citizens who are particularly concerned with the good organisation and functioning of certain essential services should have the right to participate, on a self-management basis, in the management of those services. Thus responsibility for management falls not on the State as the official representative and guardian of general social interests but on the people directly concerned in each particular sphere of activity.

Such communities of interest may be established in all fields of work. However, the most important communities of this nature are those set up for public utilities and social services. They are set up to run public utilities in such fields as energy, transport and water supply, where the laws of the market cannot be used as the sole foundation for the co-ordination of labour and needs. The communities of interest in these fields are founded by the organisations of associated labour that provide such services and by those that use them. For example, the self-managing community of interest for energy in a given region is formed by the association of all the organisations in the region dealing with the production and transmission of energy, and the organisations of associated labour in industry, mining and other sectors of the economy that need a continuous and stable supply of energy. By joining the self-managing community of interest, organisations from two different spheres of activity guarantee the direct co-ordination of their interests in the process of managing the essential service concerned. The members of the community take decisions and manage its affairs on a basis of equality and mutual responsibility, through their elected delegates to the community's assembly, who, as in other cases, are guided by the instructions of the organisations which elected them. The self-management principle thus embraces the major utilities serving the common interests of the economy. As regards social services, self-managing communities of interest are obligatory for education, science, culture, health and social welfare. Their members are, on the one hand, organisations of associated labour engaged in one of these fields, and, on the other hand, the organisations of associated labour that finance their activities. Thus, for example, the self-managing community of interest for education in a given area includes all the production organisations located in the area and all organisations of associated labour, i.e. schools and other institutions, providing education in the area. In addition, all workers and other citizens who contribute out of their own income towards the provision of these social services for the satisfaction of individual and collective needs may, independently or through their organisations, associate themselves with these communities.

The organ through which management of the community's affairs is carried out is the assembly, which is made up of two chambers, one composed of delegates from the organisations providing the service in question and the other of delegates of workers and organisations that use the services provided and have helped to finance them. The two chambers have equal rights, obligations and responsibilities under the self-management agreement constituting the community; decisions must be taken by agreement and not by one group imposing its will on the other. The members of a self-managing community of interest are responsible to society for the quality of services provided and for their general state and their financial situation.

Within the framework of these communities, workers from the different spheres of activity concerned co-ordinate their interests and needs, determine their joint interests in relation to the interests of the society, and take joint decisions with regard to priorities, work programmes, prices, the evaluation of results and the determination of development policy in a given field of social activity. This process of joint decision-making in the context of the socio-economic relations established within the self-managing communities of interest is known concisely as the "free exchange of labour". The creation of this particular form of self-managing community has been aimed at the attainment of a certain number of social goals. In the first place, it eliminates the function of the State as mediator between the production of goods and the provision of services, and limits the powers of the socio-political communities to that of co-ordinating development policy in these fields by means of social plans. Secondly, it establishes direct bonds of common interest between workers in these two spheres, who have in the past been separated and often brought into mutual opposition by the intermediary role of the State. In the third place, it allows workers who contribute part of their income for social and public services to have a say in decisions as to how this income is to be used. And, fourthly, the income of workers in organisations providing social and public services is derived from the free exchange of labour, which means that their position is essentially similar to that of workers engaged in the production of goods. The development of workers' management in the sphere of social and public services thus acquires its own stable financial foundation.

The first forms of self-managing communities of interest appeared in the mid-1960s, but a broader legal foundation for them was provided only through subsequent constitutional amendments. Nevertheless, the integration of social and public services into the workers' management system in this way already plays an important role in the organisation of society. Given the scope and depth of the changes involved, some problems have inevitably arisen in the practical operation of these self-managing communities. One such problem is a tendency to form within the community an administrative apparatus that exceeds real needs and tends in practice to play a greater role in decision-making than is necessary. Another problem is that of ensuring greater involvement and influence of the community's spokesmen in the organisations on which their financing depends. Problems also occur in guaranteeing the necessary co-ordination among various communities of interest, in order that the development of services may be related to economic possibilities. It is for this reason that the assemblies of the socio-political communities are still required to supervise the distribution of income in this respect, as explained above. Certain significant positive results of the establishment of these communities have also been observed. For example, it has been noted that current problems in education, science, social welfare and other fields of service have become the subject of much more widespread and better-qualified discussion and criticism. It would also appear that the direct connection between organisations of associated labour engaged in production and those providing social and public services has strengthened those services and prompted initiative and a search for higher efficiency, whereas in the past they tended to suffer from the administrative routine of government machinery.

Association with persons working with privately owned resources

Farmers and other workers who engage in economic activities using their own labour and resources may also associate in various forms of self-managed co-operation and association. While the self-managed organisations of associated labour working with socially owned resources account for over 80 per cent of the total national income of Yugoslavia, there are still some important sectors of activity where individual work with private resources prevails, in particular, in agriculture, in which 80 per cent of arable land is in the hands of small farmers, although the maximum size of private landholdings is limited to 10 hectares; and also in small-scale craft production and services, which were for a long period on the decline but have nevertheless retained a significant place in the economy that is likely to expand to meet the needs of producers and consumer demand. It was therefore a matter of some importance to the Yugoslav authorities to find a means of linking the activities of independent workers using their own private resources with the various forms of associated labour on self-management foundations. The new Constitution and the Associated Labour Law provide a legal basis for the free and voluntary association of labour and resources by workers using privately owned resources and for the linkage of this sphere of private endeavour with the self-managed organisations of associated labour. Thus, independent farmers may freely decide to associate their labour, land and financial resources in co-operatives and other forms of agricultural association. Farmers retain their right to ownership of the land or of the funds they contribute to the farming co-operative, unless specified otherwise in the self-management agreement on association or other special contract to which they are parties. Similarly, craftsmen engaged in production with privately owned resources may associate freely and voluntarily in craftsmen's co-operatives or other forms of association. Farmers and craftsmen have essentially the same rights, on the basis of their labour, in the co-operative associations they found, as do workers in organisations of associated labour.

It is also provided that farmers and craftsmen may, either directly or through their co-operatives, associate their labour and their other resources, voluntarily and on a basis of equality, with the workers in organisations of associated labour by establishing various forms of long-term business co-operation with them. Self-management agreements or contracts are concluded in such cases, laying down how the joint affairs of the parties are to be managed, how decisions on jointly created income are to be made and how it is to be distributed. The principle that all parties shall share in the distribution of income proportionately to their contribution to its creation is guaranteed in the agreement or contract. This method of linking private ventures with associated labour under the system of self-management has been widely applied in practice, and most private farmers are already included in various forms of self-management association and long-term co-operation with organisations working with socially owned resources.

THE SOCIO-POLITICAL COMMUNITIES

The expansion of workers' management throughout the various sectors of the economy has, as explained above, provided the basis for the development of new relations in the socio-political field. Under the Yugoslav system worker-managers, as members of basic organisations of associated labour, take decisions in matters directly affecting their working and living environment; as citizens, they participate in the management of the affairs of their local community, along with all other residents; and they share the responsibility for satisfying their personal and family requirements and those of the community at large with regard to education, health, culture and other social services, through the participation of their basic organisations in the corresponding self-managing communities of interest. Parallel with the development of the workers' rights and obligations in those fields, their political rights have been steadily extended through the closer integration of organisations of associated labour and self-managing communities of interest into the political decision-making process at every level. The purpose of this integration is to enable a plurality of interests, organised on a self-managing basis, to be freely expressed in the political process, to reduce gradually the still considerable direct influence of government agencies and professional politicians on decision-making on all social affairs, and thus to achieve a comprehensive form of socio-political organisation based on the self-management principle.

The means through which this integration is achieved is the delegate system, that is, the creation of a wide network of delegations, elected by the workers in the basic self-managing organisations and communities, from which delegates are elected in turn to the assemblies of the communes, provinces, republics and federation (see diagrams 5 to 7, on the structure and composition of the assemblies, and tables 10 and 11, on the number and composition of delegations). By virtue of their composition the assemblies of those socio-political communities are workers' management bodies, but they are also supreme organs of authority, responsible for ensuring the co-operation and integration of the various self-management institutions in the territory they cover. They determine social policy, and adopt development plans as well as laws and other statutory and self-management instruments. The executive councils of the assemblies and all the other agencies carrying out public functions are responsible to the assemblies, in particular for implementing the policies determined by them.

The intimate connection between the assemblies of the socio-political communities and the basic organs of associated labour and of other self-managed organisations and communities, through their delegations, makes it possible and necessary to take account of all the basic interests of working people in the determination of political and social policy. In fact, no decision affecting the essential interests of the workers in associated labour may be taken legally against the will of the workers concerned. Thus the Constitution provides that no assembly of a socio-political community may take a decision "calling for the allocation of part of income for common and general social needs or concerning the purpose and volume of resources earmarked for such needs" if "it has not been approved by the chamber of associated labour" of the assembly.[3] The influence of the basic organisations and communities in the assemblies is further strengthened, as has already been noted, by the fact that their delegates are required to follow the instructions they have received and to reach decisions that strike a balance between the co-ordinated special interests and needs of the various groups of workers they represent and the broader, general social interests of the community. The assemblies of the socio-political communities are thus both organs of political authority and a means of exercising workers' management rights at every level in the community generally.

The institutional framework for the exercise of these rights, as laid down in the Constitution, provides for the election of delegations to participate in the assemblies of socio-political communities—

(a) in basic organisations of associated labour and work communities;

(b) in co-operatives and other forms of association of farmers, craftsmen and other persons working with their own private means;

(c) in work communities in government agencies, expert services of the self-managing communities of interest, banks, insurance institutions, socio-political organisations and associations; they are also elected by military and civilian staff of the armed forces on active service;

(d) in "local communities"; and

(e) in socio-political organisations.

Most of the delegations are elected by workers from among themselves, by direct and secret ballot, for a term of four years. The normal representative bodies of the socio-political organisations act as delegations on their behalf for the purpose of representation in the assemblies of the socio-political communities. Every delegation has the following rights and duties:

(a) to follow the proceedings of the assemblies of the socio-political communities and inform the workers in the organisations or communities they represent on the matters under discussion in the assemblies, on the content of any proposals made, and on the views expressed, by the delegates of other basic self-managing organisations or communities;

(b) to judge which questions are of particular concern to the workers who elected them and to submit those questions to those workers for consideration, and help them to examine the subject fully before decisions are taken by the assembly;

(c) to issue basic policy instructions for the delegates who are to participate in the work of the assembly, following the instructions given by their electors but taking into account also the interests of other self-managing organisations and communities and general social interests and needs;

(d) to initiate the consideration of issues through the delegates and to submit proposals for adopting decisions in the assemblies in keeping with the needs and interests of the workers they represent;

(e) to participate through the delegates in the general proceedings and decision-making of the assemblies;

(f) to follow the work of its delegates in the assemblies and to let the basic self-managing organisation or community concerned know whether or not delegates have acted in the process of decision-making in accordance with the basic policy instructions given; and

(g) get in touch with other delegations and co-operate with them in order to achieve the aim of joint, democratic decision-making.

In 1974 over 70,000 delegations, with over 780,000 members were elected in Yugoslavia; the next elections, in 1978, produced about 200,000 delegations, with about 2.5 million members.[4] This means that at least one in every 15 adult citizens of the country was a member of a delegation formed to participate in the proceedings of assemblies of the socio-political communities. Delegations thus occupy an important position in the process of identification of the entire political system as an emanation of society.

The delegations elect delegates from their own ranks to participate in the work of the appropriate chamber of the assembly. They act and vote individually, but they are, as indicated, expected to follow the directives of their organisations and delegations and to express views corresponding to those directives and with the joint interests of all the groups represented and the general social needs. Delegates are required to inform the delegation and organisation that elected them about the proceedings of the assembly and their own activities, and they are responsible to those bodies.

As shown in diagrams 5 and 6, the assemblies in each commune, republic and autonomous province are composed of—

(a) a chamber of associated labour, made up of delegates of workers in basic organisations of associated labour and other self-managing organisations and work communities;

(b) a socio-political chamber of delegates from the socio-political organisations; and

(c) a chamber of local communities in the assemblies of communes, and a chamber of communes in the assemblies of the autonomous provinces and republics.

The same delegations elect delegates to the assemblies at these various

Diagram 5. Composition of the assembly of a commune

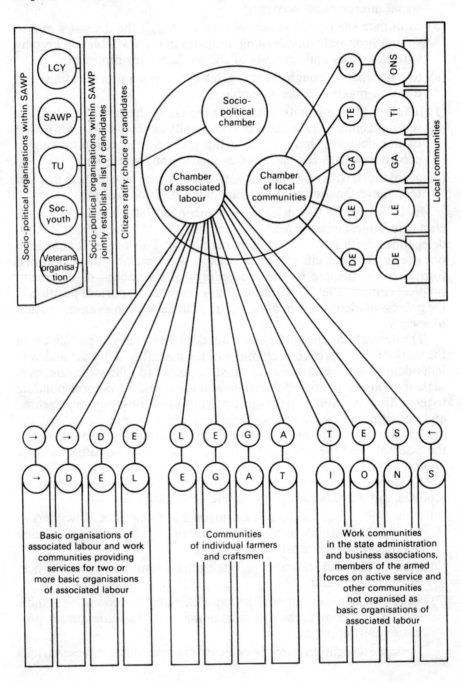

Diagram 6. Composition of the assembly of a republic or autonomous province

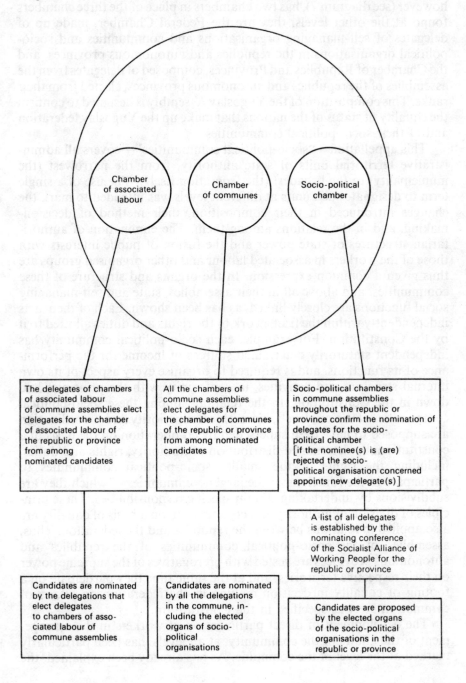

The delegates of chambers of associated labour of commune assemblies elect delegates for the chamber of associated labour of the republic or province from among nominated candidates

All the chambers of commune assemblies elect delegates for the chamber of communes of the republic or province from among nominated candidates

Socio-political chambers in commune assemblies throughout the republic or province confirm the nomination of delegates for the socio-political chamber [if the nominee(s) is (are) rejected the socio-political organisation concerned appoints new delegate(s)]

A list of all delegates is established by the nominating conference of the Socialist Alliance of Working People for the republic or province

Candidates are nominated by the delegations that elect delegates to chambers of associated labour of commune assemblies

Candidates are nominated by all the delegations in the commune, including the elected organs of socio-political organisations

Candidates are proposed by the elected organs of the socio-political organisations in the republic or province levels, as well as to the Yugoslav Assembly at the federal level. The latter, however (see diagram 7), has two chambers in place of the three chambers found at the other levels; they are the Federal Chamber, made up of delegates of self-managing organisations and communities and socio-political organisations in the republics and autonomous provinces, and the Chamber of Republics and Provinces, composed of delegates from the assemblies of the republics and autonomous provinces, elected from their ranks. This composition of the Yugoslav Assembly is designed to confirm the equality of status of the nations that make up the Yugoslav federation and of their socio-political communities.

This appellation—"socio-political communities"—covers all administrative territorial units of state authority, from the narrowest (the municipality) to the broadest (the federation itself). The use of a single term to designate such units at different levels was intended to mark the changes introduced in their composition, their method of decision-making, and in the relations among them. The elimination of authoritarian structures of state power and the fusion of public interests with those of the workers in associated labour and other organised groups are thus given a common expression. In the organs and structure of these communities, and above all in their assemblies, state and self-managing social functions are closely linked, as has been shown. Each of them acts independently within the framework of the rights and duties allotted to it by the Constitution. For example, each socio-political community has independent statutorily determined sources of income for the performance of its functions, and is required to organise every aspect of its own internal structure and activities, in conformity with the principles laid down in the Constitution. In the relations among these socio-political communities at various levels, hierarchical superiority and subordination are supposed to have been superseded by co-operation on the basis of a constitutionally determined distribution of authority, rights and duties, including the rights of the smaller socio-political communities to participate in the functions of the larger communities of which they are subdivisions by undertaking certain specific responsibilities. These principles of division of authority and co-operation on a basis of equality are also applied in relations between the republics and the federation. Thus, assemblies of the socio-political communities of the republics and autonomous provinces are vested with prerogatives of the supreme power on their respective territories, and at the same time they participate on a footing of equality in decision-making in the federation on affairs of common interest as specified in the Constitution.

The development of direct participation of workers in the management of the affairs of the community, at all levels, has been particularly marked at the level of the commune. As has already been explained, the

Table 10. Number of delegations to the assemblies of socio-political communities in 1978, and distribution of delegation members by sex and age and by nature of groups represented

Groups represented	No. of delegations	Members		
		Total number	Percentage of—Women	Young people
Basic organisations of associated labour and work communities	43 652	469 459	33.6	18.6
Workers operating with privately owned resources	4 722	53 702	5.1	9.2
Professional people working on their own account	178	1 849	21.1	12.8
Working communities of government organs and socio-political organisations	3 149	39 037	38.0	16.3
Local communities	12 402	130 735	9.9	17.0
Socio-political communities[1]	2 200	92 434	19.9	29.2

[1] Statistics from the Socialist Republic of Slovenia not available.

Source: *Statistički bilten SZS*, 1978, No. 1140.

process of integrating self-managing organisations of associated labour into the process of political decision-making was begun at that level, during the first decade of the development of workers' management, and today it still constitutes an essential element of the development of workers' management into a social system. The Constitution provides that the commune, as the basic socio-political community that is closest and most accessible to the workers and citizens as a whole, shall exercise all functions of authority in the management of social affairs that are not specifically assigned to the larger socio-political communities. This gives the commune a particularly strong position in the entire political system. Assemblies of communes, linked by a network of delegations with all the self-managing organisations, local communities and socio-political organisations, are the focal points where the initial integration of different interests, demands and needs expressed through the delegates of those various organisations is carried out.

Although this integration of interests at the level of the commune is essential, there is a danger that it may lead to an overemphasis on exclusive local interests, as opposed to those of the larger social community. Such tendencies are countered, in practice, by the unitary delegate system through which the socio-political communities at all levels are linked by a common delegate base: the chambers of the communal assemblies elect delegates to the provincial, republican and

Table 11. Geographical distribution of delegations to the assemblies of the socio-political origin and nature of groups represented

Item	Bosnia and Herzegovina[1]	Croatia	Macedonia[1]	Montenegro
Delegations	5 655	14 260	5 196	2 233
Delegation members representing—	84 298	127 187	52 007	26 179
Basic organisations of associated labour and work communities in organisations of associated labour	47 525	74 438	30 336	18 518
People working in agriculture, handicrafts, catering and transport	10 436	11 700	4 789	1 791
People engaged in cultural, artistic, scientific and other professional activities on their own account	—[1]	288	—[1]	—
Work communities of government agencies and socio-political organisations, and military and civilian personnel of the Yugoslav armed forces	3 575	5 364	2 190	920
Local communities	22 762	35 397	14 692	4 950

[1] Data refer to 1974. Members of the delegations who are engaged in cultural, artistic, scientific, research, legal or other professional activities on their own account are shown together with members in the previous line.

federal assemblies, and are thus concerned with the issues and interests relating to the country as a whole. The formation of inter-communal regional communities is another means of overcoming local isolationism. Established by the free association of communes, such regional communities do not restrict the independence of communes as the basic socio-political communities, nor do they limit any of their rights. The assembly of a regional community is composed of an appropriate number of delegates from communal assemblies within the regional community, and it performs only the duties and functions of co-ordination and joint supervision that are assigned to it by agreement among the associated communes. Such communities may, for example, provide a broader foundation for the organisation of services in such fields as health, culture and education, wherever this appears to be conducive to more efficient organisation of such services: the association of communes in regional communities thus facilitates integration.

communities in 1978, and distribution of delegation members by geographical

Serbia				Slovenia	Yugoslavia	Under-developed areas	More developed areas
Total	Excluding autonomous provinces	Kosovo	Vojvodina				
19 616	13 029	1 840	4 747	5 797	**52 757**	*14 924*	*37 833*
208 608	138 771	25 016	44 821	46 178	**544 457**	*187 500*	*356 957*
119 521	76 629	13 060	29 832	31 476	**321 814**	*109 439*	*212 375*
28 427	19 283	4 303	4 841	1 478	**58 621**	—	—
243	145	—	98	698	**1 229**	—	—
8 198	5 049	1 280	1 869	1 973	**22 220**	*7 965*	*14 255*
52 219	37 665	6 373	8 181	10 553	**140 573**	*48 777*	*91 796*

THE SOCIO-POLITICAL ORGANISATIONS

Under the Yugoslav workers' management system the socio-political organisations, as a political form of organisation of the working people, play a very important role both in the basic self-managing organisations and communities and at the level of society as a whole. As already indicated, the establishment of a new form of production and social relations, linking equal, mutually dependent and responsible workers voluntarily and freely associated in the production process and in other forms of work and in all decision-making connected with their management is the object of the whole workers' management system.[5] The pursuit of that objective is governed by the provisions of the 1974 Constitution, which formally prohibits any kind of relations and socio-economic and political organisation that would aim at establishing a different socio-economic and political system.

In view of the different forces operating in society and the conflicts of interests that emerge, it appears essential that the workers should be

Diagram 7. Composition of the Assembly of the Socialist Federal Republic of Yugoslavia

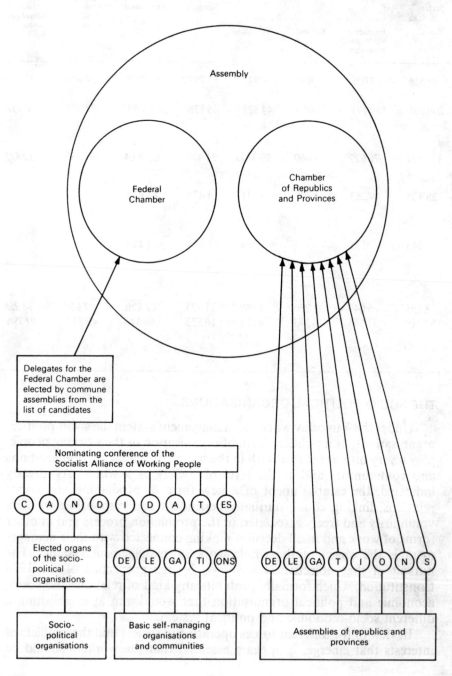

organised politically as well as through self-managed organisations of associated labour. The relationship between self-management and political forms of organisation is of fundamental importance in the construction and functioning of the system. In Yugoslav theory and experience, a breakdown of this relationship, either because the role of the socio-political organisations is underestimated or because they assume a full guardianship of workers' management decision-making, may lead to serious disturbances and difficulties. Every step in the evolution of workers' management is of necessity accompanied by corresponding changes in the organisation and work of the socio-political organisations. The main direction of these changes has been to transfer the focus of the activities of those organisations from the management of social development through the power of the State to action from within the self-managing organisations and communities, by influencing decisions taken in workers' management bodies by workers and their delegates.[6]

The League of Communists

Neither the development nor the present characteristics of the political system of Yugoslavia can be explained without keeping in view the leading ideological and political role of the League of Communists. The position of that organisation is based on the historical role of the Communist Party in the early struggle for independence and in the war of national liberation that gave birth to the new Yugoslavia. The League is considered to be the embodiment of the aspirations of the working class towards the full achievement of self-management in the organisation of society. As a militant political organisation, the League exercises a strong ideological influence on the self-managing organisations and communities and on the socio-political communities at all levels. But being in a sense the guardian of workers' management rights and committed to the development of autonomous decision-making by the workers in their work organisations and political bodies, its function "is not to exercise direct control over social, economic and political life, but to bring its influence to bear in all bodies and institutions . . . above all by persuasion . . .".[7] This slant to its activities was introduced at its Sixth Congress, in 1952, when the name of the organisation was changed from Communist Party to League of Communists.

The aim of this change of approach was designed to avoid a potential clash with the social aspirations and increasing independence of the workers under the workers' management system—a clash that might have occurred had the organisation continued to act as a fount of political power and authority; the organisation was therefore obliged to develop more flexible methods of retaining ideological control. An important part of its activities is of an educational nature, directed mainly towards the

Table 12. Occupations of members of the League of Communists of Yugoslavia, 1946–66
(Percentages)

Year	Workers n.e.c.	Administrative personnel and other employees	Farmers	Others
1946	27.6	10.3	50.4	11.7
1948	30.1	23.6	47.8	8.5
1950	31.2	19.0	43.4	6.4
1952	32.2	18.9	42.8	6.1
1954	28.3	29.8	22.6	19.3
1956	31.9	32.6	17.2	18.3
1958	32.7	34.8	14.7	17.8
1960	36.1	32.0	13.0	18.9
1962	36.7	36.4	9.6	17.3
1964	36.6	39.0	7.6	17.4
1966	33.9	39.0	7.4	19.5

Source: *Komunist*, 31 Mar. 1968.

younger members of the labour force. Members of the League of Communists are also frequently elected to membership of workers' councils, managerial organs of organisations of associated labour[8] and delegations to the assemblies of the socio-political communities at the communal, republican and federal levels. It is noteworthy, for example, that according to recent statistics, 73 per cent of the general managers of organisations of associated labour were members of the League in 1976. The proportion of League members is generally higher in managerial organs and in delegations than among the workers who elect them. Membership in the League is, in fact, a criterion for election to such bodies in some cases, since League members are deemed to be more motivated to defend and develop the management rights of workers.

It has been estimated that some 1.7 million citizens are members of the League.[9] The occupational distribution of its membership has changed considerably during the past three decades, as shown by tables 12 and 13.)

The widespread presence of the League of Communists provides continuity, cohesion and awareness of social responsibility to a system that might otherwise suffer from fragmentation. The fact that the League, as well as other socio-political organisations, has an over-all vision of the system as well as a deep-rooted concern for its importance may help to mobilise people and to avoid possible distortions of self-management and particularly its conversion into group capitalism. On the other hand, the

Table 13. Occupations of members of the League of Communists of Yugoslavia, 1968–77
(Percentages)

Year	Workers n.e.c.	Farmers, agricultural workers	Engineers, technicians	Intellec- tuals[1]	Administrative workers	Civil servants	Armed forces	Others[2]
1968	31.1	7.4	4.4	11.3	12.2	7.2	7.8	18.6
1969	31.1	7.3	4.9	11.9	12.4	6.1	8.0	18.2
1970	29.9	6.5	5.0	12.9	12.0	7.1	8.2	18.5
1971	28.8	6.3	5.2	13.0	12.1	7.5	8.1	18.9
1972	28.7	6.0	5.5	13.3	12.3	7.4	8.0	18.7
1973	29.1	5.6	5.8	13.7	12.0	7.3	7.7	18.7
1974	28.9	5.3	6.1	13.6	11.9	7.1	7.3	19.8
1975	28.7	5.1	6.4	13.9	11.9	7.2	7.0	19.8
1976	28.8	4.9	6.6	14.1	11.7	6.9	6.7	20.3
1977	29.2	4.8	6.7	14.1	11.5	6.7	6.4	20.3

[1] Including economists, attorneys, scientists, educational and health-care workers, and artists. [2] Including craftsmen working on their own account, persons with private means, dependants, unemployed persons and Yugoslav citizens working abroad.

Source: Federal Bureau of Statistics.

League's emphasis on commitment and political loyalty may sometimes obscure the need for critical analyses of the system. As a Belgian sociologist has put it, the party is an invisible actor which paves the way for self-management and sets the limits of its operation.[10] Most Yugoslav observers, however, feel that the role of the League of Communists in the system of self-management is quite visible and precisely defined in conformity with the democratic principles of the system as a whole.

The Socialist Alliance of Working People

The Socialist Alliance of Working People, like the League of Communists, grew out of the Yugoslav fight for independence. Its origin was the grouping of patriotic forces, regardless of political, national or religious affiliation, in the National Liberation Front during the Second World War. When the war ended the Front developed under the new name of the Socialist Alliance as a mass organisation for the promotion of the new society embodied in the workers' management system. The Alliance is the broadest political organisation in the country. It embraces the other socio-political organisations, including the League of Communists, the trade unions, the youth organisation, the women's organisation and the federation of veterans of the National Liberation Front, and co-ordinates their activities. Individual citizens are also members; indeed, it is the role of the Alliance to act as a cohesive force in society by involving the largest possible proportion of the population in political action, overriding national or other differences that may make for division and the pursuit of narrow or selfish group interests.

The focus of activity of the Alliance is the socio-political communities, particularly at the communal level. Since the introduction of the delegate system, constituting more direct links between self-management in basic organisations of associated labour and the political decision-making process, the activities of the Alliance have gained in importance. For example, the Constitution emphasises the role of the Alliance, along with that of the trade unions, in the election of delegations to the assemblies of the socio-political communities. The Alliance is also instrumental in ensuring political communication from the basic self-managing organis-ations and communities to the delegations, the delegates, and the assemblies and back.

The Alliance is responsible, along with the other socio-political organisations, for striking a balance among various group interests in accordance with the common and long-term interests of associated labour. It does this in the socio-political chambers of the assemblies of the socio-political communities, and also by exerting its influence through delegates in other chambers. The Alliance is represented and takes part in the proceedings of meetings of delegations, and exercises a strong influence over political decision-making and the general development of public opinion on all important public issues. Among its main activities in this regard are the following:

(a) organising democratic discussion of all matters concerning society as a whole, taking political initiatives and making proposals, reconciling different points of view and issuing statements for the guidance of delegates in the assemblies of the socio-political communities and as a democratic basis for the entire process of political decision-making;

(b) supervising and criticising the work of government agencies, organs of management, and persons invested with self-management, public and other social functions;

(c) keeping working people and citizens informed, and safeguarding the democratic role of the press and other means of mass communi-cation; and

(d) attempting to open up even wider opportunities for the participation of young people in management and in political life (this is a particularly important task of the Union of Socialist Youth, which operates within the framework of the Socialist Alliance, as well as of the Alliance as a whole).

The trade unions

To a large extent the trade unions perform an educational function, endeavouring to raise the level of understanding and social consciousness of workers so that they may effectively direct and control the entire process of the maintenance and development of society as a whole. At the same time, they also take part in this process themselves, as parties to self-management agreements and social compacts, and as mediators among the various groups of workers and organisations of associated labour in cases of conflict or dissension. As has already been indicated, the role of the unions in inducing individual workers to identify with the organisations of associated labour in which they work is of considerable importance in dealing with problems arising from the discrepancies and conflicts of interest that occur in the economic sphere. The unions are instrumental in co-ordinating various individual, group, common and general interests not only in organisations of associated labour but also within sectors of the economy, including production and other sectors, and within socio-political communities. Every aspect of their activities serves the purpose of strengthening social cohension. However, their role is basically that of defending the individual and collective interests of their members when they are threatened by other individual or group interests. Far from becoming superfluous, as was initially feared in some quarters, trade unions occupy an important place in the workers' management system as guardians of the workers' interests both in organisations of associated labour and in society as a whole. They are not an arm of the State but autonomous organisations, providing the most comprehensive collective representation of workers within the framework of the Socialist Alliance of Working People of Yugoslavia. In organisations of associated labour the trade unions participate in the entire decision-making process, from the initiation of proposals to supervision of the implementation of decisions. On the political plane, the organs of the State are required to consult the trade unions on matters of social policy, and the unions may put forward proposals, although their views and suggestions are not necessarily followed.

Structure and membership

The trade unions operate on three different levels: in basic organisations of associated labour, at the level of broader self-managing organisations and communities for economic and social activities, and in the assemblies of the socio-political communities. Their organisation (see diagram 8) is adapted to the structure of the workers' management system; thus as a rule a union is formed in every basic organisation of associated labour and work community. Several trade unions may,

167

Diagram 8. Trade union structure in organisations of associated labour

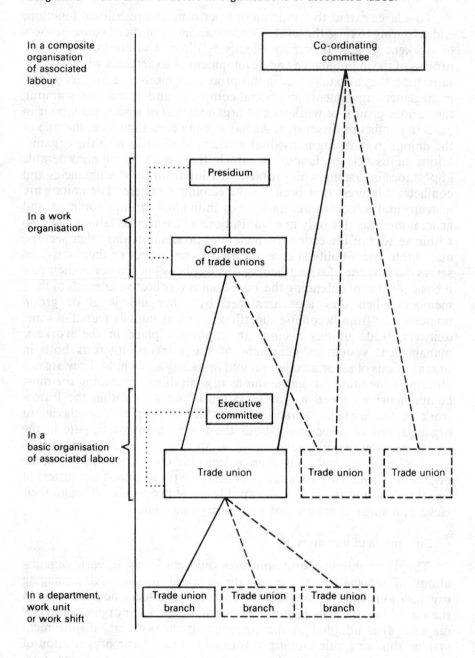

however, be set up in units located in different places though belonging to the same basic organisation of associated labour or work community, and organisations of that type that consist of many units and have many shift workers may also have a number of unions. Conversely, the workers in several small basic organisations or work communities may form a single trade union.

The organs of a trade union are the general meeting, the executive committee and the supervisory board. In a work organisation that has several basic organisations of associated labour a conference of trade unions is formed. The conference is formed on the delegation principle and is composed of delegates from the various constituent unions. The conference elects a presidium as its executive organ, a supervisory board, and other standing or special committees. In a composite organisation of associated labour, all the unions elect a joint body, the co-ordinating committee, on which each one of them is represented by the same number of delegates.

The structure of trade union organisation in Yugoslavia is both industrial and territorial. Thus, individual trade unions belong to the appropriate industrial federations that are organised at the communal, regional, provincial, republican and federal levels, and they also belong to trade union confederations at those levels. In local communities where a large number of workers and several trade unions exist, a co-ordinating body for joint action may be set up on a delegate basis. Trade union members elect the executives of their respective trade unions and of the territorial confederation at all levels. These executives are elected for a period of four years. They may set up various committees and other bodies to help them. For the country as a whole, organs of the industrial federations, known as federal committees, are formed on the basis of equal representation of each republican and provincial trade union federation. There is some duplication of effort between the industrial federations and the territorial confederations, both of which deal with the same problems; and an attempt is being made to arrive at a clear division of competence between the two kinds of bodies.

The Council of the Central Confederation of Trade Unions is the highest organ of the Confederation between two congresses. It is composed of delegates of the confederations in the individual republics and provinces. Republican confederations each have 18 delegates on the Council, while the provincial confederations have 15 each. The Council elects the Presidium as its political and executive organ, on the basis of five delegates from each republican and four from each provincial conference, and the Presidium in turn elects the Secretariat, which is its executive organ.

Trade union membership is voluntary. About 95 per cent of all workers are members, and by the end of 1978 the Confederation of Trade Unions had nearly 5 million members. Members of the Confederation may be workers in basic organisations of associated labour or work organisations, workers in contractual organisations of associated labour, workers who are employed by persons working on their own account with their own labour and resources, civilians working for the armed forces, or self-employed or professional workers who do not employ other workers, and who co-operate on a steady basis with an organisation of associated labour (unless otherwise specified by the by-laws of the republican or provincial trade union confederation). Trade union activities are financed by union dues, which are fixed at a uniform rate of 0.6 per cent of net personal income. They are usually collected through a check-off system.

The concept of collective work and responsibility is applied in all union bodies. All of the members of such bodies have the same rights, obligations and responsibilities, and among them there are no hierarchical relations whatsoever. The chairman of a trade union body is elected from among the members of that body for one year, after which another person is elected for next year, and so on. This principle applies to the function of Chairman of the Council of the Central Confederation of Trade Unions as well, with the additional proviso that each year the Chairman must be elected from a different republic or province.

Main fields of activity

Trade unions are active in every sphere of social life in Yugoslavia, since their activities extend beyond the defence of workers' interests at work and includes the protection of workers' rights in all respects and of the entire position of the worker in society. The following account is a highly selective one, highlighting activities or policies that distinguish Yugoslav trade unions from those in other countries. So far the trade unions have been predominantly concerned with the production and distribution of income in organisations of associated labour, but more attention is now being paid to their political role as the workers in associated labour themselves become more closely integrated into the political decision-making process.

Workers' education

As has already been indicated, the trade unions are particularly active in training workers for management and public functions, and in raising their general level of education, promoting their cultural progress and developing their sense of social responsibility. A significant part of their activity in the educational field has to do with the training of workers for the discharge of workers' management responsibilities: various forms of workers' education and training organised by the unions serve this purpose. The unions also encourage and support the work of worker-managers' clubs, "workers' universities", schools for skilled workers, educational centres within organisations of associated labour and all other educational institutions engaged in training workers for workers' management functions. The unions also pay particular attention to the training of workers elected to various workers' management bodies, and have, for example, organised special seminars for delegates elected to workers' councils and to assemblies of self-managing communities of interest, as well as for members of workers' supervisory commissions. At the same time, they promote the continuing education of all workers who are called upon to take part in various forms of decision-making as managers of their own organisations. A few figures may be cited in this respect. In 1976, for example, 272,000 workers took part in various forms of training for workers' management in the Republic of Bosnia and Herzegovina, and 310 workers' management schools were either organised or assisted by the trade unions, in addition to their own 158 trade union schools. In Slovenia trade unions were directly engaged in the training of 17,630 members of various workers' management bodies. In Serbia about 60 per cent of all workers took part in various forms of training for workers' management, double the number of two years earlier. In Croatia the trade unions took part in the organisation of workers' management training courses through the media, which were taken by 30,000 workers in 1977.

The trade unions also monitor the whole system of general education, demanding that it should meet the workers' requirements, correspond to their best interests and provide an adequate preparation for workers' management. They also organise congresses and conferences for the exchange of experience and the determination of future courses of action, which play an important part in the training of workers for their workers' management functions. The unions are also instrumental in the development of various types of cultural and artistic activities for workers. On the whole, however, their action in the field of education is eminently practical, being primarily concerned with the everyday experience of workers' management, in an effort to improve the ability of workers to exercise effective control over the maintenance and development of the country as a whole.

Crystallisation and expression of workers' views

In order to facilitate decision-making by the workers on all matters pertaining to their work and life, the unions try within organisations of associated labour to explain the meaning of every proposed decision to every worker, and to ensure that those decisions will truly reflect the workers' needs and interests. In addition, and as explained earlier, in preparation for decision-making through referendums or workers' general meetings the unions co-operate with the workers' councils in organising preliminary public discussions of the issues involved. In the course of those discussions the unions are instrumental in harmonising the workers' various views and proposals. The unions also take part in the entire decision-making process within the workers' councils, especially when matters of particular importance to workers are discussed. Trade union policy is determined by agreement in union bodies, after discussions in which all members may participate on an equal footing and which are open to the public. The unions are constantly endeavouring to help workers to express themselves freely and to arrive at co-ordinated statements of their interests and needs. Nevertheless the unions sometimes fail to achieve their objectives in this regard: for example, in a basic organisation of associated labour the union sometimes fails to communicate the workers' views effectively to the workers' council and the managerial organ, and conversely, the union may have no real influence on its members' thinking and decisions. Efforts are being made to develop a more democratic approach within the unions to allow for criticism and free confrontation of ideas.

Establishment of organisations of associated labour

One of the basic problems with which workers in organisations of associated labour are faced is how to organise their activity on a truly self-managing basis. The trade unions organise exhaustive discussions on this matter in an effort to develop the most efficient forms of self-managing organisation and to enable all workers to take an active part in decision-making with regard to the formation of organisations of associated labour. In this respect the trade unions are entitled and required by law—

(a) to initiate and participate in the process of organising a basic organisation of associated labour;

(b) to participate in the establishment and constitution of a work organisation and to propose to the assembly of the commune to make the necessary preparatory arrangements for the constitution of such an organisation;

(c) to institute proceedings in a court of associated labour, in cooperation with the social attorney of workers' management, when workers are precluded from establishing a basic organisation of associated labour; and

(d) to participate in the conclusion of self-management agreements and social compacts laying down detailed rules concerning the setting up of basic organisations of associated labour and work organisations.

Self-management agreements and social compacts

The trade unions play an important role in the initiation and conclusion of the self-management agreements and social compacts that play a large part in regulating social and economic relations. The unions may, for example, make proposals for negotiating self-management agreements concerning the association of workers in basic organisations and work communities, or the pooling of labour and resources in work organisations, composite organisations, banks and other financial institutions, life and property insurance communities, self-managing communities of interest and other types of organisations. They may also initiate agreements concerning outline plans, principles and scales for the allocation of income and the distribution of resources for personal incomes and collective consumption, rules for the self-management regulation of prices, the regulation of the free exchange of labour between production and non-production workers, and the regulation and exercise or discharge of mutual rights, obligations and responsibilities of workers in associated labour. The trade unions organise discussions among workers leading to the conclusion of such agreements, and endeavour to reconcile the various interests represented. The trade unions are themselves signatories of self-management agreements through which workers associate their labour in basic organisations, as well as of agreements regulating labour relations or laying down principles and scales for the distribution of net income and the allocation of resources for personal incomes and joint consumption. They also have the right to initiate proceedings for the revision of agreements already concluded if they consider that such agreements violate workers' management rights or socio-economic relations established by the Constitution.

Personnel selection

The trade unions have a very extensive part to play in ensuring that as many workers as possible will take on management duties in organisations engaged in production and in other spheres of activity, as well as responsibility for the management of public affairs. For example, the unions participate in the determination of criteria for the nomination of candidates for public office, and take care that these criteria are met and that democratic procedures are followed in the nomination of candidates for workers' management organs and delegates to the assemblies of socio-political communities.

In an organisation of associated labour the trade union takes the preliminary steps for the nomination of candidates for membership of the workers' council. It may also propose the recall of elected members of the workers' council. It exercises similar rights with regard to the election and recall of general managers and members of boards of management, members of disciplinary commissions, workers' supervisory commissions, assemblies of self-managing communities of interest, assemblies of communities of associated labour for mutual business and planning co-operation, and the managerial organs of business communities, banks and insurance communities, as well as the delegates to chambers of associated labour in assemblies of socio-political communities. For appointments to posts of general manager and as members of boards of management the unions are entitled to designate representatives to sit on the selection committees, and they may also initiate proceedings for the dismissal of general managers or of other persons in positions of authority.

The workers' council, which decides on all of these appointments and dismissals, is required to give consideration to the trade union proposals, take a decision on them, and inform the trade union of the action taken. For elections to the workers' supervisory commission it is the union that draws up the list of candidates and makes the other electoral arrangements.

Representation and defence of workers' collective interests

The self-management organs of all organisations of associated labour are required by law to enable the trade unions to participate in all their discussions whenever a decision is to be taken on issues pertaining to workers' management rights and the economic position and interests of workers and of their organisations of associated labour, and whenever it is necessary, in the process of decision-making, to reconcile the interests and views of a particular group of workers with those of the majority of workers in associated labour. Those organs are required to examine every trade union demand and take a decision in regard to it. If such a demand is rejected, they must inform the union of the reasons for the rejection.

The workers' council and other organs are also obliged to keep the unions fully informed about the entire business activity of the organisation, its economic and financial position, the income earned and its distribution, the use made of resources placed at their disposal and preparations for workers' defence and social self-protection, as well as about all other questions relevant to decision-making and to the supervision of the working of the management system. They must inform the unions about decisions taken by the workers' council and its executive organs and the implementation of those decisions, as well as about the activities of the managerial organs, in all types of organisations of associated labour. The workers' council and the managerial organs are also bound to inform the union, on request, of all the warnings, findings and decisions of the social attorney of workers' management, the social accountancy offices and other organs and services of the socio-political community. If they fail to inform the union in such circumstances, they are regarded as violating workers' rights, and sanctions may be taken against them. If workers' management in an organisation of associated labour has been seriously disrupted or if serious harm has been done to the interests of society, the trade union concerned may initiate proceedings to impose temporary measures of social protection on the organisation of associated labour in which such occurrences have been noted.

The trade unions have also been given extensive duties in connection with the new workers' supervisory commissions. Indeed, many features of those commissions reflect action proposed or taken by the unions in the subject of workers' supervision of management. The unions' duties include helping workers' supervisory commissions in improving their methods of work, submitting proposals and reporting any irregularities to them, and making sure that they report regularly to the workers on their proceedings and findings. Conversely, the commissions are entitled and required to turn to the trade unions for help and advice, and to inform them about all irregularities observed in the performance of workers, organs and services in organisations of associated labour. The unions are particularly vigilant with regard to any techno-bureaucratic and other forces that resist the development of workers' management; for example, they waged an intensive campaign against the abuse of new constitutional provisions by technocrats who usurped the decision-making rights of workers. This action by the trade unions was broadly supported by workers and has largely contributed to the elimination of such abuses. The trade unions are also involved in the settlement of disputes between a Yugoslav organisation of associated labour and a foreign partner over the investment contract governing their joint venture.[11]

The unions also play an effective role in the assemblies of the socio-political communities, in which they are represented by delegates to the socio-political chambers of communes, provinces and republics. They prepare briefs and position papers for delegates from organisations of associated labour to these assemblies, and they may also submit directly their own proposals and views on the issues discussed. The assemblies and chambers are required by statute and by their standing orders to consider the views of the unions before decisions are taken on subjects of particular interest to them.

Grievance procedures

As already indicated, under the workers' management system the protective functions of trade unions remain extensive, although rather different from what they are in other types of society. There are many areas where the vigilance of the trade unions is still required, in order to counter threats to workers' management rights arising, for example, from vestiges of centralised state planning and control with regard to the production and distribution of income, inequalities in the economic situation of different groups of workers, trends towards technocratic and bureaucratic monopoly of decision-making power, abuses of power by individuals for personal reasons, conflicts of interest and other weaknesses and shortcomings that inevitably occur.

Within organisations of associated labour the first aim of protective action by the trade unions is to establish good relations so that controversies or disputes will be dealt with by the workers themselves before management organs of the organisations of associated labour or the socio-political communities are called upon to intervene in their settlement. When grievances and disputes nevertheless arise, the unions have the right to defend a worker's rights and interests subject to his or her request and concurrence, and they may institute proceedings for an individual worker's defence, as a matter of principle, even if the worker does not formulate a grievance or refuses trade union intervention. Such proceedings are instituted before the competent organs of the basic organisation of associated labour and before the court of associated labour. Most of the trade union councils at the communal and municipal levels have a special department that gives legal assistance to workers and trade union organs and represents them in court.

In recent years there has been a gradual increase in the number of workers' grievances recorded. This trend probably reflects both the difficulties encountered by organisations of associated labour and the increased effectiveness of trade union action in this field, a factor which has undoubtedly encouraged workers to bring out into the open not only their personal grievances, but also various other shortcomings and irregularities of a more general nature. It would appear, in fact, that it is these latter types of complaints, which tend to emphasise workers' insistence on the sharing of responsibility of all workers in associated labour, that are on the rise.

If grievances cannot be settled with the help of the trade union at shop-floor level, they may be, and often are, taken to higher levels in the trade union organisation: quite a number of petitions and complaints reach the Central Council of the Confederation of Trade Unions and the republican or provincial councils, although most of them are dealt with by the trade union councils at the level of the commune. From 1974 to 1977 the Central Council of the Confederation of Trade Unions and its organs received 3,390 written petitions and statements of grievances and 1,598 verbal complaints from the workers. During the same period, the republican and provincial councils received a total of 7,185 petitions and complaints. In 1978 the Council of the Confederation of Trade Unions received 1,957 petitions and statements of grievances.[12] Most of them referred to problems in the area of labour relations (465). Petitions and statements of grievances concerning the distribution of personal incomes (350) came second, followed by complaints relating to housing (306), pensions and disability insurance (112), violations of the workers' management rights and of the principles of social ownership (241), and other subjects. Most of the petitions and complaints concerning labour relations referred to problems regarding the establishment of such relations. In the first place, workers pointed out violations of social compacts concerning work opportunities; they also denounced cases of arbitrariness and nepotism in the selection of workers, particularly in organisations of associated labour that were not a parties to social compacts on employment. The number of petitions and grievances concerning the assignment of workers to other jobs grew in 1978: there were cases of unnecessary transfers, favouritism and unjustified transfers to lower work positions. On the other hand the number of petitions concerning the termination of work relations in associated labour decreased. This decline was largely due to the Associated Labour Law and other statutory provisions, and particularly to the activity of the social attorneys of workers' management and the courts of associated labour as well as to the preventive work of the commune councils of the Confederation of Trade Unions.

Petitions and grievances with regard to the distribution of personal incomes indicated difficulties and anomalies in the adoption of rules and measures concerning distribution in accordance with work done. It appears that certain jobs were inadequately assessed, often according to the persons performing them: there were inequalities in the standards and methods of measurement of work; certain standards were not set objectively, and in some organisations of associated labour the same jobs performed under similar conditions were assigned different basic ratings.

In the field of housing, criticisms were made concerning the established rules for the distribution of flats, failure to observe the established principles and rules for the distribution of flats and the grant of credit for individual housing construction, as well as favouritism toward individuals in allocating flats and credit.

In 1978 the number of petitions and complaints not referring directly to the rights of individuals but to failure to defend the general interest (93) showed an over-all increase, as did those concerning the protection of social ownership (78), and the appearance of bureaucratic and technocratic conduct and behaviour, inconsistent with the principle of workers' management, on the part of individuals, groups and organs of management. It was evident, however, that some of the complaints recorded arose from the ignorance of workers in regard to the internal self-management rules of their own organisations of associated labour and how particular subjects were dealt with under those rules. About 20 per cent of the petitions and complaints requested explanations from the Council of the Central Confederation of Trade Unions and its organs with regard to matters exclusively governed by the self-management rules of organisations of associated labour.

Production and distribution of income

The trade unions pursue a policy of raising living standards through the improvement of productivity and a corresponding increase in income. They endeavour to help eliminate bottlenecks both in individual work organisations and in the economy as a whole, and they also play an important role in all phases of planning, both in organisations of associated labour and in socio-political communities.

Within organisations of associated labour the trade unions endeavour to promote the various forms of association of labour and resources on the basis of interdependence of income, and to encourage efforts to maximise income. They defend the principle of distribution of income according to the contribution made to its creation by each worker and by each basic organisation of associated labour, and they are actively engaged in the development of rules and scales for the allocation of net income on the basis of these principles. As regards personal incomes, the trade unions support differentials based on individual work results, as a means of stimulating increased productivity; they are opposed to any equalisation of incomes that would reward lack of effort. On the other hand, they advocate the improvement of general standards of living rather than personal consumption, with a view to compensating for differences in personal incomes based on work performed, and to strengthening the solidarity and social security of workers; thus they are particularly active in promoting services designed for joint consumption, such as canteens and catering services to supply hot meals for production workers; the design and construction of workers' housing; devising old age and disability insurance policies; and the provision of rest and recreation facilities and child-care centres.

Trade unions are also concerned with the improvement of the working environment and the humanisation of working conditions. They launch campaigns to raise standards of safety at work and protect the workers' health, improve the organisation of work and the arrangement of time schedules (with reduced working hours, particularly on hazardous work), and transfer older workers to lighter work without loss of income.

PROTECTION OF WORKERS' MANAGEMENT RIGHTS AND SOCIAL OWNERSHIP

The protection of workers' management rights and of social ownership, as the fundamental values of Yugoslav society, is the duty of society as a whole and of each of its parts. All working people and citizens and all basic and other organisations of associated labour, workers' councils, self-management organs, workers' supervisory commissions and sociopolitical organisations are responsible for this function. They are both entitled and required to protect social ownership and workers' management.

There are also special institutions for the protection of these values, namely the social attorneys of workers' management and the courts of associated labour. Special functions in this respect are also assigned to the assemblies of the socio-political communities and to the constitutional courts. The social accountancy offices also play a role in this regard. The numerous and varied forms of action of these different bodies have a common emphasis on prevention.

Social attorneys of workers' management

The social attorneys of workers' management are a new institution, established by the Constitution of 1974. As independent agents of the community, the social attorneys are entrusted with the duty and the legal means of ensuring the protection of workers' management rights and social ownership. They carry out their functions in two ways.

In the first place, they point out violations of the workers' rights and of the principles of social ownership and the conflicts that may arise from these anomalies. They encourage the workers to settle disputes by self-management means and to prevent breaches of the principles of workers' management and social ownership. They carry out these duties in co-operation with the organisations of associated labour, the self-managing communities of interest, the workers' supervisory commissions and the socio-political organisations.

In the second place, the social attorneys may, if necessary, institute proceedings before the courts of associated labour, the assemblies of the socio-political communities and the constitutional courts, with a view to enabling those bodies in the statutorily prescribed way to take steps to rescind actions, decisions or regulations that are contrary to the principles of workers' management or social ownership. The social attorneys may take such action on their own initiative or at the request of the workers, the workers' supervisory commissions, or the organs of organisations of

179

associated labour or other self-managing organisations or communities, or of the socio-political communities.

The social attorneys of self-management concentrate on preventive measures. They do not themselves take decisions, but rather initiate action for the settlement of problems in organisations of associated labour on a self-management basis, by assisting their workers and their self-management organs to deal with their particular problems themselves. Only when they fail to find an adequate solution in this way do the social attorneys turn to the courts of associated labour or to the assembly of the appropriate socio-political organisation (usually the commune) for a decision.

On the basis of the experience of the past few years, it would appear that these attorneys are frequently effective; in 1976 and 1977, in some 80 per cent of the cases, their interventions resulted in the elimination of the weaknesses indicated on a voluntary basis, by the workers concerned. As table 14 shows, the majority of requests made by workers for the intervention of a social attorney have referred to the protection of their rights in respect of the establishment and termination of work relationships, the distribution of resources for personal incomes and joint consumption, and housing questions.

A more recent analysis of the work of the social attorneys of workers' management, carried out in the Socialist Republic of Montenegro in 1978, indicates that the attorneys directed their activity primarily toward the application of the Constitution and the Associated Labour Law, particularly with regard to the formation and structure of basic organisations of associated labour and other forms of organisation and the implementation of internal self-management rules and their conformity with the Constitution and the Associated Labour Law. Parallel with those activities, the attorneys acted to eliminate violations of workers' management rights and of the principles of social ownership. The greatest number of violations of workers' management rights in Montenegro in 1978 related to the establishment or termination of labour relationships (855), income, particularly the distribution of resources for personal incomes (496), housing (235), disciplinary measures imposed on account of violations of work obligations and other breaches of work discipline (85) and violations of the principle of social ownership (39). The bodies and organisations to which the attorneys turned in order to protect workers' management rights and social ownership adopted 1,077 of their proposals and suggestions in full and 154 in part, and rejected 180. The number of requests for the intervention of a social attorney of workers' management increased from 1,559 in 1977 to 2,354 in 1978. The attorneys took action on their own initiative 156 times in 1977, and 306 times in 1978.

Table 14. Action taken on reports concerning violations of workers' management rights and of the principles of social ownership received by the social attorneys of workers' management in 1979

Subject	Level					
	Communes or groups of communes		Republics and provinces		Federation	
	Reports received	Action taken	Reports received	Action taken	Reports received	Action taken
Labour relations	41 301	30 375	1 186	597	135	63
Distribution of personal incomes	21 318	16 047	609	290	90	50
Housing	18 219	13 804	863	321	162	64
Earning and distribution of income	5 070	4 530	282	92	7	6
Use and distribution of resources for joint consumption	4 345	3 308	37	23	—	—
Workers' right to form self-managing organisations	3 818	3 472	171	84	9	4
Violations of the principles of social ownership	3 239	3 711	144	88	8	8
Right to the free exchange of labour[1]	1 166	800	10	4	—	—
Association of farmers	76	47	6	—	—	—
Other	12 972	8 213	630	211	41	19
Total	111 524	84 307	3 938	1 710	452	214

[1] Relations with self-governing communities of interest.
Source: Savezni Zavod za Statistiku: *Statistički godišnjak SFRJ*, 1981, p. 110.

Courts of associated labour

The courts of associated labour are also a new institution; their jurisdiction, procedure and aims are established by the Constitution of 1974 and by a law of the same year.[13] These courts are required to safeguard the rights of working people and the self-managing status of their organisations and communities, and to ensure the constitutionality and legality of relations in the area of associated labour.

The courts of associated labour decide whether the prerequisites for the formation of basic organisations of associated labour and work communities have been met. They also rule on such matters as requests for the protection of the right to work with social resources, other workers' management rights, and social ownership; on disputes concerning the formation and mergers and divisions of organisations of associated labour, the conclusion and implementation of self-management agreements in those respects, and the founding and operation of self-managing communities of interest. These courts are also responsible for settling disputes on the establishment and termination of work relationships in associated labour, as well as on other workers' management rights and obligations in organisations of associated labour and in other socio-legal entities.

Most of the judges of the courts of associated labour are elected from the ranks of the workers: more than 90 per cent of the judges act in an honorary capacity and continue to work in their basic organisations after their election to the bench, performing this judicial function as a social obligation. In 1979 there were about 3,000 judges who performed this function in an honorary capacity as non-professionals, and about 250 professional judges who were permanently employed in these courts.

Courts of associated labour are autonomous bodies, and retain this autonomy in decision-making. Because their jurisdiction is based on the problems of everyday self-management practice, these courts are better suited to requirements in this particular field than are courts of the traditional type. Their decisions are taken on the basis of the Constitution and statutory provisions but also, to an increasing degree, on the basis of the general self-management rules and by-laws of the basic and other organisations of associated labour, self-managing communities of interest and other self-managing organisations and communities. The facts of a case are usually established in the organisation of associated labour in which the dispute in question occurred. The courts attempt to settle disputes by conciliation, but if an agreement cannot be reached they will make a ruling, which is legally binding.

From 1975 to 1978, 113,898 disputes were brought before the courts of associated labour[14], mostly (about 90 per cent) by workers, whose applications were upheld by the courts in more than 60 per cent of the cases. Most of the disputes brought before the courts resulted from the violation of workers' management rights in respect of the establishment and termination of work relationships, the distribution of resources for personal incomes and joint consumption, and housing. The law specifies the types of disputes on which decisions may be taken by a court of associated labour, acting on the proposal of a social attorney of workers' management, in order to ensure the workers' exercise of their rights and the fulfilment of their obligations and responsibilities.

Constitutional courts

Acting on the proposal of a social attorney of workers' management or at the request of individual workers or of groups of workers, the constitutional courts may abrogate or annul any self-management decision made by an organisation of associated labour, a self-managing community of interest, bank or other financial institution, or by any other self-managing organisation or community, if the decision is incompatible with statutory or constitutional provisions.

Assemblies of socio-political communities

The assembly of a socio-political community, acting on the proposal of a social attorney of workers' management, may take statutorily prescribed temporary measures to protect social property, such as changing the composition of the managerial organ; relieving of duty individual workers holding posts of authority and responsibility; dissolving the workers' council and calling elections for a new one; dissolving the executive committee of the workers' council, for a maximum period of one year, and setting a time-limit for the election of a new one; temporarily restricting the exercise of specified workers' management rights; making temporary appointments in an organisation of associated labour. Such temporary measures are compulsory if workers' management in an organisation of associated labour has been fundamentally disrupted or if serious harm has been done to social interests, or if an organisation of associated labour does not fulfil its statutorily determined obligations. The law defines the circumstances that determine whether those conditions have been met.

Social accountancy offices

Other important Yugoslav institutions are the social accountancy offices, which are responsible for ensuring lawful use of social resources and for providing data on all the financial operations involved in social and economic activity. They are an independent group of organisations established by the Constitution and by statute,[15] and comprise the Social Accountancy Office of Yugoslavia, which is responsible to the Assembly of the federation, and social accountancy offices for each of the republics and autonomous provinces, which are responsible to the assemblies of those socio-political communities.

In furtherance of the requirements of an integrated country-wide market and the aim of implementing a common economic policy, the Social Accountancy Office of Yugoslavia applies a uniform methodology to the performance of specified functions on behalf of all users of social resources, throughout the federation. Those functions enable the Office to supervise and control the use of social resources, and fall into the following four groups:

(1) Record-keeping, analysis and provision of information on the use of social resources.

(2) Monitoring the accuracy of data and legality in the use of social resources as well as fulfilment of obligations to the community by users of social resources.

(3) Economic and financial auditing.

(4) Payments transactions within the country.

1. The Office supplies financial returns to the organisations of associated labour and other entities that use social resources. On the basis of that information workers, workers' management organs and workers' supervisory commissions gain an insight into the economic performance and financial operations of their organisations as well as into the planning and orientation of economic and social development in general. The data and analyses supplied by the Office cover the management and use of social resources; the results of workers' labour; the business operations of the basic organisations of associated labour and expenditure on personal incomes, joint consumption, general obligations and investment; the legality of the use of socially owned resources; the attainment of the targets set in development plans, the implementation of self-management agreements and social compacts, the implementation of economic policy measures, and so forth.

2. In its supervisory capacity, the Social Accountancy Office confirms the accuracy of the data which it provides to the users of social resources, the legality of the disposal and use of social resources, and the proper and timely execution of mutual obligations as well as obligations to the socio-political communities by users of social resources. The Office carries out this supervision through preventive inspection and financial control. When a social accountancy office establishes the existence of an unlawful situation or a criminal offence, it is required to bring charges against the responsible worker or beneficiary of social resources through the competent public prosecutor.

3. Through economic and financial auditing, the offices examine the aggregate financial operation, establishing the accuracy of financial statements, the source of funds and the results of business operations as given in annual and other balance sheets. The offices carry out audits at the request of the users of social resources and the socio-political communities.

4. All movements of the funds (except foreign exchange) of holders of social resources have to be made through accounts with the Social Accountancy Office.[16] They make all their payments through these accounts, except those that are made on their behalf by an internal bank. The Office provides daily reports of the changes in these accounts to the users of social resources as well as to the banks where they have deposited funds. Organisations of associated labour and other users are required to provide the Office with all data required for the adjustment of relations in social "reproduction" and development and to provide the workers with timely and exact information, in accordance with their constitutional rights. (In the event of bankruptcy the sequence of payments to be made is established by the law relating to the Social Accountancy Office: in such a case the payment of personal incomes to workers is one of the very first to be made.) The Office informs the socio-political communities and socio-political organisations of all economic developments, as well as of the measures that it takes to put a stop to unlawful use of social resources.

Notes

[1] See, for example, an article on "A democratic co-ordination of interests", in *Yugoslav Trade Unions*, Jan.-Feb. 1979, p. 3, in which attention is drawn to certain weaknesses in the adoption of agreements on association and their implementation, particularly as regards the equality of the signatory parties.

[2] For further details on the foundation and operation of these types of banks, see *Financial institutions in Yugoslavia* (Belgrade, Jugoslavenski pregled, 1977), pp. 51–76.

[3] Art. 154, para. 5. The composition of the assemblies of socio-political communities is dealt with on p. 156.

[4] *Yugoslav Trade Unions*, May-June 1978, p. 7.

[5] On the principles of associated labour see p. 20

[6] The position of the socio-political organisations was summarised thus in a resolution adopted at the Second Congress of Self-Managers of Yugoslavia, held in Sarajevo in 1971:

"In the past years, parallel with the changes in the socio-economic and political system and the democratisation of social relations, the League of Communists, Confederation of Trade Unions, Socialist Alliance of Working People, Union of Socialist Youth, and the Federation of Veterans of the National Liberation War, have invested visible efforts to transfer the focus of their influence from the state mechanism to self-management organisation and decision-making. In this process, these socio-political organisations have further affirmed themselves as the internal moving force of the development of our self-management socio-political system and as a factor in resolving social contradictions and realising social unity. For the working person and citizen, they are an irreplaceable instrument for the organised expression and synthesis of basic interests and needs, a powerful weapon in the struggle to realise these interests and socialist social relations on the basis of self-management distribution according to the results of labour solidarity."

[7] From a resolution adopted at the Sixth Congress of the League. See *Les nouvelles yougoslaves* (Paris, Agence yougoslave d'information), 15 Nov. 1952.

[8] See table 4.

[9] cf. Tito, op. cit., in *Review of International Affairs* (Belgrade), 5 May 1979. p. 22.

[10] Albert Meister: "Problèmes et réalités d'une expérience autogestionnaire", in *Dirigeant* (Paris), Jan. 1978, p. 24.

[11] On the legal procedure for settlement of such disputes see p. 80; and on the contents of the contracts and their implications for workers' management, pp. 77–80.

¹² *Sindikati*, 1979, No. 2, pp. 36–44.

¹³ *Službeni List*, 10 May 1974, pp. 749–755.

¹⁴ Figures produced at a conference on the work of the courts of associated labour held in Belgrade on 14 and 15 May 1979.

¹⁵ *Službeni List*, 7 Jan. 1977, pp. 38–53.

¹⁶ Users of social resources may have the following accounts with the Social Accountancy Office: a giro or drawing account, an account for allocated resources, a transitional account, and other such accounts. According to the Associated Labour Law (Art. 146), and the rules governing the opening and closing of accounts (*Službeni List*, No. 59/77), all beneficiaries of social resources are required to open a giro account.

ACHIEVEMENTS AND SHORTCOMINGS 6

In introducing workers' management as the general rule, Yugoslavia was breaking new ground. Apart from some general philosophical ideas that had gained currency in the nineteenth century, and a few isolated experiments, there were no precedents or models available. Indeed, one story relates how, when the law of 1950 was applied to the steel mills at Jesenice, the manager convened a meeting of delegates elected by the workers and proceeded to read out the relevant provisions of the law. This reading was followed by complete silence, and the meeting was promptly adjourned because no one knew what to do next.

During the three decades of its existence immense strides have been made in developing and spreading the system of workers' management to every sphere of activity, and it has now become part and parcel of Yugoslav life. Today workers' management is not only a most advanced form of workers' participation in decision-making, but also the cornerstone of an entire social system based on the over-riding role played by workers both in the establishments where they work and in society at large.

This radical transformation of Yugoslav society into a self-managing social system has brought radical changes on the economic, social and cultural planes and in the socio-political life of the country. The continuous development and expansion of workers' management over the past three decades has coincided with a period of considerable economic growth, industrialisation, and rising standards of living. It is hard to assess to what extent the latter developments may be due to the former, or how far they have been facilitated by the general economic expansion that has occurred in most countries since the Second World War. Many Yugoslav observers of the system, however, are convinced that workers' management has played an important role in Yugoslavia's economic development through the participation of working people in management decision-making and in the entire socio-political process. In their view, it is this mobilisation of creative initiative on a broad, democratic basis that has enabled the country to pursue its development without affecting its social stability even when serious difficulties and problems have arisen.

Admittedly, workers' management has not always been an unqualified success. At times its spread has been retarded by its own intrinsic weaknesses or other handicaps, and these difficulties have been reflected in a momentary stagnation of the economy as well as in other areas of social life. The workers' management system provides for the planning of economic and social development, the pooling of labour and resources, the distribution of income, financial and credit policy and all other matters of joint interest to be decided upon by the workers directly, or through their delegates, by means of self-management agreements and social compacts concluded among all the parties concerned. However, the articulation of the interests of the working people and the adjustment of their opinions on immediate or long-term measures and decisions is an extremely complicated and delicate process, as regards both self-management decision-making in organisations of associated labour and political decisions in the broader socio-political communities. It has also been noted that the complex self-management machinery and rigorous procedures, requiring preliminary general debate and individual expression of views by workers on all important matters, may sometimes slow down the process of decision-making. While workers in general may understand the philosophy of workers' management and be committed to its values, the mechanics of its functioning can quite often be beyond their reach, or they may not be prepared to accept the full implications of their responsibilities under its rules.

Although consistent efforts have been made to involve workers in decision-making by personal expression of views through referendums and meetings, or through their elected delegates to workers' councils in organisations of associated labour, some difficulties have inevitably appeared in practice. One of the basic problems, according to Yugoslav observers, appears to lie in the lack of adequate preparation of workers for decision-making. For example, information concerning questions to be decided upon at a general meeting or by referendum is not circulated well enough in advance; the practice of organising preliminary discussions on such questions is not always followed; and decisions are frequently put forward without alternatives and explained in a manner difficult to understand.

Other difficulties spring from a tendency observed in some organisations to resist workers' management and an attempt to maintain a dominant influence in decision-making, and privileged status, for bureaucrats and technicians. This resistance may come from the managerial teams and specialised staff that play an important role in the preparation and drafting of decisions taken by the workers. This staff prepare the documents for general meetings and for the workers' councils, select the items to be discussed and prepare draft decisions and proposals. The temptation is no doubt strong, particularly for experts, to attempt to impose their own views, or the views of the individuals or groups that have the strongest influence among them, under the guise of advice or assistance in the preparation of proposals. They may, for example, submit long indigestible documents, generally without providing alternative proposals, clear explanations or arguments for and against that would give the workers a rational basis for decision-making.

On the other hand workers themselves may act in accordance with selfish interests and group-ownership tendencies, ignoring the principles of workers' management, when taking decisions by referendum. In one basic organisation, for example, the workers voted three times by referendum against the association of their organisation with a work organisation and a composite organisation of associated labour, thus blocking the project. In the view of Yugoslav observers, it is undeniable that the failure of some referendums held after the adoption of the Associated Labour Law can to some extent at least be attributed to group ownership tendencies and an undercurrent of economic isolationism, especially in the organisations that are better off. Unsuccessful referendums may also be the result of insufficient ideological and political preparation and inadequate preliminary disucssions: in most cases when a referendum fails the trade unions, the League of Communists and socialist youth organisations have not been active and have not done their job of preparing the workers for decision-making by referendum.

Weaknesses have also been noted in the practice of expression of personal views by workers at general meetings as provided for in the Associated Labour Law. In many organisations workers still decide at general meetings on questions that fall within the competence of the workers' council or should be submitted to a referendum. In a large number of organisations preparations for general meetings, the questions to be decided by them and their procedure are not regulated by self-management rules with the result that managerial and specialised staff retain their predominant influence over the decisions taken, as was often the case in the past.

In the practical functioning of decision-making by workers through their delegates to the workers' council, some weak points are also visible. It is taking time to put into practice the principle that delegates shall take decisions on the basis of the instructions and views of the workers whom they represent. It often happens, for example, that the documents to be considered at a meeting of the workers' council are sent out just before the meeting or even circulated at the meeting itself, which makes it practically impossible for delegates to consult the workers and to act according to their instructions. The question of the delegates' responsibility has also been neglected. Some delegates rarely inform the workers who provide their instructions about decisions of the workers' council and the part that they have played in reaching such decisions.

Owing to the self-seeking attitude of workers in some basic organisations, difficulties appear to have arisen in some organisations of associated labour in striking a balance between the interests of different groups and drawing up joint instructions for delegates to the workers' council of the work organisation, composite organisation or other form of association. Or, again, it has been observed that delegates have made up their minds and taken decisions solely on the basis of consultations with specialised and managerial staff, neglecting to consult the workers in the basic organisation who elected them.

One interesting practice which has emerged in some areas in an effort to remedy these weaknesses is that of electing temporary delegates. The influence of managerial or technical staff on the decisions taken by the councils tends to be greater when the delegates are permanent. Therefore instead of electing permanent delegates to the workers' council of the work organisation or composite organisation to which they belong, the workers in some basic organisations elect delegations from which they appoint delegates to attend certain sessions of the council. The practice of appointing temporary delegates has the advantage of enabling a larger number of workers to participate in the proceedings of the workers' councils, and thus reducing to some degree the influence of managerial and technical staff. It also ensures more qualified participation in decision-making by workers since it is possible to delegate to specific meetings the members of the delegation who are best acquainted with the problems to be discussed. The appointment of temporary delegates is not always effective, however, since a variety of problems may come up at any one meeting and delegates may not be qualified to participate in decisions on them all. Increasing emphasis is therefore being laid on the importance of drawing up the agenda of meetings well in advance, arranging for similar or related subjects to be discussed together, and providing the fullest possible information with regard to agenda items.

In decision-making through delegates in organisations of associated labour, special importance is attached to co-operation between delegations and the workers' councils in the basic organisations of associated labour. On the whole, in the opinion of Yugoslav observers, this co-operation has still not become effective in all organisations. There is a tendency for the workers' council of a basic organisation to behave as an organ that commands its delegation; conversely, there are cases in which the delegations do not understand their job and take on the authority of the workers' council. Joint meetings at which the particular questions that come up could be discussed and instructions for the delegates drawn up are rarely held. Co-operation between the two has been reduced to the presence of representatives of the delegations at meetings of workers' councils and vice versa.

In a great number of organisations of associated labour the rights and responsibilities of the delegates and delegations have been established only in skeleton form, in terms of general rules in the by-laws. In many cases there are neither prescribed modes of operation nor programmes of action; instead, delegates follow the programme of the assembly of the socio-political community.

Intensive efforts are being made to overcome these shortcomings in organisations of associated labour, through more precise regulation of workers' decision-making by general self-management rules that are discussed, adopted and applied by the workers in the organisations concerned. The provisions of the Associated Labour Law seem to be increasingly implemented in this respect. The trade unions and the League of Communists are playing a leading part in this endeavour.

As has already been noted above, attention was drawn to these and other weaknesses in the functioning of the workers' management system and in the application of the Associated Labour Law at the Eleventh Congress of the League of Communists of Yugoslavia, in 1978. That Congress reaffirmed the role of the League in establishing in practice the rights, obligations and duties of workers in basic organisations of associated labour, through the means established by the law, so that decision-making by workers might become a reality. It also proclaimed that the duty of the League of Communists was "to constantly struggle against monopolistic, technocratic group ownership and other non-self-management tendencies that directly contradict self-management and threaten its foundations and development."

A detailed statement of action to improve decision-making in accordance with the principles of workers' management was adopted at the Eighth Congress of the Confederation of Yugoslav Trade Unions, in 1978.[1]

Beyond these specific measures there is a determined will to strengthen and improve the system. The Yugoslavs refuse to seek a remedy for this difficulty by shortening or simplifying the decision-making process or reverting to more centralised procedures, but rather try to facilitate workers' management, particularly by improving the information and communication system and by direct and regular consultations of delegates with the workers who have elected them, as well as by developing the activities of self-management organs and socio-political organisations. No observer can fail to note the Yugoslavs' critical approach to their own weaknesses and shortcomings and their constant efforts to overcome these failings and to bring the system closer to its original ideal.

It must also be borne in mind that the political environment is an important factor in the workers' management system. As has been shown in the present volume the work organisations and communities are far from isolated, but on the contrary are closely linked with, and influenced by, the political and other bodies on which all sections of the community are represented. As was pointed out in the earlier ILO study, "this 'social pressure' (which can greatly modify the impact of economic incentives) is all the more effective because under a single-party system it operates within the framework of a single ideology whose foundations are not open to question. The system of workers' management now operating in Yugoslavia followed upon a complete reorganisation of the political and economic structure of the country and can hardly be dissociated from it".[2]

Contemporary Yugoslavia is certainly not free from disputes and conflicts of interest, whether in its basic organisations or at the level of society as a whole. However, the country's workers' management system appears to have demonstrated its vitality, resistance and capacity to overcome serious social conflict in a democratic way. The history of the past 30 years also seems to show that such workers' management is possible not only in a poorly developed and poorly integrated economy but also in a rapidly industrialising economy in which steadily increasing reliance is placed on contemporary scientific and technological developments and which is becoming more closely integrated in national and international patterns of production, trade and technical progress. The extension of workers' management to every area of activity including the political decision-making process does not appear to have impeded the planned development of productive forces and of society as a whole.

Notes

[1] According to the text published in *Sindikati*, Jan.–Feb. 1979, the organisations of the Confederation of Trade Unions should—

(a) ensure the political preparation of workers for decision-making;

(b) organise workers' discussions to enable them to express and compare their views, strike a balance between different interests and take policy decisions that will serve as a basis for decision-making on particular questions;

(c) in the course of decision-making, from the launching of an initiative to the adoption of a decision, point out various possible solutions to a specific question, so as to encourage the most rational adoption of the decisions;

(d) encourage workers to decide through referendums and other forms of the personal expression of views on general workers' management rules and all other matters that require such decision-making;

(*e*) monitor the implementation of the decisions of the workers and the workers' management bodies and initiate changes in those decisions that fail to produce the expected results;

(*f*) promote a responsible relationship toward work and workers' management obligations, against one-sided emphasis on rights to the exclusion of obligations, against techno-bureaucratic and group ownership resistance to workers' management, and in favour of a responsible relationship of the workers' councils, managerial organs, specialised staff and others toward all decisions that are made by the workers directly;

(*g*) institute proceedings to determine socio-political, financial and criminal responsibility in cases of failure to comply with socially agreed norms of behaviour and anti-social attitude to work, stubborn adherence to personal views and usurpation of the management rights of workers, and unlawful use of social property;

(*h*) strive for the consistent application of the principles of delegate decision-making in the workers' councils and other bodies that are constituted on the delegation principle; and

(*i*) oppose the adoption of any decision, regardless of the identity of its sponsor, unless it has first been discussed under the delegate system.

[2] ILO: *Workers' management in Yugoslavia*, op. cit., p. 294.

This index gives definitions of terms describing specifically Yugoslav institutions and concepts, or references to pages where they are described.

Table 15. Number and population of communes in 1981

Area	Number of communes					
		By number of inhabitants in thousands				
	Total	< 10	10–30	30–50	50–100	⩾ 100
Bosnia and Herzegovina	109	7	48	27	22	5
Croatia	113	11	46	25	23	8
Macedonia	34	—	15	4	9	6
Montenegro	20	5	9	3	2	1
Serbia	186	3	76	42	44	21
Excluding autonomous						
provinces	*114*	*2*	*53*	*20*	*26*	*13*
Kosovo	*22*	*—*	*1*	*7*	*9*	*5*
Vojvodina	*50*	*1*	*22*	*15*	*9*	*3*
Slovenia	60	3	36	10	10	1
Yugoslavia	**522**	**29**	**230**	**111**	**110**	**42**

Source: Savezni Zavod za Statistiku: *Statistički Godišnjak SFRJ*, 1981, pp. 586–587.

Delegate. See *delegation principle*.

Delegation principle. 29–30, 152–157. Refers to the system whereby workers in organisations of associated labour elect delegations, from which members are designated to represent them on various socio-political and other bodies.

Disciplinary commission. 90–91.

Free exchange of labour. 23–24. Characteristic of a self-governing *community of interest* for the provision of public and social services.

General associations for particular sectors of industry and commerce. 143–145.

Income. 22–23, 105–125.

Insurance community. 148–149.

Internal bank. 146–147.

Investment contract, foreign. 75–80.

Joint consumption. Refers to the allocation of income to projects of common interest to workers in a basic organisation of associated labour, such as canteens, welfare services, housing or recreational facilities, as distinct from allocation to personal incomes.

Local community. Local communities are a self-managing form of organisation of workers and citizens at their place of residence, that is, with their neighbours and sometimes with residents in neighbouring population centres. In the local community the residents decide jointly on such matters as housing, communal services, child and social welfare, education, culture, physical recreation, consumer protection, the safeguarding and improvement of the environment, national defence, social self-protection, and other matters of joint interest affecting their life and work. These matters are decided on in general meetings, through referendums, in meetings of

Table 16. Number, area and population of local communities in 1976

Area	Local communities			Percentage distribution by number of inhabitants				
	No. of local communities	Average area (km²)	Average population	< 500	500–1 000	1 001–2 000	2 001–4 000	≥ 4 001
Bosnia and Herzegovina	1 358	38	2 967	11.8	13.9	24.9	30.0	19.4
Croatia	3 761	15	1 204	40.3	23.9	17.0	9.3	9.5
Macedonia	1 360	19	1 312	47.8	23.6	14.5	7.2	6.9
Montenegro	238	58	2 374	—	—	—	—	—
Serbia	3 945	22	2 246	16.4	25.0	25.3	17.0	16.3
Excluding autonomous provinces	*3 106*	*18*	*1 748*	*20.1*	*30.2*	*27.0*	*12.0*	*10.7*
Kosovo	*319*	*34*	*4 533*	*0.3*	*1.9*	*17.2*	*45.2*	*35.4*
Vojvodina	*520*	*41*	*3 815*	*5.6*	*10.0*	*20.7*	*27.5*	*36.2*
Slovenia	1 040	19	1 723	22.0	23.9	24.2	18.2	11.7
Yugoslavia	**11 702**	**22**	**1 842**	**26.7**	**23.0**	**21.6**	**15.5**	**13.2**

consumers and users of the services provided by the organisations of associated labour, or through agreements with those organisations reached by consensus and through their delegates to the council of the local community and to the organs of management of *self-managing communities of interest* that operate in fields of interest to the local community. The residents of a local community also consider and discuss questions that are submitted for decision to the assemblies of the municipalities, the autonomous provinces, the republics and the federation, and draw up instructions for their delegates on those questions.

Reproduction complex. 112.

Self-management agreement. 27–28, 42–44.

Self-managing community of interests. See *Community of interests, self-managing, Social accountancy office.* 183–185.

Social attorney of worker's management. 179–181.

Social compact. 27–28.

Social ownership. 19–20.

Social plans. 126–128, 133–136. This term reflects the new system of planning in general.

Social reproduction is the process of the maintenance and development of society as a whole; it refers both to production and to other activities aimed at the satisfaction of the interests and needs of the workers and the community, including educational, scientific, cultural, health, welfare and other activities; "simple reproduction" refers to the continuation of production on an unchanged scale and "expanded reproduction" refers to the expansion of production in line with the increase in society's needs.

Social resources. The means of production, capital assets, investment funds, and so forth belonging to the community as a whole, which are placed at the disposal of workers organised in associated labour. In institutional terms, the users of social resources include basic and other organisations of associated labour and their communities, contractual organisations of associated labour, banks and other financial organisations, agricultural and other co-operatives, self-managing communities of interest, socio-political organisations and local and other socio-political communities.

Social self-protection. Activities performed by workers and organisations of associated labour and other bodies with a view to protecting constitutional order and safeguarding socially owned means of production and workers' rights and personal security of workers and citizens.

Socio-political community. 152–158.

Socio-political organisation. 159–178.

Work community, for the administration of affairs of common interest. 78–80. Self-managing work unit consisting of workers performing the administrative and related functions (planning, analytical, book-keeping, legal, etc.) in a *work organisation* or in a *composite organisation of associated labour*. In certain circumstances, a work community may be converted into a *basic organisation of associated labour*.

Work organisations. 34–35.

Workers' councils. 47–52.

Workers' supervisory commission. 58–62.